T0330465

Field Guide to Leadership Development

Field Guide to Leadership Development

Edited by

Steve Kempster

Professor of Leadership Learning and Development, Lancaster University Management School, UK

Arthur F. Turner

Senior Lecturer, University of the West of England, UK and Visiting Fellow of the University of South Wales, UK

Gareth Edwards

Associate Professor of Leadership Development, University of the West of England, UK

ELGAR FIELD GUIDES

Cheltenham, UK • Northampton, MA, USA

Published by
Edward Elgar Publishing Limited
The Lypiatts
15 Lansdown Road
Cheltenham
Glos GL50 2JA
UK

Edward Elgar Publishing, Inc.
William Pratt House
9 Dewey Court
Northampton
Massachusetts 01060
USA

A catalogue record for this book
is available from the British Library

Library of Congress Control Number: 2017941897

This book is available electronically in the **Elgar**online
Business subject collection
DOI 10.4337/9781785369919

ISBN 978 1 78536 990 2 (cased)
ISBN 978 1 78536 991 9 (eBook)

Typeset by Servis Filmsetting Ltd, Stockport, Cheshire

Contents

Contributors

Scott J. Allen, John Carroll University, USA

Andrew Armitage, Anglia Ruskin University, UK

Simon Bainbridge, Lancaster University, UK

Stewart Barnes, QuoLux, UK

Ralph Bathurst, Massey University, New Zealand

Jon Billsberry, Deakin University, Australia

James Campbell Quick, Goolsby Leadership Academy, University of Texas at Arlington, USA / The Alliance, Manchester Business School, University of Manchester, UK

Philippa Chapman, University of Cumbria, UK

Keri DeCay, Goolsby Leadership Academy, University of Texas at Arlington, USA

Gareth Edwards, University of the West of England, UK

Carolyn P. Egri, Simon Fraser University, Canada

Sigrid Endres, University of Hagen, Germany

John L. Goolsby, The Howard Hughes Corporation, USA

Jonathan Gosling, University of Exeter, UK

Eric Guthey, Copenhagen Business School, Denmark

Beverley Hawkins, University of Exeter, UK

Carol Jarvis, University of the West of England, UK

Daniel M. Jenkins, University of Southern Maine, USA

Steve Kempster, Lancaster University Management School, UK

Fiona Kennedy, New Zealand Leadership Institute

Donna Ladkin, Plymouth University, UK

Janice MacInnes, University of the West of England, UK

Navadha Modha, Goolsby Leadership Academy, University of Texas at Arlington, USA

Doris Schedlitzki, University of the West of England, UK

Arthur J. Schwartz, Widener University, Philadelphia, USA

Wadii Serhane, University of Hagen, Germany

Sue Smith, University of Central Lancaster, UK

Arthur F. Turner, University of the West of England / University of South Wales, UK

Mary Uhl-Bien, Texas Christian University, USA

Emma Watton, Lancaster University Management School, UK

Jürgen Weibler, University of Hagen, Germany

Simon Western, Analytic-Network Coaching Ltd, UK

1. Beyond the 'spider's web': an introduction to *The Field Guide to Leadership Development*

Steve Kempster, Arthur F. Turner and Gareth Edwards

Whilst reviewing and editing the chapters for this book we have recognised that most of the authors have had previous experience with 'planks and barrels' type experiential interventions.[1] By this we mean outdoor physical experiential development exercises. One of us, Steve, for example, recalls an incident with a 'spider's web' exercise with a group (ropes tied together and stretched between two poles to form a spider's web – teams challenged to get through the holes without touching the rope, with each closed after an attempt):

> I was called up by the client (I was programme director). Much anxiety and concern. One of her colleagues in undertaking the spider's web had dislocated his shoulder. So the story goes: the facilitator moved away to answer a call on his mobile phone. The manager in question had 'seized the day' and dived through a high-up 'hole' in the web. In part the client's anxiety was for the chap; but also that the manager was suing the company for making him undertake such an activity. Her question: 'Does the university's insurance policy cover this?'

Such activities as this, and the barrels and planks to cross metaphoric 'shark-infested swamps', have been key components or mainstays of many leadership development interventions for a number of decades. Many training companies have been set up to deliver programmes with these types of interventions as a central element. Physical experiential activities tend to be exciting and far from the occasional dullness of classroom didactic teaching and death by PowerPoint slides. Indeed, how could declarative knowledge distilled into colourful PowerPoint slides provide insight into individual practices of leading? The experiential 'spider's web' enablers facilitators to probe participants' problem-solving skills, or team communications displayed. However, even this mode of learning has similar problems of transference to the organisational setting. Often the insights of the high-octane activity are very tangential from everyday complexity of organisational leadership. Issues of institutional power, politics, unstated assumptions, histories of practice, emerging identities, or aspects such as emotional labour and emotional dissonance do not cross over into the metaphoric leadership task of safely crossing the 'shark-infested swamp' with the barrels and planks. But a good time, apparently, has been had by all (except the manager with the dislocated shoulder).

Yet we do not want to lose the excitement of experiential learning, and all the fun that goes with that. We assert, from the voices of all chapter authors herein, that our collective evidence speaks to experiential learning being most efficacious in leadership learning transference. We argue that such efficacy is enhanced by connecting experiential activity with three interrelated aspects: reflection, theory and practice (most similar to Kolb's early work (1984), which has been recently updated to offer a more complex and nuanced interpretation: Bergsteiner and Avery, 2014). We suggest that these three aspects have not been well served by barrels and planks, or indeed didactic classroom pedagogies. We suggest that 'experiential activities' in the main tend not to follow the full route of experiential learning as advocated by Kolb, but instead remain decontextualised activities. Too often the use of experiential projects is limited in viewing the activity as merely metaphoric (Belling et al., 2004). It is simply an opportunity to reflect and explore on experiences, assumptions and practices; unless of course you are faced with a 'shark-infested swamp', or your way is blocked by a giant spider's web.

Creative methods of seeking to develop leadership practice have been gaining precedence over more conventional classroom methods (see Edwards et al., 2013, 2015). Although these standard and conventional methods can be used to impart knowledge for its own sake – and are certainly a common necessity for meeting needs of accreditation – they can fail to enable leadership development through not addressing how leadership practice is learned. Leadership cannot be taught as if someone was coming cold to the topic for the first time, as for example might be the case with accounting and finance. Evidence suggests it can be learned from an early age, even as early as the age of three (Barnes et al., 2015). It is broadly understood that lived experience shapes our practice of leading. It has been mostly unconsciously learned, from moments that are hard to recall and are absorbed into a tacit store of practical knowledge. In addition, we also recognise that leadership is a relational phenomenon (see Cunliffe and Eriksen, 2011; Uhl-Bien, 2006). Seen through a relational lens, leadership is learned interpersonally through observation, participation and enactment that forms relational identities and practices anchored to specific contexts (Kempster, 2009) – a dynamic that is never-ending. In this way we offer up the notion of leadership learning and development as a process of situated leader as an incomplete or never-ending journey. This is in contrast to the process of leadership learning and development as having a destination, or end or final outcome – the notion of becoming a leader. Becoming has a forward trajectory that is always drawn from the past. Importantly, the becoming is interconnected with others – it is a relational process that similarly has a past and an ongoing trajectory. In this way, leader becoming is not a singular process, but rather an interconnected and malleable dynamic. Leadership development of an individual needs to be considered as situated leadership development of a greater system (a point developed by Day, 2001, who distinguished between leader and leadership development).

We recognise that becoming is gradual, and learning in this way is rarely noticed, occurring imperceptibly through life's course. Major moments – such as critical incidents, episodes, hardships, trigger points – can be recognised, yet so much of what occurs in the becoming is most difficult to access and recognise. Intervention methods that can help reveal something of this process of becoming seem most critical if leader and leadership development is to be constructive and effective. The methods need to be able to enable someone to explore such hard-to-retrieve experiences of being led and leading, emergent implicit theories of leading, everyday tacit practices of leading, and a related sense of relational identity associated with leadership. This is the challenge we have given to all chapter authors.

The common theme that connects all aspects within this book is the central mechanism of reflection.

The reflective aspect is fundamental if the relational, contextual and emergent aspects of leadership practice are to be brought into focus. Reflective leadership, then, is making visible the underlying influences that shape activity in order that individuals can consciously shape their everyday practice. Thus, however exciting barrels and planks might be, if they do not speak to revealing the complexity of leader becoming through reflexive engagement then the ability to enact purposeful change relevant to a person's context will be heavily restricted. The emphasis we give throughout this book to reflection speaks to the central orientation of making sense of experience. Without conscious and organised reflection, the experience of everyday activity that imperceptibly shapes who we are and how we behave remains for the most part out of reach. We continue to be shaped by the contexts and the experiences we engage in. Mechanisms of how to make this conscious, and shape reflection, is what each and every chapter seeks to do.

At this point we wish to define some terms with regard to reflection. Reflection, critical reflection and reflexivity are interrelated terms that need to be clarified as these will be important lenses through which to make sense of the various chapters and the approaches outlined therein. Mike Reynolds (1998) has helpfully offered a distinction between reflection and the notion of critical reflection. Reflection is a process of making thoughtful and productive use of experience for future action, while critical reflection is seen as enriching our sense-making of the experience to 'an analysis of power and control and an examination of the taken-for-granted within which the [experience] is situated' (1998, p.189). In essence, critical reflection is concerned with questioning assumptions, paying particular attention to power relationships, and is concerned with emancipation (Mezirow, 1985; Reynolds, 1998). Using Goffman's (1969) work, reflexivity focuses on an individual making sense of themselves, positioned and impacted by underlying power relations. Goffman's assertion is that an individual needs to be able to stand 'outside the stage' in order to understand and interpret how meaning and activity is being shaped on the 'front stage and back stage' (1969, p.107) in which she/he is a participant.

The depth of conscious awareness of appreciating the different aspects of reflection from critical reflection and personal reflexivity can be seen through Burgoyne and Hodgson's (1983) work that adapted Bateson's (1973) three levels of learning: level one reflects naturalistic learning drawn from everyday experience related to undertaking a specific activity – it is not usually transferable; level two is similarly naturalistic learning but is recognised by an individual as capable of being transferred to another situation, but does not recognise the underlying features that influence the learning; level three learning sees an individual as being able to make sense of the world around them, including the underlying influences (Burgoyne and Hodgson, 1983). Connecting with Argyris and Schon's (1978) concept of single- and double-loop learning, the single loop represents habits and everyday practices connected to the background situational consciousness (arguably levels one and two); and the deeper double-loop learning relates to changes affecting underlying values and general orientations (reflect level three). It is to double-loop level three that various approaches in this volume are seeking to stimulate within leadership development. It is argued that such reflection at level-three learning does occur naturalistically as a consequence of transformative incidents or episodes. Mezirow (1985) argues that significant triggers such as marker events or disorientating dilemmas (Mezirow, 1981) enable an individual to question their historic interpretation of their learning biography. These critical moments open up questions of taken-for-granted assumptions of events, and people within events, in order to generate critical reflection and personal reflexivity. It is through such critical reflexivity that an individual is capable of seeing and understanding the world they are part of and constructed within (similarly developed by Reynolds, 1998) and arguably allows an individual to see afresh how situations influence thought and action. As a consequence, embracing reflexivity can offer a new perspective and an individual can take control in terms of their own development. Returning again to the 'spider's web' incident, we speculate on the manager suing the company. His reflection might be something like this:

> The company had sent me on the course and it is their fault that I am injured. I mean the exercise is about taking the lead after all – that was the purpose of the course!

However, a very different reflection could have been drawn. If the manager was enabled to undertake a critical reflection of the incident, he might have been able to explore his desire to perform in front of others, his desire to take the lead – was this part of a moment of release from constraining instructions that limit his sense of himself? Did he wish to challenge his narrative identity by demonstrating possibilities of being heroic? Being heroic or tragic are discourses that permeate our lives and shape us in daily acts. If any of these questions were explored there would be a revealing of underlying structures and powers, unstated but pervasive assumptions that impose limits and expectations on people. Using a reflexive orientation the incident could have been reframed as a powerful moment for sense-making that reaches beyond the painful shoulder. We are not, of course, suggesting that designs for leadership development should inflict pain – physical or mental – far from it. However, it does illustrate how experiential moments can trigger insight into the taken-for-granted aspects that play out in shaping our pathways of leader becoming.

SO WHY A FIELD GUIDE?

We have developed this edited collection of reflections on leadership learning and development practice as we believe there are few books that have been written with this overt orientation. Few books have been written explicitly on leadership development. Rather, it is left to the leadership studies textbooks to try to incorporate this large field of practice into one or two chapters. Of notable exception is the *Handbook of Leadership Development* (McCauley et al.,1998), which we think is a most useful contribution. Its central argument is a triple lock of: challenge, assessment and support – all three needing to be designed into an intervention to develop a leader. We shall draw on these principles in this book. The distinctiveness that we seek to achieve here is to place emphasis on the following elements: reflection, dialogue, creativity, relationality and a practice orientation.

Debates on the necessity for leadership development to draw on these five aspects are often buried in academic texts and periodicals, remarkably inaccessible to the commissioners of leadership programmes. Authors and academics – some of whom are in this volume – have been researching into creative methods of development for many years. Their findings hint at a cornucopia of methods that would enhance and enliven the delivery of leadership development. The evidence-based understanding of the effectiveness of approaches that are relational-oriented have also been well documented – see for example the LEAD programme (Barnes et al., 2015). So rather than this being a handbook of 'nice' or wishful ideas, it is based on research and practice of many interventions applied and refined over many years. Although some of the methodological approaches may appear rather unconventional, what is evident in the chapters to follow is the effect that can occur on participants and the impact that the techniques can have on practice.

The book is laid out as a 'field guide' because we want it to be used in the 'field' – used by designers of leadership development in crafting their programmes. We offer plenty of possible approaches in order to provide scope for the multiplicity of contexts that leadership development programmes are challenged to address. We have sought a variety of contributions that draw from a plethora of backgrounds. All have been tested, evaluated and revised.

A most impressive range of academics, practitioners and 'actioners' have contributed to this field guide, both in academically rigorous extrapolations of theory and research but also in the wide-ranging practical application of these and other ideas evolving from their use in workshops and organisational development settings. These colleagues of ours have enthusiastically offered up their considerable knowledge, experience and insight into leadership development. We have requested that every chapter follows Peters and Waterman's (1982) old adage of a loose–tight structure – tight with regard to asking all chapter authors to follow a structure that has three (and a bit) elements:

- First, to consider the theoretical underpinnings of the approach. We have taken the view that however good the process might be its success relates in no small part to drawing on a firm foundation. For all authors there was a great sense of clarity for the underpinning ideas that shaped their specific pedagogy. In this volume there is a rich array of theories. In part this provides an unconventional introduction to debates and perspectives that explore leadership, learning, reflection and development; but also we hope it will provide a stimulus and resource for further reading and reflection.

- Second, to explore the process being offered up in the chapter. The intent here was to create sufficient detail that someone would be able to use the ideas to frame a design. Most authors have sought to achieve this by writing most candidly of the process – the successes and failures, the changes, aspects dropped and new parts included – as they have travelled their learning journey. For the most part this is undertaken in the first person and seeks to make the experience being described as graphic and insightful as possible. It is anticipated that the approaches seem possible, realistic and enticing; inviting a sense of imagining the possibilities of undertaking the processes within a leadership development programme. We hope for many readers that the ideas will be a 'hit'; they may resonate and open avenues of experimenting and reshaping what is being suggested in terms of contextual practicalities.

- Third, the need to reflect on the learning journey of designing the leadership development intervention. With the anticipated readership of leadership development practitioners, or human resources (HR) managers, or researchers curious about the topic, we wanted to provide a space in which other practitioners could share their reflections. The tightness of the editorial policy was to provoke the authors to be reflexive of their process, themselves and the potential of their designs. For some authors the reflections are on the learning resulting from undertaking the process. For others the attention is forward to the possibilities of change that the process might bring – for the leaders, teams, organisations and even communities they serve. But also some authors reflect on topics that they feel have been underutilised in the leadership development field thus far.

The 'bit' is a summary (in bullet points) of tips, or must haves, for the process to be successful. This is deliberately brief and practical. We hope that it provides space in the book for any reflections, insights, comments or questions that a reader might have. In this way we want the book to have potential as a field resource – capable of being scribbled on and personalised – for use in design meetings or indeed in the 'to connect to field' during and after activity. And, of course, we would like to hear back on experiences gained from the use of the field guide, so that we too can continue to learn from experience.

The final element of the 'tight' writing structure has been the restricted word length. All authors have been up against it trying to distil their wonderful work down to 5,000 words (which we have kept to in this opening chapter). This is simply to fulfil a desire to include a rich variety of leadership development interventions – hence the relatively large number of chapters (17).

Within this 'tightness' the evidence of the 'looseness' in this volume will be so very evident on reading the eclectic range of chapters. Most notable is the breadth of style and orientation. We have clustered authors into particular themes. This is in order to allow readers to select the area of most interest and to see the variety of different methods within each theme. Part I is about relational-based approaches. Part II is centred on narrative-based approaches. Part III examines the use of artefact-based approaches. Part IV considers place-based approaches. Part V is reflective practice-centred approaches. We provide a brief glimpse of the 'looseness' with an overview of the chapters clustered within each of these themes.

In Chapter 2 Donna Ladkin pursues the idea of practice-based approaches to developing ethically responsible leaders. Five design elements are explained and described as integral elements for developing 'offline' ethical approaches to real-time ethical dilemmas.

In Chapter 3 Scott Allen, Arthur Schwartz and Daniel Jenkins outline the collegiate leadership competition whereby there is an opportunity for deliberate practice on the road to expertise. This collegiate leadership competition engages students in practice, which includes declarative knowledge, understanding group dynamics and skilful intervention.

In Chapter 4 Stewart Barnes, Sue Smith and Steve Kempster look at leadership development through a quasi-non-executive board in the context of the small to medium-sized enterprise. The use of the prism of non-executive leadership, as a form of a community of practice, opens out development of capacity and confidence.

In Chapter 5 James Campbell Quick, Keri DeCay, Navadha Modha and John Goolsby describe a technique called biographical inquiry. This follows a belief that skilled performance can be learnt from masterful descriptions of people's journeys through leadership as well as amassing their own experience through research and interviews.

In Chapter 6 Andrew Armitage explores leadership development using the poetic voice of care ethics. He examines the role of poetry in understanding both context and settings as well as developing imaginative ideas to deal with chaotic environments. This work helps to develop an alternative paradigm to standard leadership development programmes through open and reflexive dialogue.

In Chapter 7 Doris Schedlitzki, Carol Jarvis and Janice MacInnes describe their use of Greek mythology in instilling deep and critical self-reflection in leaders. This chapter evaluates the usefulness of working with Greek mythology to enhance self-reflection and, through the discussion of an example, seeks to outline the role of archetypes in self-reflective practice.

In Chapter 8 Steve Kempster retells the story of his 'tent' exercise in constructing a narrative of leadership learning through detailed examination of a timeline. Steve's research shaped an intervention design to allow participants to gain access to unexplored, unrecognised and tacit knowledge. He offers us the notion of leadership development as narrative identity.

In Chapter 9 Emma Watton and Philippa Chapman run through their use of leadership artefacts, which relates to a process of storytelling within groups. Their technique is often used as a warm-up with newly formed groups but has lots of potential for customisation. Little attention has been paid to artefacts in learning and this chapter prompts us to think about how artefacts enable striking insights into the leader's sense of values, identity and purpose.

In Chapter 10 Jon Billsberry and Carolyn Egri describe their technique for leadership development through videography that engages participants in close observation of human behaviour, and that creates a strong resonance in retention, interpretation and experiences of leadership. The practical instructions on how to set this up liberate the opportunity for videography in many leadership development courses.

In Chapter 11 Arthur Turner expands on his use of multi-ethnic, contemporary and historical puppets. These mediating objects have been used across a wide range of leadership development activities, including introductions, action learning, and reflective practice and coaching. Their use is both stimulating and unusual, which often creates a visceral learning atmosphere within the dynamics of the group.

In Chapter 12 Wadii Serhane, Sigrid Endres and Jürgen Weibler articulate their method called 'seeing beyond the usual', using the notion of a social photo matrix. It is a socioanalytical method of experiential leadership development and it draws on expressive and creative work-related media. By using photographs this method helps to reach more deeply held ideas on sociocultural functions and associations that shape our daily practice.

In Chapter 13 Fiona Kennedy and Ralph Bathurst offer us examples of their leadership development work in developing the practice of sense framing. They describe an approach to the practice of framing that engages participants to firmly appreciate the socially constructed and experienced nature of leadership.

In Chapter 14 Beverley Hawkins and Gareth Edwards highlight the ways in which they embrace liminality – the anthropological concept describing human learning spaces that are experienced at times of transit in a human life. The concept of liminality allows for insights into learning about leadership through the experience of space and moments of being neither here nor there.

In Chapter 15 Jonathan Gosling and Simon Western describe their 'Lead2Lead' programme, which uses observational learning as a means of learning about leadership from each other. Having received initial coaching and training in observational skills, pairs of delegates shadow each other and then use this experience to debrief and learn from the experience through reflection.

In Chapter 16 Steve Kempster and Simon Bainbridge draw on Wordsworth's *The Prelude* as a way of exploring leadership as purpose within leadership development. By creating a multi-disciplinary approach, the autobiographical poem of Wordsworth acts as both a physical and metaphoric journey allowing for leadership learning that generates a profound sense of purpose and vocation to everyday leadership practice.

Finally, in Chapter 17 Steve Kempster, Eric Guthey and Mary Uhl-Bien highlight the use of an approach called leadership development as collaboratory. This approach seeks to engage leaders in addressing societal challenges. It draws on the notion of design science to organise leadership influence in tackling current world leadership issues. A series of case study vignettes are offered; for example, working with the Danish Red Cross and the engagement of major businesses in supporting social integration of refugees. We have positioned this chapter last as it opens up discussion on the research possibilities for leadership development, to help stimulate debate on linking leadership development with leadership research – a form of research and development (R&D) of the leadership field.

The great variety of creative approaches contained within this volume will hopefully provide insight, reflection and creativity for advancing the field of leadership development. It has been the collective endeavour of all contributors that a focus on leadership practice can be enhanced through stimulating reflection on the lived experience of leadership – the raw material that has shaped how we learn to lead. Without enabling those who lead to obtain a rich reflective access to the building blocks of practice, they are captured by their pasts to repeat historic orientations without a realisation of such reoccurrence. Practices of leading are difficult to recognise by the owner, yet the impact is profoundly recognised by all those they seek to lead. It is a cruel asymmetry – those leading being so unaware of what they do every day, but yet having such detailed insights to offer. If we were speaking of sport, for instance, it is common for the practice to be observed and detailed feedback offered, usually by a recognised 'expert'. In a sense it is what is developed through deliberate practice – as Scott Allen, Arthur Schwartz and Daniel Jenkins (Chapter 3, this volume) so wonderfully articulate. It would be developed on the 'practice field'.

What then are the 'practice fields' of leadership? How can Allen et al.'s argument for deliberate practice be undertaken within everyday organisational leadership? What is palpably clear is that leadership practice needs attention, and as such has to become highly salient to those who lead. The leadership development industry has this task as its central purpose. The related question must surely be: how can we enable those who lead to practise leading in the same way as they might rehearse to become better at, for example, playing a musical instrument? There is the notion that 10,000 hours of practice creates a master (Ericsson et al., 1993). Yet so few managers can describe in any detail how they practise to become better at leading. How can a manager expect to be able to effectively lead others if they do not set about practising? Drawing on a golf analogy, the professional golfer practises for a few hours, going through a deliberate practice drill, before hitting the first ball off the tee. The amateur turns up at the last minute, grabs a driver, swings it around a few times and hopes to be able to hit this straight down the fairway. The outcome is, usually, notwithstanding an occasional lucky connection, a wasted round of golf as the ball has been hit off the fairway. In the same way, why should managers be able to deliver a commanding speech – one that raises the confidence and levels of motivation in their team to come together to move collectively towards a desired outcome – by simply standing up and speaking? The leaderful moment, like the tee shot, has been wasted. For much of the rest of the day the negative repercussions flow as a result of the lack of preparation. Reflection is (or needs to become) a significant aspect of a manager's everyday practice. An important step is learning how to practise reflection and, in the spirit of deliberate practice, becoming better and better at reflection.

In this way the book is but a start in this direction. The variety of approaches outlined herein are perhaps opening up principles and approaches that might migrate to an organisational practice field. We hope that colleagues engaging in leadership development may greatly enhance this first step towards developing leadership practice fields.

NOTE

1. This term 'planks and barrels' is a catch-all phrase that is in common use in and around outdoor learning and refers to the many exercises and approaches that are physical in nature. These exercises might include moorland walking, building rope bridges or solving challenges through the use of unfamiliar equipment in the outdoors. Frequently, such organised exercises are followed by reflective sessions and/or theoretical classroom exercises and are part of an overall approach to learning.

REFERENCES

Argyris, C. and D. Schon (1978), *Organisational Learning: A Theory of Action Perspective*, Reading, MA: Addison-Wesley.

Barnes, S., S. Kempster and S. Smith (2015), *Leading Small Business: Business Growth Through Leadership Development*, Cheltenham: Edward Elgar.

Bateson, G. (1973), *Steps to an Ecology of Mind*, New York: Ballantine Books.

Belling, R., K. James and D. Ladkin (2004), 'Back to the workplace: how organisations can improve their support for management learning and development', *Journal of Management Development*, 23(4), 234–55.

Bergsteiner, H. and G.C. Avery (2014), 'The twin-cycle experiential learning model: reconceptualising Kolb's theory', *Studies in Continuing Education*, 36(3), 257–74.

Burgoyne, J.G. and V.E. Hodgson (1983), 'Natural learning and managerial action: a phenomenological study in the field setting', *Journal of Management Studies*, 20(3), 387–99.

Cunliffe, A.L. and M. Eriksen (2011), 'Relational leadership', *Human Relations*, 64(11), 1425–49.

Day, D. (2001), 'Leadership development in the context of on-going work', *Leadership Quarterly*, 11(4), 581–613.

Edwards, G.P., C. Elliott, M. Iszatt-White and D. Schedlitzki (2013) 'Critical and alternative approaches to leadership learning and development', *Management Learning*, 44(1), 3–10.

Edwards, G.P., C. Elliot, M. Iszatt-White and D. Schedlitzki (2015), 'Using creative techniques in leadership learning and development: an introduction', *Advances in Developing Human Resources*, 17(3), 279–88.

Ericsson, K.A., R.T. Krampe and C. Tesch-Romer (1993) 'The role of deliberate practice in the acquisition of expert performance', *Psychological Review*, 100, 363–406.

Goffman, E. (1969), *The Presentation of Self in Everyday Life*, London: Penguin Press.

Kempster, S. (2009), *How Managers have Learnt to Lead: Exploring the Development of Leadership Practice*, Basingstoke: Palgrave Macmillan.

Kolb, D.A. (1984), *Experiential Learning*, Englewood Cliffs, NJ: Prentice Hall.

McCauley, C., R.S. Moxley and E. Van Elsor (1998), *Handbook of Leadership Development*, San Francisco: Jossey-Bass.

Mezirow, J. (1981), 'A critical theory of adult learning and education', *Adult Education*, 32(1), 3–24.

Mezirow, J. (1985), 'A critical theory of self-directed learning', in S. Brookfield (ed.), *Self Directed Learnings: From Theory to Practice*, San Francisco: Jossey-Bass, pp.17–30.

Peters, T. and R. Waterman (1982), *In Search of Excellence*, New York: Harper & Row.

Reynolds, M. (1998) 'Reflections and critical reflections in management learning', *Management Learning*, 29(2), 183–200.

Uhl-Bien, M. (2006), 'Relational leadership theory: exploring social processes of leadership and organizing', *The Leadership Quarterly*, 17, 654–76.

PART I

Relational-based approaches

2. A practice-based approach to developing ethically responsible leaders

Donna Ladkin

PURPOSE

The purpose of a practice-based approach to developing ethical leaders is that it focuses on actions rather than individuals' intentions or personality traits. In this way it provides those aiming to develop ethical leaders with pragmatic possibilities for fostering ways of being in the world, which are aligned with ethical astuteness such as moral perception, the ability to reflect on the larger system, and the capacity to live with uncertainty. Most importantly, this approach suggests that ethical capabilities can be developed 'offline' rather than in the midst of ethical dilemmas and thus promotes a key role that developers can play in achieving ethically responsible leadership.

DEFINITIONS AND CONTEXTUALIZATION

What is Meant by 'Ethics'?

In the context of this chapter, the practice of ethics is seen to encompass the means by which social relationships are regulated such that an individual's wants, needs, aspirations and rights are balanced against those of another (Clement, 1996). In this way, ethics are conceptualized as essentially relationally based.[1]

A number of different frameworks exist that aim to guide behaviour in regulating these relationships. Deontological, or principle-based approaches (such as the 10 Commandments), provide rules that those aspiring to act ethically can follow. Utilitarian, or consequentialist, approaches take into account the ends towards which certain actions lead, and the extent to which others are harmed, or enjoy pleasure from certain acts.

Virtue-based approaches ask the question, 'what would a virtuous person do in this situation?' in order to find the best way forward in ethically questionable situations. Care-based approaches consider the relational aspects of a situation, and work to maintain caring relations between those affected by judgements and choices.

The practice-based approach offered here is informed by the understanding that action, rather than intention, plays a central role in the determination of ethical outcomes. Furthermore, ethics are seen to be embedded in certain habits and practices, rather than being a separate domain of activity. In particular, one's habits of perception, way of relating to others and manner of decision taking lead to outcomes that can be judged as ethical or not, even if one's intentions are indeed to act ethically (Ladkin, 2015). As so vividly demonstrated by Dennis Gioia's work into Ford's decision to continue to manufacture Pinto cars without life-saving equipment – even after it was determined that rear-end collisions could be fatal due to a design fault – the way in which situations are framed and interpreted plays a critical role in exercising ethical judgement (Gioia, 1992).

The Inherent Ethical Challenges of Leading Ethically

Leaders face particular challenges when attempting to exercise their role ethically. They owe followers moral consideration to treat them well and not to lead them, literally or metaphorically, over cliff edges. Additionally, their position often places them at the intersection of their organization and the wider community. Consequently, the leader's ethical responsibility should extend beyond 'what is good for their organization' to broader society as well. Difficulties can often arise as leaders attempt to balance the needs of these differing stakeholder groups. Indeed it is often impossible for leaders to provide equal ethical consideration to all of those affected by their decisions.

Additionally, leaders often have to make judgements of an ethical nature with imperfect knowledge. When former prime minister of the UK Tony Blair decided to join the USA in invading Iraq because of the suspicion that the country was harbouring 'weapons of mass destruction', his decision was supported by incomplete data. Leaders often have to make difficult decisions based on limited knowledge, and in this way the conditions through which they are forced to make ethically charged decisions are imperfect. This can be exacerbated if the power asymmetries inherent to their role mean that followers withhold information that could be helpful in making key decisions.

Finally it is virtually impossible for leaders to know whether decisions they take will be judged unequivocally as ethically correct or not. More than 70 years after the dropping of the atomic bomb in Japan, the question of whether or not Harry Truman acted 'ethically' in detonating the bomb is still debated. Although utilitarian approaches may suggest that the number of lives saved by dropping the bomb far outweighed those lost in the attack, principle-based approaches might suggest that unleashing military force on civilians in the way it occurred in that attack is never acceptable. This example vividly demonstrates the extent to which leaders' decisions are often indeterminate in terms of their ethical correctness.

These three aspects – the difficulties associated with balancing the needs of the organization and those of the larger community, the impossibility of having access to perfect information, and the indeterminate nature of ethical decisions – make the question of how to lead ethically a tricky one! The next section considers how others have tackled the challenge of developing leaders capable of responding to these challenges.

UNDERPINNING RESEARCH

Developing Ethical Capabilities

There is a relatively small body of research devoted to how developing ethical leaders might best be approached. Even within the broader field of business ethics, there are few conclusions about how managers can best be prepared for the ethical dilemmas they will face. One of the most cited models of ethical behaviour used within the business ethics literature is that of James Rest (1986), who suggests four stages of ethical decision making: moral sensitivity, moral judgement, moral intention and moral behaviour. In order to answer the question of how these capacities might be developed, there is a trend in the literature towards attending to single stages of Rest's model. For instance, Werhane (1998, 2002), Moberg and Seabright (2000) and Hargrave (2009) explore ways of developing moral perception (aligned with moral sensitivity in Rest's formulation) whereas Comer and Vega (2011) and Christensen et al. (2007) focus on the means by which moral courage (aligned with Rest's notion of 'moral intent') might be fostered.

Perhaps the literature that most applies to the development of ethical leaders relates to the notion of authentic leadership. As theorized by Avolio et al. (2004), 'internalized moral perspective' is one of the four components of authentic leadership (along with self-awareness, relational transparency and balanced processing). Although the extent to which an internalized moral perspective should be a constituent of authentic leadership has been questioned (Ladkin and Taylor, 2010; Eilam-Shamir and

Shamir, 2015), for the purposes of this chapter it is interesting to consider the way that authentic leadership theorizing suggests such a capacity might be developed. Those authors dwelling with ways of developing 'authentic' leaders focus heavily on reflective activities, with Sparrowe (2005) proposing a narrative approach in which leaders recall and reflect on the story that has brought them to leading, and Shamir and Eilam (2005) contributing a similar approach. All of these authors stress the importance of leaders tracing the way in which they have resolved conflicting demands and the contradictions that occur between their espoused and enacted values as a way of bringing criticality to their moral behaviours.

Pedagogical Approaches

Along with considering how particular ethical capacities might be developed, there are a range of pedagogical approaches that are proposed to enable ethical responses to organizational issues. Hartman (2006) and Falkenberg and Woiceshyn (2007) promote case studies as means of developing ethical character, whereas Abowitz (2007) and Koehn (2014) propose the use of arts-based methods as a novel means of enhancing students' reflexivity (that is, their capacity to notice the way in which their own perspective inherently contains bias, which influences their way of perceiving) and to increase their capacity to perceive situations from an ethical perspective. It must be noted that there are few empirical-based evaluations of the effectiveness (or not) of such pedagogical interventions. However, of the empirical studies that do exist, the great majority investigate student populations who have not actually faced the type of ethical dilemmas that leaders of organizations, or even leaders of workgroups, face. In this regard the direct applicability of these studies to those in leading roles is questionable.

Towards a Practice-Based Approach to Developing Ethical Leaders

For the most part, those cited previously conceive of ethics as the application of certain rules, and propose that identifying the prevailing 'rule' and applying it to oneself achieves ethical leadership. An alternative rendering highlights the role that context plays in ethical enactment. Rules are still important, but the way one applies the rule is more sensitive to contextual demands (Cummings, 2000; Loacker and Muhr, 2009). It is this appreciation of the role context plays in ethical engagement that leads to a 'practice-based' approach.

The practice-based approach has its roots in post-structuralist accounts of ethics, as conceptualized most notably by the French philosopher

Michel Foucault. For Foucault, the 'ethical self' is 'continually constituted within power–knowledge relations' (Foucault, 1997). From this perspective, ethics is always a 'personal choice' (note: not free choice!), which lies in 'specific acts of responding to norms and rules according to singular demands' (Loacker and Muhr, 2009, p.265). Key to acting ethically from this practice-based understanding are a range of 'self' practices: self-reflection, self-examination or self-aesthetics, and decipherment of the self (Cummings, 2000, p.212).

This approach sees the cultivation of the 'self' as crucial to ethical engagement. This is a kind of cultivation, however, which goes beyond common understandings of 'self-awareness'. Instead, active critical interrogation of the self seeks to uncover blind spots, to question assumptions and to extend one's boundaries of perception. As well as developing such critical self-reflexivity, this approach demands interrogation of the system in which one is situated and the underlying power dynamics that hold in place certain ways of relating to others (Crane et al., 2008).

In order to work effectively from this perspective there are certain 'habits of the self' that can be cultivated. It is these habits of the self that are introduced here as a means of developing leaders who can cope well with the ethically grey areas their roles demand. The remainder of the chapter describes a module taught at one of the UK's leading business schools in a practice-based approach, offering it as a first step in the development of an intervention grounded in a practice-based understanding of ethical engagement.

DESIGN

What follows is a summary of the key design aspects of an MBA elective taught at Cranfield School of Management in the UK, which was underpinned by a practice view of ethical development.[2] Taught over a six-week term, the module introduced participants to a range of practical activities aimed at helping them to develop habits of perception, inquiry and systems awareness, which they could practise as part of their day-to-day lives in order to develop their 'ethical muscles'. A key message at the module's heart was that almost every situation leaders find themselves in has an ethical component. Acting ethically requires active sensitivity to those aspects in their nascent form rather than waiting for them to blow up into full-scale ethical problems.

Five key design features of the course are described below: building bridges, extending perception, fostering negative capability, developing inquiry and reflexivity, and creating an immersive form of assessment.

Although this programme was delivered to MBA students, the design elements would be equally applicable to other populations of executives and organizational leaders.

Building Bridges

A practice-based approach to developing ethical astuteness is not common. Faced with the issue of 'ethics', most people think of 'compliance'; that is the need to abide by an organization's code of conduct or a profession's rules of practice. The kinds of ethical issues leaders face, however, can seldom be through reference to such guidelines and codes. They often rely on judgements that lie in a grey area of competing values between different stakeholder groups. For instance, what is more 'ethically sound' – sourcing wood for a UK-based construction firm from an African community that depends on sales for its livelihood, or a more local community that does not involve the same level of carbon footprint? The first step in establishing the importance of the module was to find ways of connecting this way of thinking about ethics with participants' experiences.

Two approaches to building bridges between participants' often black-and-white understanding of ethics and this more nuanced understanding were employed. First, one of the school's leading finance professors opened the module by showing how accounts could be created and interpreted very differently, depending on the story you wanted to tell. She very carefully took the students through ways in which they were normally taught to read and balance accounts, and then considered alternatives. The point was made that the accounts is a creative endeavour in terms of how items are listed (for instance: is training considered a cost or an investment? How should a shareholder dividend be decided? How do you decide how much to pay senior executives?) Every choice tells a different story and offers different ethical issues. Whereas participants often begin the module by thinking that the distinction between what is ethical and what is not ethical is clear-cut, this session begins to demonstrate the ambiguity at the heart of financial reporting. Participants began to be sensitized to the possibility of more than one way of reading a situation, and that different interpretations and choices have different ethical implications.

A second means of bridge building was to invite a well-known leader to share his own ethical choices and issues along the journey of his career. The individual chosen was a respected member of the academic community, and he spoke about early career decisions that began to lead him down a questionable path. This 'true confessions' session indicated how easy it is for individuals to find themselves in moral slippage. His story showed the way in which one small decision, which doesn't seem so bad, can lead to another one, which doesn't seem so bad, which leads to another, until one finds oneself in a situation that is decidedly ethically incorrect. Many course participants considered this talk alone to be the most powerful aspect of the module. It alerted them to the fact that, if this highly respected individual could have found himself in ethically question-able situations – it could happen to them as well.

Having established the relevance of thinking of ethics 'beyond compli-ance', the stage was set for the next design element, expanding perception.

Expanding Perception

The second key design element of the course was to open students' perceptions to the myriad possibilities for both seeing and interpreting interpersonal and organizational events. I wanted to bring home the idea that ethics start with the way in which we perceive the world around us and our place in it. Two key means for fostering this understanding were employed: art and mythology.

Looking at art and talking with others about what one sees is a powerful way of demonstrating the range of perceptions and interpretations avail-able to any situation. An art historian joined the class to take us through a 'crash course' in perceiving art: through the exploration of a range of artworks (both fine art, but also dance and opera) he vividly demonstrated the depth to which particular instances can be analysed. Inviting discus-sion about the range of interpretations in the room served to emphasize the extent to which perception is fluid and is heavily influenced by one's own background, position and even mood!

A second means by which perception was expanded was through working with mythology and other forms of resonant stories. These are the type of stories that invite those hearing them to ask questions of themselves: when faced with the issue of fighting one's cousins, as in the Krishna tale, for instance, how does one know what is right? Participants were encouraged to view the film *The Scent of a Woman* (1992), in which the protagonist is presented with a range of ethical decisions. Such stories pose the meta-level question of 'how do I make a decision of this type?', rather than providing pat answers. These activities served to open up the ethical territory, to indicate that there is always more than one way of viewing a situation. Faced with a new appreciation of the complexity involved, participants needed to have some sense of a way forward, and the paradoxical response was helping them to foster the capacity to sit with the complexity, as represented in the concept of 'negative capability'.

Developing Negative Capability

One of the counter-intuitive capabilities that the course was designed to foster includes negative capability, that ability to wait, rather than jump to conclusions or answers. This notion is encompassed in John Keats's words: 'the ability to live with uncertainty and not knowing and to do so without grasping after action, without irritability' (Keats, 1970, p.43). Negative capability contradicts the notion that action – and indeed swift action – is central to effective leadership. Applying this capacity to the organizational context, British management scholars Peter Simpson, Robert French and Charles Harvey conceive of it as 'reflective non-action' (Simpson et al., 2002). Rather than doing 'nothing', acting from this orientation involves stepping back, weighing up opposing possibilities, actively inquiring and sometimes just waiting to see what will happen next before launching into action mode. This capacity is vital in handling ethically difficult issues well.

The module introduced 'really listening' as an activity aimed at developing negative capability. 'Really' listening, rather than 'active' listening, involves two individuals speaking with one another, with one person listening and the other speaking. The listener just listens, rather than asking probing questions or responding with empathetic body language, as one is encouraged to do when 'active' listening. He or she doesn't say anything, and is also encouraged to keep their face in a neutral position. Because the listener is not tasked with showing that he or she is listening, they can, actually, listen. Participants often report a sense of calmness when engaged in these listening encounters. Often the speaker finds that they say much more than they intend to say; through not being directed in any particular way they are able to open up in ways they might not have imagined. This experience can foster an appreciation for the power of not doing or reacting, but just being, in a way aligned with the notion of negative capability.

Of course when taking the leader role, there are times when coming to a judgement quickly is important, but circumstances may occur much less frequently than is imagined. Even when taking action is important, the nature of that action can be nuanced through being based in inquiry and reflexivity, as described in the next section.

Encouraging Inquiry and Reflexivity

Being able to ask good questions concerning the situation at hand is a vital ethical capability. 'Good' questions have two important qualities. First, they aim to open up the territory in question rather than to close it down. Such questions attempt to elicit as much diversity of opinion and affect as possible. This is counter to habits of leading aimed at achieving agreement and consensus. Instead, such questions invite people to contribute their unique perspectives of a given situation.

A second important aspect of 'good' questions is that they seek to reveal the underlying, often unspoken, assumptions that underpin views and perceptions about a situation. An appreciation that the way a situation is framed can have important consequences for the way it is viewed from an ethical perspective is critical. For instance, asking why people consider a way forward as essential, and the extent to which alternatives have been articulated, can reveal biases that overlook ethically questionable issues.

The way in which questions are asked plays a large role in how much information they evoke. We have all been asked questions in a way that indicates the answer being sought. Eliciting truthful responses can be particularly difficult when power differences are in play; few people want to tell the boss that something he or she is committed to doing is problematic. Cultivating trusting relationships with followers is essential in order to glean the range of perceptions and understandings that are essential to understanding the diversity of effects of certain decisions.

Finally, it is essential that leaders spread their range of inquiry as far as possible. Increasingly the importance of leaders understanding the breadth of impact of their decisions from an ethical standpoint is apparent through corporate social responsibility agendas and calls for 'responsible' leadership. Unless there is a broad view of how that responsible leading operates, however, there can be missed opportunities for real impact. For instance, one participant from the course spoke of how he now realized that the publicity he generated about the way in which his organization was being 'responsible' in the community could have been better spent on more donations and material support for the community, and made a commitment to changing his own practice as a result of this insight.

As well as inquiring with a broad range of others who might be affected by decisions, self-inquiry in the form of reflexivity is also critical. Within this course of study, participants kept reflective journals to chart the way in which their thinking about ethics changed, as well as any actions they took to engage differently with ethical territory. These journals were read by course tutors, who through their feedback encouraged participants to engage in deeper levels of self-questioning and criticality.

It is important to note that this kind of reflexivity goes beyond notions of self-awareness. Knowing that one has certain habits and predilections is perhaps a starting point for ethical astuteness. However, extending one's ethical capabilities requires actively interrogating one's actions and motives and constantly seeking better ways of balancing the needs of others with those of the self.

Immersive Assessment Activities

A final distinctive design element of this module concerns the type of assessment activities used. It was important to see the assessments for this module as themselves opportunities for learning, rather than merely testing participants' knowledge. The assessments were 'immersive' in that they encouraged participants to engage emotionally as well as intellectually.

There were two elements of the assessment process: the reflective journal mentioned earlier and a group project in which participants worked together to focus on a particular ethical issue of their choice, analyse it, apply techniques from the course to it and present their deliberations to the rest of the group.

One of the most powerful forms of presentation incorporated role plays, in which students took different parts within an ethically challenging scenario. In the most effective of these role plays, the larger student group was invited to make a decision about the ethical choice to be made, based on a cursory summary of the situation. The presenters then acted out the viewpoint of each person involved in the particular case, providing a more elaborate back story for their actions, as well as their perceptions of the larger situation. Those watching were asked to re-evaluate their choice on the basis of the further information. The significant number of those who changed their views served as stark evidence of the importance of gaining a deeper perspective concerning individuals involved in ethical dilemmas.

In particular, those watching learned that their first 'gut reaction' was perhaps limited in its response. By waiting and questioning more deeply their own and others' assumptions they were able to arrive at ways forward that they had not considered previously. This approach helped them to be more self-critical in analysing their own prejudices and assumptions, and through that criticality to search for more robustly informed responses.

The second form of assessment was an individually based learning journal, through which participants reflected on an ethical issue they had faced in the workplace, or were currently facing in the workplace, and applied ideas introduced during the module to find ways of resolving. It was interesting to see how participants' framing and assessment – both of the issue they were facing and the possible responses to it – shifted over the course of the module. Comments such as, 'I never thought of this situation from this perspective before' were common.

REFLECTIONS

A practice-based approach to developing ethical astuteness is not without its challenges. For instance, this approach does not provide a set of 'answers' to 'common ethical dilemmas'. Instead it offers a *process* of engagement that relies on sensitivity to the emerging dynamics of a situation and how it is being construed. This orientation itself is in opposition to prevailing business-school cultures in which answers and recipes are valued. Indeed, much current business ethics literature seems to assume that it is possible to find 'answers' to ethical issues, or that being ethical within the leader role is merely a question of doing what is 'right', without questioning the difficulty associated with figuring out what 'right' is.

A second difficulty in this approach is its challenge to assumptions about how ethical dilemmas arise. Dilemmas are rarely neatly packaged as 'ethical', especially early on. The case of British MPs overstepping their expenses allowances, which arose during the summer of 2008, serves as a helpful case in point. Whereas media accounts represented the scandal as an issue of 'unethical' MPs swindling the British public, closer inspection reveals a range of motivations and issues behind MPs' actions, including an assumption that in return for not receiving pay rises their expenses would be considered generously. The seed of what was later labelled as 'unethical' was planted many years earlier, in a decision that was viewed as inconsequential at the time. This is often the case, and leaders must be alert to the ethical dimensions of practices as they unfold.

Implications for Leadership and Leader Development

Perhaps the most important implication for this understanding of how ethical leaders can be developed is that, from this perspective, 'ethics' is not seen as an 'add on' but rather at the heart of all interactions between leaders, their followers and the wider community in which they are situated. This approach fosters an appreciation that all human interactions have ethical components to them, and that these components can unfold as situations and contexts change.

This orientation is radical in that it argues for inquiry as a crucial and ongoing leader activity: inquiring into how others are perceiving a situation, how they are affected by decisions, as well as how situations are changing. Seeking information that contests one's views, rather than bolsters them, would be part of this inquiring orientation. Consider how differently Tony Blair would be judged had he robustly interrogated available intelligence about weapons of mass destruction, rather than using it (rather uncritically) to support his own stance. From this perspective, he would have actively sought critique and robust discussion with those of alternative views before taking such a significant and damaging decision. It is interesting, for instance, to contrast Blair's response to that of President John Kennedy during the Cuban Missile Crisis, in which Kennedy waited and actively sought more information, rather than hastily moving into armed combat.

The practice-based orientation also limits the role of 'personal values' in ethical engagement. Certainly, the motivation to 'do the right thing' is a starting point. However, one's own values and perspective must be subject to critique and inquiry in the same way that one would evaluate another's, in order to hope to find 'the best' balancing point between them.

Finally, leaders working from a practice-based appreciation of ethics would understand the ability to respond ethically as an ongoing and continual process of development. Growing in one's capacity to respond ethically is a constant 'work in progress', a commitment to generosity of heart, which itself is a fundamental aspect of leading well.

KEY TIPS

In creating leadership development interventions based in a practice-based view of ethics, the chapter ends by offering the following key tips:

- Begin by establishing the difference between a practice-based perspective and a compliance-based perspective to ethical engagement. Remember that the compliance-based perspective is often the starting point for the way ethics is conceptualized, so it is important to make this distinction clear.
- Finding ways of showing that acting unethically can happen to 'anyone' is also important. Often people come to 'ethics' programmes with the notion that acting unethically could never happen to them. Indicating the way that habits of perception are critical in the recognition of ethical aspects to situations is a critical aspect of fostering such understanding.
- Engage a range of other professionals (such as colleagues from finance, marketing) and practitioners to contribute their perspectives and open up debate.
- Model the ability to actively inquire, to work with uncertainty and indeterminacy and to be self-reflective. Participants learn from the way their course leaders behave, and engage with them and issues as they arise.

ACKNOWLEDGEMENTS

This chapter is largely based on an elective taught at Cranfield School of Management from 2010–12. I would like to thank my co-tutors: Ruth Bender, Paul Hughes, Andy Logan, Leo Murray and Claus Springborg for their contribution to that elective and therefore to the thinking upon which this chapter is based.

NOTES

1. Here, I am primarily concerned with human-to-human relationships, but it is important to allow the possibility that ethical regard can also be extended to other creatures, as well as to the natural world itself.
2. The elective upon which these design ideas are drawn is elaborated in the text *Mastering the Ethical Dimension of Organizations*, written by myself and published by Edward Elgar in 2015.

REFERENCES

Abowitz, K.K. (2007), 'Moral perception through aesthetics: engaging imaginations in educational ethics', *Journal of Teacher Education*, **58**(4), 287–98.

Avolio, B.J., F. Luthans and F.O. Walumbwa (2004), *Authentic Leadership: Theory-building for Veritable Sustained Performance*, Lincoln: Gallup Institute.

Christensen, D., J. Barnes and D. Rees (2007), 'Developing resolve to have moral courage: a field comparison of teaching methods', *Journal of Business Ethics Education*, **4**, 79–96.

Clement, G. (1996), *Care, Autonomy and Justice: Feminism and the Ethic of Care*, Boulder, CO: Westview.

Comer, D.R. and G. Vega (2011), *Moral Courage in Organizations: Doing the Right Thing at Work*, Armok, N.Y.: M.E. Sharpe.

Crane, A., D. Knights and K. Starkey (2008), 'The conditions of our freedom: Foucault, organization, and ethics', *Business Ethics Quarterly*, **18**(3), 299–320.

Cummings, S. (2000), 'Resurfacing an aesthetics of existence as an alternative to business ethics', in S. Linstead and H. Höpfl (eds), *The Aesthetics of Organization*, London: Sage, pp.212–27.

Eilam-Shamir, G. and B. Shamir (2015) 'Life stories, personal ambitions and authenticity: can leaders be authentic without pursuing their "higher good"?', in D. Ladkin and C. Spiller (eds), *Authentic Leadership: Clashes, Convergences and Coalescences*, Cheltenham: Edward Elgar, pp.93–119.

Falkenberg, L. and J. Woiceshyn (2007), 'Enhancing business ethics: using cases to teach moral reasoning', *Journal of Business Ethics*, **79**(3), 213–17.

Foucault, M. (1997), *Ethics*, ed. P. Rabinow, London: Penguin.

Gioia, D.A. (1992), 'Pinto fires and personal ethics : a script analysis of missed opportunities', *Journal of Business Ethics*, **11**(5), 379–89.

Hargrave, T.J. (2009), 'Moral imagination, collective action and the achievement of moral outcomes', *Business Ethics Quarterly*, **19**(1), 87–104.

Hartman, E.M. (2006), 'Can we teach character? An Aristotelian answer', *Academy of Management Learning & Education*, **5**(1), 68–81.

Keats, J. (1970), *The Letters of John Keats: A Selection*, ed. R. Gittings, Oxford: Oxford University Press.

Koehn, D. (2014), 'Ethical darkness made visible: Michael Moore's Roger and Me', in D. Koehn and D. Elm (eds), *Aesthetics and Business Ethics*, Dordrecht: Springer, pp.83–101.

Ladkin, D. (2015), *Mastering the Ethical Dimension of Organizations*, Cheltenham: Edward Elgar.

Ladkin, D. and S.S. Taylor (2010), 'Enacting the "true self": towards a theory of embodied authentic leadership', *The Leadership Quarterly*, **21**(1), 64–74.

Loacker, B. and S.L. Muhr (2009), 'How can I become a responsible subject? Towards a practice-based ethics of responsiveness', *Journal of Business Ethics*, **90**(2), 265–77.

Moberg, D.J. and M.A. Seabright (2000), 'The development of moral imagination', *Business Ethics Quarterly*, **10**(4), 845–84.

Rest, J. (1986), *Moral Development: Advances in Research and Theory*, New York: Praeger.

Shamir, B. and G. Eilam (2005), '"What's your story?" A life-stories approach to authentic leadership development', *Leadership Quarterly*, **16**(3), 395–417.

Simpson, P.F., R. French and C.E. Harvey (2002), 'Leadership and negative capability', *Human Relations*, **55**(10), 1209–26.

Sparrowe, R.T. (2005), 'Authentic leadership and the narrative self', *Leadership Quarterly*, **16**(3), 419–39.

Werhane, P.H. (1998), 'Moral imagination and the search for ethical decision-making in management', *Business Ethics Quarterly*, 75–98.

Werhane, P.H. (2002), 'Moral imagination and systems thinking', *Journal of Business*, **38**(1/2), 33–42.

3. Collegiate leadership competition: an opportunity for deliberate practice on the road to expertise

Scott J. Allen, Arthur J. Schwartz and Daniel M. Jenkins

PURPOSE

The purpose of collegiate leadership competition (CLC) is to create a practice field for leadership learning and education by incorporating the fundamentals of deliberate practice as a theoretical base. Our work is grounded in two assumptions. First, that students engaging in deliberate practice (Ericsson et al., 1993; Ericsson and Pool, 2016) will greatly accelerate their learning, both in and out of the classroom. A second assumption is that students like to compete, and competition can serve as another high-impact educational practice (Kuh, 2008). These two fundamental assumptions set apart CLC from other leadership learning opportunities.

In addition to a focus on deliberate practice, CLC uses the KNOW, SEE, PLAN, DO model of development (Allen et al., 2014):

- KNOW: obtaining declarative knowledge of terms, concepts, facts and theories.
- SEE: identifying and recognizing the concepts in others or the environment.
- PLAN: integrating existing knowledge to develop a plan of action.
- DO: intervening skillfully when carrying out the plan of action (p. 30).

Intentional and deliberate opportunities for reflection throughout help individuals make sense of their experience and develop schemas (as in mental representations) that aid in their future work (Schwandt, 2005; Ericsson and Pool, 2016).

EXPERTISE AND DELIBERATE PRACTICE

What Separates an Expert From a Novice?

> "Leadership development is therefore closer conceptually to what it takes to become an expert rather than acquiring a particular skill."
> Day et al. (2009)

The theoretical foundation of our work is heavily rooted in the expertise literature that has focused in two primary areas – what separates an expert from a novice, and *how* expertise is trained or developed. While Ericsson et al. (1993) identify many dimensions that separate an expert from a novice (for example, motivation to learn/energy, location relative to resources and coaching, available time, parental/institutional support), we focus on four primary differences, as set out below.

First, the expert will *know* more about the domain than others (Bransford et al., 2000; Sternberg, 1995). There is a great deal of declarative knowledge on the topic – information, facts, theory, history and so forth. Many would suggest that declarative knowledge must be present before "higher order" learning can occur (Bloom, 1985; Kraiger et al., 1993). Combined with experience and practice, the knowledge and behaviors required of a leader become more procedural, which aids in speed and automaticity (Ericsson and Pool, 2016; Glaser and Chi, 1998; Day et al., 2009).

A second difference between experts and novices is their ability to see patterns and chunks of information while engaging in an activity (Merriam and Cafarella, 1999; Glaser and Chi, 1998). To the untrained eye, these stimuli may appear random or confusing (Ericsson and Pool, 2016). Experts have the ability to rely upon their knowledge and experience to draw upon mental models (or mental representations) that help them to understand better the problem or challenge (Mumford et al., 2009). For instance, Clarke and Mackaness (2001) found in their exploratory study that senior professionals relied more heavily than younger professionals on experience and previous outcomes. Such mental representations "make it possible to process large amounts of information quickly [. . .] one could define a mental representation as a conceptual structure designed to sidestep the usual restrictions that short-term memory places on mental processing" (Ericsson and Pool, 2016, p.61).

A third difference is that experts often have superior planning skills (Ericsson et al., 2007; Mumford et al., 2009). Because of their knowledge and diagnostic abilities, they often spend more time defining the problem and scenario planning different options (Glaser and Chi, 1998; Simon, 1973). Thus, "declarative knowledge becomes proceduralized through practice and experience" and "knowledge about situations, responses, and outcomes is integrated in ways that provide context-specific rules for application" (Day et al., 2009, pp.177–8). When faced with ill-structured (Voss and Post, 1998) or adaptive challenges (Heifetz and Linsky, 2002) the planning process becomes a critical ingredient for success or failure.

Finally, expertise yields concrete results (Ericsson et al., 2007). Experts not only bring forth better decision-making processes than novices, they yield better results on a consistent basis (Johnson, 1988).

How is Expertise Developed?

> "Not all practice makes perfect. You need a particular kind of practice –
> *deliberate practice* – to develop expertise."
> Ericsson et al. (2007)

A natural question in the dialogue about what separates experts from novices is "*how* did they attain the highest levels of performance?" Some of the earliest work on the topic stemmed from the work of Bloom (1985) who, through a series of retrospective interviews with world-class performers, found that:

> Exceptional levels of talent development require certain types of environmental support, special experiences, excellent teaching, and appropriate motivational encouragement at each stage of development. No matter what the quality of initial gifts, each of the individuals studied went through many years of special development under the care of attentive parents and the tutelage and supervision of a remarkable series of teachers and coaches [. . .] All the talented individuals we interviewed invested considerable practice and training time, which rivaled the time devoted to school or any other activity. (p. 543)

Building on the work of Bloom, in 1993 Ericsson et al. (1993) concluded that it is *deliberate practice* that separates world-class performers from novices. The authors concluded that deliberate practice involves components such as motivation to learn, access to coaching and feedback, a structured curriculum, considerable time (upward of four to five hours each day), and engagement in activities outside of one's current ability level. In 2016, Ericsson and Pool published several criteria for an intervention to be considered deliberate practice. We highlight below the most essential components and after each item we provide a short comment that, based on our experience, highlights how traditional approaches to leadership development converge or diverge from the deliberate practice tenets described by Ericsson and his colleagues.

Deliberate Practice . . .

1. "requires a field that is already reasonably developed – that is, a field
    in which the best performers have attained a level of performance that
    clearly sets them apart from people who are just entering the field"
    (p. 98). Ericsson and Pool also emphasize the need for objective criteria
    upon which superior performers can be judged.

    Comment: While there are individuals who have attained "roles" at the
    highest levels of societal and organizational life, there are currently no
    widely agreed-upon "objective criteria for superior performance" or
    archetypes for leadership. Thus, it is challenging to set apart experts
    from novices.
2. "requires a teacher who can provide practice activities designed to help
    a student improve his or her performance [. . .] in particular, deliberate
    practice is informed and guided by the best performers' accomplish-
    ments and by an understanding of what these expert performers do to
    excel. Deliberate practice is purposeful practice that knows where it is
    going and how to get there" (p. 99).

    Comment: Because the field lacks a clear understanding of objective
    criteria, it is difficult to determine *who* the ideal models are when dis-
    cussing leadership. As a result, it is often difficult to define "where it is
    going, and how to get there."
3. "develops skills that other people have already figured out how to
    do and for which effective training techniques have been established"
    and has "teachers to provide beginners with the correct fundamental
    skills in order to minimize the chances that the student will have to
    relearn those fundamentals skills later when at a more advanced level"
    (p. 99).

    Comment: Consensus on a widely understood and agreed-upon set
    of skills has not yet been determined (Riggio, 2013). While a number
    of studies have identified themes of content (for example, decision
    making, emotional intelligence, communication skills, transforma-
    tional leadership), training techniques are underdeveloped and rarely
    result in expert levels of performance. Likewise, the "fundamentals"
    have not yet been outlined and agreed upon. Ask 30 theorists "where
    development is going, and how to get there" and one will likely get 30
    different answers.
4. Requires a practice regimen "that should be designed and overseen
    by a teacher or coach who is familiar with the abilities of expert
    performers and how those abilities can be best developed" (p. 99).

Comment: A practice field for leadership development does not exist. Most "practice" occurs in teams, groups, organizations and communities while an individual is engaged in the work. As a result, there is rarely an educated "teacher" to guide development and growth on a consistent basis.

5. "takes place outside one's comfort zone and requires a student to constantly try things that are just beyond his or her current abilities. Thus, it demands near-maximal effort, which is generally not enjoyable" (p. 99).

Comment: Without a clear picture of superior performance, a list of the subsequent skills, representative "ideal" performers, a practice field, and educated coaches to build skill, it is difficult to push individuals to work beyond their current abilities.

6. "involves well-defined, specific goals and often involves some aspect of the target performance; it is not aimed at some vague overall improvement. Once an overall goal has been set, a teacher or coach will develop a plan for making a series of small changes that will add up to the desired, larger change" (p. 99).

Comment: In addition to the items listed in the *Comment* to 5, above, leadership development rarely has a specific target for development and growth. Unlike swimming, diving, or track and field, it is difficult to objectively measure an individual's decision-making abilities or communication style. However, some organizations such as Toastmasters have attempted to do so.

7. "requires a person's full attention and conscious actions. It isn't enough to simply follow a teacher's or coach's directions. The student must concentrate on the specific goal for his or her practice activity so that adjustments can be made to control practice" (p. 99).

Comment: In the current context, rarely does an individual have the luxury of focusing solely on a specific goal or practice activity.

8. "involves feedback and modifications of efforts in response to that feedback. Early in the training process much of the feedback will come from the teacher or coach, who will monitor progress, point out problems, and way to address those problems" (p. 99).

Comment: Without a clear picture of superior performance, a list of the subsequent skills, representative "ideal" performers, a practice field, and educated coaches to build skill, it will be difficult to provide expert feedback on performance.

9. "both produces and depends on effective mental representations. Improving performance goes hand in hand with improving mental

representations; as one's performance improves, the representations become more detailed and effective, in turn making it possible to improve even more. Mental representations make it possible to monitor how one is doing, both in practice and in actual performance. They show the right way to do something and allow one to notice when doing something wrong and to correct it" (pp. 99–100).

Comment: Without a clear picture of superior performance, a list of the subsequent skills, representative "ideal" performers, a practice field, and educated coaches to build skill, it will be difficult to produce effective mental representations.

While some could view the current state as "bleak" we would suggest that the opportunity for exploration is an exhilarating proposition. Leadership educators have an opportunity to build and develop learning interventions that truly develop leadership capabilities across multiple dimensions (cognitive, behavioral, humanistic, constructivist).

COLLEGIATE LEADERSHIP COMPETITION

Some reading this text might wonder if it is even possible to develop expertise in an area as broad as leadership. Ericsson and Pool (2016) themselves suggest:

> [P]retty much anything in which there is little or no direct competition, such as gardening and other hobbies, for instance, and many of the jobs in today's workplace – business manager, teacher, electrician, engineer, consultant and so on. These are not areas where you're likely to find accumulated knowledge about deliberate practice, simply because there are no objective criteria for superior performance (p. 98).

The sentiments of Ericsson and Pool, along with the seemingly paltry alignment with their requirements for deliberate practice, leaves leadership development in an exciting place for exploration.

The CLC was founded to explore this underdeveloped space. In the most general sense, the CLC was founded to create a "practice field" and competitive outlet for leadership studies, training, education and development (Allen and Shehane, 2016). By doing so, we have been challenged to explore many of the required elements of deliberate practice mentioned in the previous section.

The CLC uses the KNOW, SEE, PLAN, DO (KSPD) model of development (Allen et al., 2014). Rooted in the expertise literature (for example, Ericsson and Pool, 2016; Glaser and Chi, 1998), KSPD proposes that learning and development occurs as learners: (1) acquire declarative knowledge about leadership; (2) use the knowledge to see or diagnose dynamics in the group or environment; (3) use knowledge and their diagnosis to plan a course of action, and, ultimately (4) skillfully intervene (Meissen, 2010) to achieve their objectives.

In addition, the CLC is committed to working toward the objective of providing students with an opportunity to engage in deliberate practice. While we have a long way to go, we would suggest that by creating the competition and a practice field for developing leadership we are on our way to identifying: a better picture of superior performance, a list of the subsequent skills, representative "ideal" performers, a practice field, and educated coaches who provide deliberate instruction. In addition to challenging students to work outside their comfort zone, we are allowing the time, repetition and real-time feedback necessary to (better) develop expertise.

An Overview

CLC, a non-profit organization founded in 2015, creates a dynamic practice field that stretches students and coaches to the boundaries of their knowledge, skills and abilities. CLC makes leadership a real, tangible experience for the next generation of corporate and organizational leaders. Headquartered in Ohio, USA, the CLC has one executive director and three board members who set the strategy and provide day-to-day resource development and organization. Currently, the CLC hosts four regional competitions (Great Lakes, Southern Ohio, Philadelphia, New England) of eight teams from various colleges and universities. An objective of the organization is to have an international presence by 2020.

Team Recruitment

Each fall, a team of six students at each college/university is recruited to participate. Coaches use a wide variety of techniques to recruit their teams. Representative techniques include: hand-picking excellent students; offering a "for credit" course; securing nominations from faculty; hosting tryouts; making an open call; and choosing students from intact groups on campus (for example, student clubs/organizations; student government). Coaches clearly outline the commitment and practice schedule for the winter/spring term (January–April each year).

Coach Development

At the time that a university agrees to participate, they also identify a faculty or staff member who is eager to "coach" their CLC team. Coaches are provided with opportunities for face-to-face training, one-on-one support and group phone calls. Coaches also provide support leading up to the competition as they work to prepare their team for the regional competition. CLC provides team coaches with all of the tools and resources to recruit teams, plan practice and prepare for the competition.

Team Development/Training

All teams are provided with the list of the CLC Terms & Concepts (roughly 85 unique concepts), which serve as the foundation for the competition. CLC does not endorse or prioritize any one set of theories (such as transformational leadership, servant leadership). The goal is to provide the students with an introduction to an integrated (Boyer, 1990) perspective on leadership. Practices are held on each college/university's respective campus from January through April. Over the four-month period, participants and coaches learn and practice leadership topics such as decision making, presentation skills, navigating stress, influencing others, leadership styles, followership and team dynamics.

For instance, one term, SOLVE, provides participants with a simple process for problem solving when faced with a challenge or task. As with the CLC Terms & Concepts, SOLVE becomes a focus of deliberate practice for participants. As with many other CLC Terms & Concepts, SOLVE is an integrative representation of multiple models from the decision-making literature (for example, Guo, 2008; Nutt, 1999; Hammond et al., 2002; Beyth-Marom et al., 1991). The term SOLVE and its corresponding set of concepts (items in bold) are described as follows:

> A core activity of leadership is problem solving. The SOLVE acronym provides a simple model to help the leader and team navigate the challenges ahead. First, it's critical to **Set roles** – who will lead? Who will keep time? What role will each person take in the activity? Next it's important to **Outline the problem**. This means that the group has a clear understanding of the task at hand. A hallmark of this stage is there are a number of questions as the group tries to truly understand what it's trying to accomplish. Once the group has a clear understanding of the task's parameters, it can begin **Listing strategies** for completion. Once multiple strategies have been listed, the group can **Veer toward consensus** and continue to **Evaluate results** even as they implement the chosen strategy. It's not rare that the group will need to readjust if the chosen approach is not working. It's important to note that this process does not need to take a great deal of time. A skilled leader will move the group quickly through the process and have an

acute awareness when the group (or certain members) has skipped a step or has not given a phase enough time and attention.

Another term, STYLES, is an integrated representation of several leadership styles outlined in the literature (Goleman, 2000; Vroom, 2000; Blanchard et al., 1985). As an example of how the CLC Terms & Concepts integrate with one another, a goal would be to help students practice being intentional and aware of their leadership STYLES while also moving through SOLVE when taking the team through a task or challenge. The hypothesis is that if we can help participants be more intentional (for example, using a simple problem-solving model *and* the appropriate leadership style(s) for the context) students will better perform when serving in formal and informal leadership roles. The term STYLES and its corresponding set of concepts (items in bold) are described as follows:

> There are six basic styles or approaches an individual can use when leading others. Each of these styles has benefits and drawbacks depending on the context. Skilled individuals will *intentionally choose* an appropriate style for the situation. The first style, ***Share your vision***, is an authoritative approach whereby the leader has the knowledge or a clear vision for how the group should proceed. The second style, ***Teach and coach***, requires the leader to convey their knowledge to the others on the team. This approach takes time, but builds capacity and depth among team members, which in the long run, will save time. The third style, ***Yell, tell, and the hard sell***, is a coercive style of leadership. An individual using this style, really wants *their* way and will do what it takes to ensure that the group complies with their directives. A leader who ***Listens and engages others***, is more democratic in their style. They are seeking the wisdom or knowledge of the group and building ownership in the path forward. At times leaders need to "raise the heat" and ***Energize and push*** their team to work above and beyond. This style is often associated with time constraints and high necessity for results. At times, leaders need to ***Simply delegate*** tasks and keep an eye on progress. By delegating tasks, leaders can build capacity in their teams, increase the shared workload, and accomplish more in less time. In the end, each style has benefits and drawbacks that will be important for a CLC team to explore.

Each of the 85 CLC Terms & Concepts are supported by a video of explanation, and a list of activities and support materials (such as activities, rubrics) for coaches. Curricular resources are delivered to coaches and students via the CLC Mobile App so all participants and coaches have access to the same information regarding content.

Weekly practices are a combination of team building, experiential activities/group challenges, reflection, discussions and planning. Each week the training session is designed to be challenging, fun and, most importantly, an opportunity for the students to reflect and recognize that they are developing new skills. In short, each practice should place students at the boundary of their knowledge, skills and abilities. In doing so, students and coaches work to understand the challenges they face, which include individual and team skill building, interdependence, synthesis, and the common goal/challenge of the competition.

Most teams practice about 90-120 minutes each week and there is a CLC rule that teams cannot practice for more than 45 hours between January and the date of the competition (April). The time limit is designed to provide a level playing field between the curricular (as in received course credit for participating) and co-curricular (as in did not receive course credit) teams.

A primary goal of the team development and education is building a level of *intentionality* in the students via the use of deliberate practice. For example, the goal is that students intentionally move through the problem-solving model (SOLVE), implement an appropriate leadership style (STYLE) and, in a general sense, skillfully intervene as they work to navigate the various challenges and puzzles. In other words, they engage in the KNOW, SEE, PLAN, DO process. For instance, while engaged in a challenge, a student uses his or her knowledge of potential leadership STYLES to diagnose the need, and identify an appropriate approach for the situation. Next, his or her goal is to behaviorally engage the team in a skillful manner (as in *Energize and push*).

Along with the formal learning, a goal of CLC is to build the team and energize students about the opportunity to represent their college or university. In addition, participants have mentioned that potential employers have been highly interested in learning more about their experience when interviewing for jobs and internships.

The Competition

Competitions and performances are high-impact educational experiences (see Kuh, 2008 – Collaborative Assignments and Projects). The competition weekend begins on a Friday evening with a dinner, speaker, and an opportunity for participants to mingle and build relationships. Friday evening also serves as an opportunity to set expectations and train judges who are independent reviewers assigned to monitor progress, validate results and ensure a fair process for all participants. The competition runs from 9 a.m. to 4 p.m. on a Saturday and, like the weekly practice, is a series of activities and group challenges. Coaches are not allowed to coach their teams during activities but have plenty of time to debrief with the group in between activities.

Competition Judging – What is Effective Leadership?

A major challenge we have worked to overcome is clarifying "effective leadership" for judging purposes. As per Ericsson and Pool's (2016) point, there needs to be objective criteria upon which superior performers can be judged. This brings forward an interesting conversation about the competition that we have struggled to reconcile – are we judging individual performances of "leaders" for each given task, or are we judging how the team performed? Or, are we simply recording a "winner" and assuming that the winning team's mastery of the CLC Terms & Concepts must have been superior? We have tested rubrics that focus on the individual leader, the team, and specific CLC Terms & Concepts. And while we have experimented with different tactics, we have yet to land on the approach that feels best. How we "judge" individuals and teams continues to be a puzzle that we will explore. We reflect upon this challenge in greater depth in the next section.

REFLECTIONS

Perhaps the most important reflection is the need to create a better picture of superior performance, a list of the subsequent skills, representative "ideal" performers and educated coaches to train participants. This is a ripe area for research and inquiry. Ultimately, our goal is to quantitatively and qualitatively improve performance. And while this endeavor is far from realized, our ultimate goal is to prepare men and women to lead with greater intentionality. In the coming year, we have an opportunity to identify some "best practices" in outstanding performers and begin to capture video and descriptive information on their process.

Following our most recent competition, the board and staff had time to review feedback and reflect on strengths and weaknesses of the competition. Several themes emerged as areas of focus for 2016–17. And while there is a great deal of energy and passion from coaches and participants alike, we know there is a great deal of learning and experimentation ahead:

1. *Competition judging* – the challenge around judging is threefold. First, there is a need to recruit independent and educated evaluators who can observe a team's process, ensure ethical behavior and validate results. In the first couple of years these roles were occupied by individuals from participating schools, and there is a clear need for an objective and for independent volunteers in order to ensure fairness.

Second, as mentioned, there needs to be clear and balanced judging criteria. In our first year, judges utilized a rubric that evaluated the team, the assigned leader (each student "leads" at least one activity on the day of the competition) and the results of the group's efforts. Upon completion of an activity, the judges collaborated with one another to agree upon a "winner." They also provided each team leader with written feedback. In our second year of competition, the criteria revolved around a "winner" – the team that implemented the best strategy to achieve results. In the end, both approaches had serious limitations – the first was not efficient and focused almost entirely on process, and the second focused too heavily on results. Our hunch is that results *along with* team and leader process are each important elements. We are still searching for a happy medium – judging criteria that prioritizes process and implementation of CLC Terms & Concepts *and* implementing the best strategy (results). Regardless, we have learned that clarity and fairness are *very* important to coaches and students alike – and rightfully so.

Third, we need to better train judges on the CLC Terms & Concepts, the judging criteria, their role as judges, the competition content/ activities, and potential challenges and pitfalls. This is a major area of focus that we will work to clarify in the coming year.

2. *Innovative/creative challenges* – there is a general sense among the team that we need to achieve a new level of innovation and creativity around the tasks and challenges presented to the students. Traditional team-building activities such as *egg drop* and *marshmallow challenge* have been overused. There is a need to incorporate technology and develop dozens of new and innovative challenges and puzzles for teams to work through in practice and in the competition.

3. *Managing emotions in coaches and participants* – while there were only six teams involved in the second year of competition, emotions ran high among the 36 participants. In fact, the experience was an emotional roller-coaster for many involved. We have an opportunity to better prepare participants and coaches for the highs and lows of the experience.

4. *Reflection/meaning making* – based on the previous reflection, we need to prioritize reflection and meaning making during the competition in a more intentional manner. In our first year, reflection during the competition was a major priority, but in year two, we placed more priority on "winning." As a result, during the competition, students became fixated on "winning" the challenge versus the learning. We need to ensure that participants and coaches alike have time to pause, connect their experience to the CLC Terms & Concepts, and make informed and intentional decisions about how to proceed.

5. *Ensuring ethical behavior* – in our second year of competition, organizers were somewhat taken aback at the accusations by students and coaches of unethical behavior in the other teams. As with many sports, in the heat of competition, some individuals and coaches worked at the edge of acceptable behavior and organizers were caught "flat-footed" as problems and issues arose throughout the day. Role clarity among judges and a clear process for dispelling such challenges is a key area for reflection and planning. Ethics *should* be everyone's responsibility – the coaches, students, CLC staff, judges – and the individual dynamics as well as those of the team leader and/or coach have an impact on the ethics of the team members. Conversations about sportsmanship and ethical behavior need to be highlighted before and after the competition.

6. *Coach development and training* – some areas of training and education have entire paradigms associated with *how* a coach approaches developing expertise (for example, in music there is Suzuki, Orff, Kodaly, Dalcroze). As the CLC matures and further develops its unique methodology (KNOW, SEE, PLAN, DO), we need to ensure that we adequately train and communicate our approach to coaches, participants and judges. It is likely this will be a combination of face-to-face, online and one-on-one coaching to ensure that new coaches are set up for success.

KEY TIPS

The activity of designing a leadership competition has been a challenging and rewarding experience. In many ways, the process challenges program architects to become clear on many of the attributes of deliberate practice outlined by Ericsson and Pool (2016). And while a great number of courses, training sessions and educational interventions propose to develop leadership in participants, few, if any, truly provide an opportunity for deliberate practice.

Perhaps the greatest tip we can provide is: if you choose to experiment with competitions as a way to develop leadership, be prepared to work at your edge. The work can be messy, confusing and ill-defined – much like the process of leadership itself! However, when students make comments such as – "I learned so much about myself!" or "I have never felt more challenged in my life but I learned a lot that will help me in life" – it makes it all worth it.

REFERENCES

Allen, S.J., R. Miguel and B.A. Martin (2014), "Know, see, plan, do: a model for curriculum design in leadership development," *SAM Advanced Management Journal*, **72**(2), 26–38.

Allen, S.J. and M.R. Shehane (2016), "Exploring the language of leadership learning and education," *New Directions for Student Leadership*, **2016**, 35-49.

Beyth-Marom, R., B. Fischhoff, M.J. Quadrel and L. Furby (1991), "Teaching decision making to adolescents: a critical review," in J. Baron and R.V. Brown (eds), *Teaching Decision Making to Adolescents*, Hillsdale, NJ: Erlbaum, pp.19–59.

Blanchard, K., P. Zigarmi and D. Zigmari (1985), *Leadership and the One-minute Manager*, New York, NY: Morrow.

Bloom, B.S. (ed.) (1985), *Developing Talent in Young People*, New York, NY: Ballantine Books.

Boyer, E. (1990), "Scholarship reconsidered: priorities of the professoriate" Eric Document Reproduction Service No. ED326149. Retrieved 5 May 2009 from ERIC database: http://eric.ed.gov/ERICWebPortal/custom/portlets/record Details/detailmini.jsp?_nfpb=true&_&ERICExtSearch_SearchValue_0=ED32 6149&ERICExtSearch_SearchType_0=no&accno=ED326149.

Bransford, J.D., A.L. Brown and R.R. Cocking (2000), *How People Learn: Brain, Mind, Experience, and School*, Washington, DC: National Academy Press.

Clarke, I. and W. Mackaness (2001), "Management 'intuition': an interpretative account of structure and content of decision schemas using cognitive maps," *Journal of Management Studies*, **38**(2), 147–72.

Day, D.V., M.M. Harrison and S.M. Halpin (2009), *An Integrative Approach to Leader Development: Connecting Adult Development, Identity, and Expertise*. New York, NY: Routledge.

Ericsson, K.A., R.T. Krampe and C. Tesch-Römer (1993), "The role of deliberate practice in the acquisition of expert performance," *Psychological Review*, **100**(3), 363–406.

Ericsson, K.A. and R. Pool (2016), *Peak: Secrets from the New Science of Success*, New York, NY: Houghton Mifflin Harcourt.

Ericsson, K.A., M.J. Prietula and E.T. Cokely (2007), "The making of an expert," *Harvard Business Review*, **85**, 114–21.

Glaser, R. and M.T.H. Chi (1998), "Overview," in R. Glaser, M.T.H. Chi and M.J. Farr (eds), *The Nature of Expertise*, Hillsdale, NJ: Lawrence Earlbaum Associates, pp.xv–xxvii.

Goleman, D. (2000), "Leadership that gets results," *Harvard Business Review*, March–April, 78–90.

Guo, K.L. (2008), "DECIDE: a decision-making model for more effective decision making by health care managers," *The Health Care Manager*, **27**(2), 118–27.

Hammond, J., R. Keeney and H. Raiffa (2002), *Smart Choices: A Practical Guide to Making Better Decisions*, New York, NY: Broadway Press.

Heifetz, R.A. and M. Linsky (2002), *Leadership on the Line*, Cambridge, MA: Harvard Business Press.

Johnson, E.J. (1988), "Expertise and decision under uncertainty: performance and process," *The Nature of Expertise*, 209–28.

Kraiger, K., J.K. Ford and E. Salas (1993), "Application of cognitive, skill-based, and affective theories of learning outcomes to new methods of training evaluation," *Journal of Applied Psychology*, **78**, 311–28.

Kuh, G. (2008), *High-impact Educational Practices: What They Are, Who Has Access to Them, and Why They Matter*, Washington, DC: Association of American Colleges and Universities.

Meissen, G. (2010), "Leadership lexicon," *The Journal of Kansas Civic Leadership Development*, **2**(1), 78–81.

Merriam, S.B. and R.S. Cafarella (1999), *Learning in Adulthood. A Comprehensive Guide*, 2nd edn, San Francisco, CA: Jossey-Bass.

Mumford, M.D., T.L. Friedrich, J.J. Caughron and A.L. Antes (2009), "Leadership research: traditions, developments, and current directions," *The Sage Handbook of Organizational Research Methods*, 111–27.

Nutt, P.C. (1999), "Surprising but true: half the decisions in organizations fail," *Academy of Management Executive*, **13**(4), 75–90.

Riggio, R.E. (2013), "Advancing the discipline of leadership studies," *Journal of Leadership Education*, **12**(3), 10–14.

Schwandt, D.R. (2005), "When managers become philosophers: integrating learning with sensemaking," *Academy of Management Learning & Education*, **4**, 176–92.

Simon, H.A. (1973), "The structure of ill-structured problems," *Artificial Intelligence*, **4**, 53–69.

Sternberg, R.A. (1995), "A prototype view of expert training," *Educational Researcher*, **24**(6), 9–17.

Voss, J.F. and T.A. Post (1998), "On the solving of ill-structured problems," in R. Glaser, M.T.H. Chi and M.J. Farr (eds), *The Nature of Expertise*, Hillsdale, NJ: Lawrence Earlbaum Associates, pp.261–85.

Vroom, V.H. (2000), "Leadership and the decision-making process," *Organizational Dynamics*, **28**(4), 82–94.

4. Going for gold: leadership development through a quasi-non-executive board in the SME context

Stewart Barnes, Sue Smith and Steve Kempster

BACKGROUND

It is becoming increasingly recognized that the leadership offered by the owner-manager is seen to have an impact on the performance of the business. The management and leadership capability is thus a key factor in small to medium-sized enterprise (SME) survival and growth (Barnes et al., 2015). With SMEs making up around 99 per cent of all businesses in the United Kingdom (Carter and Jones-Evans, 2006), harnessing and developing the potential of leaders of SMEs can have significant impact on the businesses, employees, communities and, more broadly, the socio-economic contexts. The challenge for the small business leader is whether to work 'in' the business, providing day-to-day management support or 'on' the business, providing strategic leadership, to enable growth (Barnes et al., 2015). Research shows that most owner-managers do the former, finding it difficult to remove themselves from the operational concerns in order to focus on longer-term strategy (Jones et al., 2007). It is well recognized that leadership development for SMEs, particularly for the owner-manager, is limited and this can constrain the potential development of the business (Kempster and Cope, 2010). Recent debates in the field of leadership learning assert that leadership development for SMEs can be achieved through social learning – that is, by, with and from other people (Barnes et al., 2015). Cope (2003) noted that owner-managers learn from experience 'on the job' and that practical learning takes place in reflecting on that experience, concluding that learning and reflective processes are inextricably linked. The GOLD programme was established to support the continued leadership development of owner-managers who had already begun to work on their leadership capabilities and it responds to the link between learning and reflection by engaging them with a network of like-minded peers from SMEs.

We focus here on one aspect within the programme, that of forming a non-executive board by making the participant owner-managers non-executive directors (NEDs). However, we emphasize that this is but one aspect of the programme. By foregrounding the NED process, we fall foul of a major flaw of leadership development programmes that we call marbles and a bird's nest. The learning from the NED process is an integrated aspect of the whole – twigs in the building of the nest. The flaw we consciously make here is to set about shining up our NED marble as a standalone thing of beauty. We return to this metaphor in our reflections.

The chapter begins with a description of NEDs and their relevance to SMEs. We follow this with detail on what the GOLD programme is bringing to life, with a rich description of a typical NED board in action. We then explore the learning processes within the NED board through the lens of communities of practice theory in order to offer a deeper understanding of how this structure affords leadership development for owner-managers of SMEs.

NEDS, LEADERSHIP DEVELOPMENT AND THE GOLD PROGRAMME

NEDs are a mandatory aspect of corporate governance and there are some indications of their value for smaller businesses (Berry and Perren, 2001). Studies of entrepreneurial networks reveal their importance, emphasizing that what occurs within networks is critical. SMEs are part of many networks. These may be formal such as Chambers of Commerce, membership to a professional body, business networking events, or informal such as friends, family and other businesses. The link between networks and entrepreneurship is not new, as many authors have recognized (see for example, Dubini and Aldrich, 1991; Jack et al., 2010; Jack 2010). Studies of networks focus on the benefit to business (Aldrich and Zimmer, 1986) and are often focused on larger organizations, inter-organizational networks (BarNir and Smith, 2002) and intra-organizational networks (Tsai, 2001). In relation to small businesses there is a general consensus about the benefit of business networks (Jack, 2005). NEDs are a specific type of potentially important network support for SME owners. The 1992 Cadbury report emphasized the benefits for all companies to utilize a NED. However, despite government encouragement for NEDs, smaller firms remain less likely to have NEDs. Interestingly, small businesses with a NED have been found to grow faster and to extract a market premium when sold (Barrow, 2001).

The GOLD programme was designed to explore and implement a

quasi-NED board among participating SME owner-managers. This is achieved by engaging them with a network of like-minded owner-managers allowing them to test the concept of having, and being, a non-executive director. Gordon (2013) outlines how the GOLD programme is constituted with non-competitive businesses that are formed into small groups, between four and six, and, through the establishment of trust, creates a supportive environment for tackling the issues faced by SMEs that often are not openly or easily discussed. Effectively, delegates act as simulated NEDs to one another. This simulation is about the role NEDs could take in the delegates' businesses, creating the benefit of a mentor and/or a critical friend who provides objective advice and asks deep, probing questions. The GOLD programme requires delegates to invest one day per month for a year to work on their business and the vision of where they want to be. The aim is both to challenge and support owner-managers as they focus on the survival, development and growth of their business, while being simultaneously mindful of the need to devote due attention to their own personal aspirations, motivations and growth. The NED board is a central element to the programme. It seeks to develop executive-director capabilities by preparing board packs, sales pipelines, dashboard indicators and budget-versus-actual reports and constructively critiquing the board papers of GOLD peers in their businesses through practising being a quasi-NED.

Long before the first NED board meeting begins there is a series of matters that must be attended to by the facilitator and, in turn, by delegates:

1. The first is axiomatic – recruitment of owner-managers onto the GOLD programme. This is not as easy as it sounds. Time pressures due to workloads, together with the commitment of a day a month for a year in the NED board, plus a few hours preparation each month in both creating their own strategic documents and reading their peers' papers, plus a further day a quarter spent in a strategic workshop all weigh heavy on potential participants' minds before making the decision to join GOLD.

2. When the quasi-NEDs have been recruited, the delegates complete a one-page budget-versus-actual (BvA) financial template in advance of the overnight experiential (OE) to present to their peers at the OE. This is the first time that the delegates will share financial information about their businesses to their peers, which is a big step for them and why trust is essential. It may be the first time ever that delegates have compared actual monthly performance to budget and to previous-year performance establishing a like-for-like. This is likely to mean that

they will need to involve their in-house financial manager or external accountant, thus requiring briefing skills. The BvA challenges their financial knowledge, appreciation of figures, understanding of trends, causes of variations. It may lead to a fear of exposure in front of others.

3. The two days and one evening at the OE are crucial for the facilitator to build bonds of trust between delegates, between delegates and the facilitator, plus for the facilitator to coach the delegates on how to construct a business plan (BP) and dashboard report (DBR) using the supplied templates and for them to be comfortable in presenting their BvA to each other, being questioned and for them acting as NEDs in questioning their peers' figures. Over the two days, delegates work on each facet of the BP and DBR so that the delegates are comfortable to complete them with their management teams back in their businesses before the first NED board meeting. Delegates have one month to complete and upload them to the online GOLD forum.

4. Delegates agree dates for the NED board meetings and the order of hosting and chairing – the host of meeting #2 chairs meeting #1 and so on. The facilitator coaches all delegates on how to use four specific NED board documents:

   a. board pack and issue that the host wishes to discuss;
   b. the agenda and how the chair constructs and agrees one with the host then shares it with the NEDs one week prior to the NED meeting;
   c. the 'minutes' template, which includes areas for NEDs to capture thoughts, ideas and observations of their visit to the host's business;
   d. the reflection log with its ten questions to be submitted by all after the board meeting.

5. The chair meets or speaks with the host, agreeing the agenda up to two weeks before the NED board meeting. The host shares the 'issue' the host wishes the NEDs to focus on during the morning of the NED board. The facilitator checks in with the chair and host that both are suitably prepared and comfortable in their board 'roles'.

6. No later than one week before the NED board meeting, the chair opens on the online GOLD forum an area for the forthcoming NED board meeting and uploads the agenda and confirms date, time and location. The host then uploads their board pack including BP, BvA and DBR. All NEDs upload their DBR. All participants then read each other's documents and come to the NED board meeting prepared

to discuss, critique, question, defend, support, advise and so on, as necessary. They will practise their strategic leadership and NED skills that over the next year will become their practice.

7.   In the month before the first NED board meeting, the facilitator liaises with each delegate on their progress, with the BP and DBR commenting on drafts as necessary. The facilitator is essentially building the delegates' self-confidence as they wrestle with the elements of the BP.

NED board meetings are facilitated by a facilitator with experience and knowledge of SME boards, balancing active observation with judicious interventions on points of process or to make an input to discussions. The facilitator also acts as secretary to the board and provides a full secretarial support function regarding meeting arrangements, and the facilitator makes research notes. Between meetings, the facilitator addresses emergent issues that are presented by board members (delegates). We give emphasis to the role of facilitation as an important aspect in our reflections. During board meetings, all board members seek to challenge the host of the meeting, whose issues dominate the agenda. They do this not as experts in the host's industry sector, but as outsiders to it. However, they each bring their own lifetime of workplace experience as well as their own owner-manager history. A given expectation is that, regardless of the host organization and the substantive agenda, every delegate brings both insights to the issues under discussion and takes away calls to action for their own situation. The act of explaining the intricacies of their business to a non-involved but interested third party can often lead to illuminating insights that enrich vision and direction of the business for owner-managers.

The above serves to illustrate the practicalities of how a board meeting takes place. However, it does not give detail to the rich learning processes that are ever present throughout. Reynolds and Trehan (2003) have argued that learning should always be understood as occurring within a social context. The NED as a board uses the social context of the board members' businesses as the premise for learning and is predicated upon the trust-based peer-to-peer learning environment where they act *as if* they were non-executive directors to each other's businesses. To give insight into the process, in Box 4.1 we outline the first day of a NED board through a rich description of observed activities made up of four NED board members, outlined in Table 4.1.

BOX 4.1   NED BOARD PRACTICE

It is the day of the first GOLD board meeting. Jane was host, Richard was chair as he was hosting next month's board meeting. Liz and Matt were present as NEDs only. They were all alumni from a previous leadership programme but only Jane and Richard were from the same cohort. All were looking to expand their network of contacts. David Chambers was the facilitator.

Not knowing what to expect, a very apprehensive Liz had spent a full day reading all the documents her peers had shared. With her own experience of marketing within her firm she could relate to Jane's business and to her 'issue' but had no experience of a company the size and complexity of Matt's or an understanding of a partnership, which was the organization Richard led.

Previously, as chief executive officer (CEO) with a minority shareholding, Jane had issues with her board and she had become overly emotional, conflicted and not dealing with the complex web of levers and barriers that were requiring her attention. Consequently, her self-confidence was once again being eroded. She was looking to her NED peers to give her the necessary support and direction.

They all arrived 20 minutes early as they were keen to catch up, swap stories and hear how each other's business trading was going.

Right on time, Richard opened the meeting and read out the disclaimer. Everyone acknowledged that this was not a meeting of the board of directors, that no one was acting as quasi-NEDs and that any action taken by the host was of their own free will. After a short tour of Jane's office, and having noted down observations, ideas and constructive comments, all were back in the boardroom probing Jane about her BP, BvA and DBR before exploring the issue she wanted her NEDs to assist with – how she could increase engagement within her own board and, in particular, the majority shareholders, who are husband and wife, both of whom work part-time.

Discussions quickly uncovered Jane's lack of confidence to take the lead in change. Initial questions centred around cold, rational, fiscal matters before exploring Jane's sense of guilt and obligation that were bound by the 'stories and myths' of the firm's past – a history she had played an active part creating during the last seven years.

Sensing this line of questioning was not assisting the host much, and drawing on his own experiences of leading the succession negotiations in his family business to a positive conclusion, Matt questioned Jane on how she could view matters from the perspective of her company's majority shareholders.

Jane admitted that she always felt slightly annoyed by an expectation that she should feel grateful and obliged to the majority shareholders, despite what she had contributed to the business. Matt immediately challenged this family/owner perspective, enquiring as to why Jane was not grateful. This stopped Jane in her tracks, who stared across the table at Matt.

'I have never thought about it like that, Matt; looking at it from the other's perspective. I need to go away and consider what you have said. Perhaps my empathy has limits, and the stories and myths as I experience them have coloured my judgement. Certainly, letting go of all the negative stories would allow me to "wipe the slate clean" and allow me to reconnect with my fellow shareholders.'

After lunch and after the NEDs feeding their observations and constructive comments via the chair back to the host, Richard opened the afternoon's part of the agenda where Jane acted as a NED helping to support the other three in exploring their DBR and whatever they want to discuss. Liz was first to speak and went through the financial summary, sales pipeline, sales and profit focus of her various divisions/outlets, key performance indicators (KPIs) and the tasks her team were focused on to improve what was featured within the DBR.

'What has been of most benefit', said Liz, 'is the fact my senior management team (SMT) have been involved in the creation of the DBR and the BP. We have many different measurements that we use in all parts of the business but we had never asked and thus not agreed what are the top five KPIs. The discussion that I already have had with my SMT has already been of immense benefit.'

'Not only are your KPIs impressive, Liz, I like how you have already measured your performance against target and shared your current status. If I may, I'll anonymize the learning and take it back to my business. My partners, or, in GOLD language, my board of directors, have been unable to agree KPIs so this will be a great incentive to see what is possible.'

'That's fine, Richard. As you know I have NEDs on my board but we do not have the tools of GOLD so my board meetings have questionable value. I am meeting the NED chair next week and I plan to show him the BP, BvA, DBR and the agenda as examples of good practice. I am keen to adopt these so that we can begin to have more effective board meetings!'

Table 4.1   Details of non-executive director board members and their companies

NED board member	Business activity	Turnover ($m)	Numbers employed
Jane	Marketing services	0.75	10
Matt	Second generation, family owned, property development and construction	21.75	70
Liz	Retail shops, online and events	6.5	59
Richard	Accountancy services partnership	3.5	42

UNDERSTANDING THE NED BOARD AS A COMMUNITY OF PRACTICE

Through the process of simulation of becoming NEDs to each other in this community, we show how GOLD enables the ongoing tacit learning and development of the leadership of owner-managers. The NED board develops as a peer learning community and theorizing it as a community of practice (CoP) helps us to understand some of the learning processes that lead to their leadership development. Much of the work on CoPs has historically focused on larger organizations and knowledge management (Brown and Duguid, 2001a, 2001b) but the concept has increasing relevance to the small business sector. Brown and Duguid (2001a) recognize that CoPs can give organizations an advantage over markets in dynamically coordinating the knowledge produced by them. This is directly applicable to the CoPs constructed in the NED board whereby the knowledge produced has a direct impact on the small businesses participating in them. Insofar as NED boards often develop into a co-mentoring network, they do so from a radically different starting point than traditional mentoring. Acting as a set of challenging–supporting mentors, they converge through self-choice; they share an extended period of intense shared experience; have established a set of formal and informal rules of operation; and are not conflicted by any form of employment or deployment contract.

A CoP involves organizing around some particular area of knowledge that gives members a sense of joint enterprise and identity (Lave and Wenger, 1991). Wenger (1998) presents three 'dimensions' that give coherence to a CoP: mutual engagement; joint enterprise; and shared repertoire. He argues that a CoP enters the experience of participants through their engagement with these three dimensions. Although he states: '[these] need not be the focus of explicit attention to create a context for the negotiation of meaning' (Wenger, 1998, p.84) they have continually been presented by other authors as the key components of a CoP and we present them as the key building blocks to establishing a NED board as a CoP.

The following is paraphrased from Wenger (1998, pp.73–85), demonstrated with examples of where this is present in the GOLD programme:

Mutual engagement Wenger describes mutual engagement as the source of coherence for the community's participants. Practice resides in a community of people and membership is a matter of mutual engagement, and the term is not a synonym for group, team or network. It is the mutual engagement of membership that defines the community, and whatever it takes to make mutual engagement possible is an essential component of any practice. In the NED board, the mutual engagement is the reciprocal process of sharing and trusting confidences with each as they share key business and financial information as well as disclosing issues at the highest level within their organizations. The board members come together to support one another for the benefit of their own leadership development and the business development of their organizations. The owner-managers use the lived experience from the NED board to improve their practice of being an executive director in their own company, their expectations of a NED if they choose to hire one at a point in the future or the enhancement of their own NED practice should they become a NED.

Before, during and after each NED board, members are encouraged by the facilitator, acting as an enabler (Kempster and Smith, 2014), to directly connect learning from the NED boards with the other elements of the programme, with themselves as well as to their business contexts. This layering of learning is akin to a bird building a nest, where each carefully selected twig is a chosen piece of learning from a GOLD element that is connected to another.

Joint enterprise   The joint enterprise of a community involves organizing around a particular area of knowledge and activity. This gives members a sense of joint enterprise and identity. The members are developing their knowledge of being a NED and developing their identity of strategic leadership within an activity that is the NED board. Members understand the joint enterprise well enough to contribute to and be held accountable for it. Members of the CoP align their engagement with the joint enterprise, becoming accountable to one another for each other's engagement. If mutual engagement is sustained over time in the pursuit of the joint enterprise, the CoP can be thought of as a practice or shared histories of learning. The joint enterprise is the facilitated process of conducting a NED board and participating within it. It is recognized that bringing any network into being involves developing structures that create mutual engagement and keep the joint enterprise in view. The practice-based learning enables them to use real situations and apply it to their respective companies. The accountability of learning from one another lies at the heart of the participative pedagogy. This binds the quasi-NEDs together within the joint enterprise. The NED board as a CoP provides the space and opportunity for the owner-managers to either provide advice or to ask open, insightful questions. For example, Matt had the knowledge and experience to proffer an opinion to Jane regarding dealing with majority shareholders, yet he used the power of open questions to let Jane consider an alternative position and come to her own conclusions. Within the NED board meetings, every month members learn how to run meetings, organize agendas, consider what to communicate and how to do it (joint enterprise and identity of a NED). Through practise and their lived experience, the role of chair becomes more salient. They review what emotions to display at any moment and how to control emotions as they explore what does and does not create responses. They observe, experience and deeply get to know more and more about each other and their businesses.

Shared repertoire   The shared repertoire is the set of resources that allow for the engagement of the practice of the CoP. For a CoP to function it needs to generate and appropriate a shared repertoire of ideas, commitments and memories. This includes routines, words, tools, stories and concepts that have become part of the community's practice. This shared repertoire contributes to the continual development and maintenance of the CoP. The shared repertoire is captured in the production of the 'board' documents. There is much emphasis on the shared repertoire of the NED board tools – board pack, dashboard report, BvA, agenda, hosting, chairing and quasi-NED role. This exposes taken-for-granted assumptions and guides members towards future action by using theories, ideas, tools and advice as prompts to the conversation. We argue that reflexive dialogue (Cunliffe, 2002) is part of the shared repertoire. The members deeply value the discussions through which they connect explicit and tacit knowledge as they reconstruct learning. This acts as a mechanism to enhance leadership development by making central this exploration of emergent leadership learning. In the rich description above, Liz and her SMT have learned to improve their company's KPIs and she is looking to connect this learning to improve her firm's own board reports to enable more effective board meetings. Within a month of being part of a NED board, Liz is changing her practice of strategic leadership and how she interacts with her own board.

Reflective judgement (King and Kitchener, 1994) is developed and honed before each board meeting, where all members reflect back on the previous month's business experiences and update DBR, BvA and BP as appropriate. Similarly, after each board the members complete a reflective learning log considering observations, learning points and what they will do differently next time, for example, reflection-for-action, an aspect that Schön (1983) does not consider. Members evidence the validity of their knowledge and how it is substantiated. In this sense, the NED board offers the owner-managers the time and space and a peer learning community to reflect on their experiences in what Gosling and Mintzberg (2006) describe as 'thoughtful classrooms', where they each learn to become a 'reflective NED'.

REFLECTIONS AND CONCLUSIONS

This chapter is an examination of the role of NEDs within a quasi-NED board and how the experience develops owner-managers through three key building blocks of mutual engagement, joint enterprise and shared repertoire in a CoP. The chapter aims to encourage SME owner-managers to consider becoming a NED as part of their own leadership development. However, this is not without its challenges. We have shown the importance of constructing a community of practice and the intricacies this entails in building and maintaining trust, open and reflexive dialogue, understanding that mutual engagement and joint enterprise is needed and that a shared repertoire will develop within the CoP. It is clear that the trust and openness that is required to enable learning and reflection to take place in the NED board is crucial and the construction and ongoing facilitation of the CoP is an essential ingredient. To create the trust and openness, the NED board involves developing structures that create mutual engagement and sustain a joint enterprise whilst nurturing a shared repertoire. The NED board develops delegates' reflexive praxis as owner-managers learning to become better strategic leaders, whether that is as executive board members within their business or, in time, non-executive directors of other companies.

Of importance within this CoP is the need for facilitators to have a strong grasp of the role and practice of NEDs. Facilitators should either have been a NED or become trained in being a NED so that they can act as an enabler (Kempster and Smith, 2014) to accelerate the leadership development of the members. As a quasi-NED, the facilitator role is a complex one, especially initially. As the enabling process commences, the facilitator has the choice of many hats to wear, depending on what is unfolding in the NED board. The facilitator acts as a coach on the completion and use of all board documents and on how to enact the various roles. The facilitator may be a mentor passing on relevant experiences, suggesting where action should be taken, or may act as a judge providing a definitive decision. The facilitator may draw from their lived experience and serve as a sage, a wise owl, or give counsel. The facilitator may judiciously intervene and act as a conductor to assist the chair and move a meeting along, or allow a point to be discussed in more depth. The facilitator may be a teacher sharing a tool, technique or process or reinforcing a point communicated on another part of GOLD. The facilitator may act as a leader and challenge the members. The facilitator should be socially aware and have empathy (Goleman et al., 2002) with the delegate's situation (SME environment) to guide and change roles as necessary. As well as actively listening and asking open questions, the members are looking in part to the facilitator for input as they seek to observe and learn from the experience (Bandura, 1986) of participating in the NED board to hasten the development of their strategic leadership practice.

Our final reflection is one of caution, and is against ourselves. We have been polishing our NED marble in front of you. Peter Checkland (1981) first coined the phrase marbles and bird's nest when examining a subsystem within a greater system – failing to see the emergent property of the whole integrated system. This is a risk and, in our experience, not an uncommon flaw present in leadership development programmes. Marbles represent a process within a programme – in our case the NED board. Marbles do not merge together; rather they stand alone, bashing into one another, and cannot generate an emergent whole, greater than the sum of its parts. The NED board's success in GOLD is as a consequence of how it is an inseparable part of the whole. We offer an example: Jane has taken learning from a GOLD workshop on culture web (Johnson and Scholes, 1999) that took place between the overnight experiential and the first NED board meeting. She has learned about the model (single-loop learning – Argyris and Schön, 1978) and applied that learning using the 'stories and myths' element of the culture web to make meaning of historical behaviours (double-loop learning – Argyris and Schön, 1978). Her thoughts were challenged by Matt and this led to a fundamental change in her assumptions of her behaviour towards the majority shareholders (triple-loop learning – Flood and Romm, 1996) which in turn leads to positive change and ultimately towards a more effective board. The importance of switching from a marbles design process to a bird's nest seems most significant and one that the facilitator must understand. Often looking at a single, perhaps ugly twig, we can fail to recognize the important part it plays on developing the emergent whole.

We have shown how a unique pedagogical approach of developing a CoP in the form of a simulated board of peers as simulated non-executive directors enhances leadership development. Underpinned with a participative pedagogy, reflective practice and accountability to the CoP, the NED board can have a remarkable impact on the lives of businesses of those participating. The NED board, as a CoP, begins to address the need for more NEDs in SMEs as executives are developed and gain practical experience of being NEDs in SMEs. We have been witness to the sustainability of NED boards with delegates from previous GOLD programmes self-sustaining their NED boards with owner-managers meeting regularly, both formally and socially, sharing progress. They are situating NED board practice within their own boards, engaging NEDs and becoming NEDs.

REFERENCES

Aldrich, H. and C. Zimmer (1986), 'Entrepreneurship through social networks', in D. Sexton and R. Smilor (eds), *The Art and Science of Entrepreneurship*, Cambridge, Mass: Ballinger, pp.3–23.

Argyris, C. and D.A. Schön (1978), *Organizational Learning: A Theory of Action Perspective*, Reading, Mass: Addison Wesley.

Bandura, A. (1986), *Social Foundations of Thought and Action: A Social Cognitive Theory*, Englewood Cliffs, New Jersey: Prentice-Hall.

Barnes, S., S. Kempster and S. Smith (2015), *LEADing Small Business: Business Growth through Leadership Development*, Cheltenham, UK and Northampton, MA: Edward Elgar Publishing.

BarNir, A. and K.A. Smith (2002), 'Interfirm alliances in the small business: the role of social networks', *Journal of Small Business Management*, **40**, 219–32.

Barrow, C. (2001), 'The role of non-executive directors in high tech SMEs', *Corporate Governance*, **1**, 34–6.

Berry, A. and L. Perren (2001), 'The role of non-executive directors in UK SMEs', *Journal of Small Business and Enterprise Development*, **8**(2), 159–73.

Brown, J.S. and P. Duguid (2001a), 'Knowledge organization: a social-practice perspective', *Organization Science*, **12**(2), 198–213.

Brown, J.S. and P. Duguid (2001b), 'Structure and spontaneity: knowledge and organization', in I. Nonaka and D. Teece (eds), *Managing Industrial Knowledge*, London: Sage, pp.44–67.

Cadbury, A. (1992), *The Committee on the Financial Aspects of Corporate Governance*, London: Gee Publishing.

Carter, S. and R. Jones-Evans (2006), *Enterprise and Small Business: Principles, Practice and Policy*, Harlow: Pearson Education Limited.

Checkland, P.B. (1981), *Systems Thinking, Systems Practice*, Chichester: John Wiley.

Cope, J. (2003), 'Entrepreneurial learning and critical reflection: discontinuous events for "higher level" learning', *Management Learning*, **34**(4), 429–50.

Cunliffe, A.L. (2002), 'Reflexive dialogical practice in management learning', *Management Learning*, **33**(1), 35–61.

Dubini, P. and H. Aldrich (1991), 'Personal and extended networks are central to the entrepreneurial process', *Journal of Business Venturing*, **6**, 305–13.

Flood, R.L. and N.R.A. Romm (1996), *Diversity Management: Triple Loop Learning*, Chichester: John Wiley.

Goleman, D., R. Boyatzis and A. McKee (2002), *The New Leaders: Transforming the Art of Leadership into the Science of Results*, London: Sphere.

Gordon, I. (2013), 'SME non-executive directors: having one and being one', *Industry and Higher Education*, **27**(6), 477–90.

Gosling, J. and H. Mintzberg (2006), 'Management education as if both matter', *Management Learning*, **37**(4), 419–28.

Jack, S.L. (2005), 'The role, use and activation of strong and weak network ties: a qualitative analysis', *Journal of Management Studies*, **42**, 1233–59.

Jack, S.L. (2010), 'Approaches to studying networks: implications and outcomes', *Journal of Business Venturing*, **25**(1), 120–37.

Jack, S.L., S. Moult, A. Anderson and S. Dodd (2010), 'An entrepreneurial network evolving: patterns of change', *International Small Business Journal*, **28**(4), 315–37.

Johnson, G. and K. Scholes (1999), *Exploring Corporate Strategy*, 5th edn, London: Prentice Hall.

Jones, O., A. MacPherson, R. Thorpe and A. Ghecham (2007), 'The evolution of business knowledge in SMEs: conceptualizing strategic space', *Strategic Change*, **16**(6), 281–94.

Kempster, S. and J. Cope (2010), 'Learning to lead in the entrepreneurial context', *International Journal of Entrepreneurial Behaviour and Research*, **16**(1), 6–35.

Kempster, S. and S. Smith (2014), 'Becoming a leader through becoming a delegate: leadership development as a community of practice through a situated curriculum', Lancaster University Working Papers Series.

King, P.M. and K.S. Kitchener (1994), *Developing Reflective Judgment: Understanding and Promoting Intellectual Growth and Critical Thinking in Adolescents and Adults*, San Francisco, CA: Jossey-Bass.

Lave, J. and E. Wenger (1991), *Situated Learning: Legitimate Peripheral Participation*, Cambridge: Cambridge University Press.

Reynolds, M. and K. Trehan (2003), 'Learning from difference?', *Management Learning*, **34**(2), 163–80.

Schön, D.A. (1983), *The Reflective Practitioner: How Professionals Think in Action*, New York: Basic Books.

Tsai, W. (2001), 'Knowledge transfer in intraorganizational networks: effects of network position and absorptive capacity on business unit innovation and performance', *The Academy of Management Journal*, **44**(5), 996–1004.

Wenger, E. (1998), *Communities of Practice: Learning, Meaning, and Identity*, Cambridge: Cambridge University Press.

PART II

Narrative-based approaches

5. Learning to lead: biographical inquiry through Goolsby interviews

**James Campbell Quick, Keri DeCay,
Navadha Modha and John L. Goolsby**

INTUITION AND SKILLED PERFORMANCE

Learning to lead is an intuitive, artful process involving practice, experience, failure and success. Leadership is a form of skilled performance in which learning from masters can be fruitful and informative. Learning to lead is not a natural scientific endeavor acquired from laboratory or field experimental research. In his seminal volume *Leadership*, Burns (1978) lamented the bifurcation of leadership and followership, seeing the two as intertwined. We could not agree more.

Nelson and Quick (2013) have viewed leadership and followership as essential companions since the early 1990s, recognizing that more research has been directed to the former. But for one to become a leader, one first must learn to be a follower. Many skills of effective followership are the same skills of effective leadership, such as communication, empathy and self-mastery. Leader development focuses on cultivating the potential within a specific leader. Leadership development concerns the broader organizational process of identifying, selecting and then developing many leaders.

The Goolsby Leadership Academy is engaged in both leader development and leadership development as well as follower and followership development. Goolsby Scholars are a very select cohort of about 30 students who study with and learn from executives and faculty. All three constituencies – students, executives, faculty – are essential to creating an opportunity for high-potential students to accelerate their development as leaders and followers.

Rather than studying theories and taking exams, one of the students' first challenges is to host a campus-wide event featuring a distinguished leader or professor with a leadership message. In previous years, these have included executives from Johnson & Johnson; general officers in a military branch; Mary Uhl-Bien from TCU's Neeley Leadership Program; Sean Hannah from West Point – United States Military Academy; and Caroline Keating from Colgate University. Goolsby Scholars expose the wider campus to different voices and points of view on leadership.

Two other early challenges are to complete The Leadership Battery® and conduct a two-person interview through which the students develop a biographical case. These Goolsby interviews are individually crafted opportunities for emergent leaders to learn through biographical inquiry by choosing role models who excite their imaginations. Wanting to know more about these individuals is a great impetus.

The biographical inquiry process parallels a self-assessment through which students come to better understand various aspects of their intrapersonal psychology. The Leadership Battery® is a set of psychological assessments designed to provide the developing leader with information about her or his intrapersonal psychological dimensions. Six instruments are used to assess these dimensions:

- Myers-Briggs Type Indicator (MBTI) (psychological preferences) (Jung, 1923);
- Fundamental Interpersonal Relations Orientation – Behavioral (FIRO-B) (interpersonal needs) (Schutz, 1958);
- Self-Reliance Inventory (SRI) (relational attachment styles) (Joplin et al., 1999);
- Emotional and Social Competence Inventory (ESCI) (emotional competence) (Boyatzis et al., 2000);
- Power Management Inventory (PMI) (use of power) (McClelland and Burnham, [1976] 2003);
- Multifactor Leadership Questionnaire (MLQ) (full range of leadership styles) (Avolio and Bass, 1991).

Knowing more about themselves enables the students to inquire about the interviewees' preferences, approaches to power, interpersonal relationships and leadership opportunities or challenges. Knowing more about oneself can leverage knowing others (Boyatzis and McKee, 2005).

Thus, leadership is more about people than things. Burns (1978) places leadership and followership squarely in the humanities, not the natural sciences. As a political scientist, he directed his attention to the study of great leaders in a range of public and civic domains. His studies were historic and biographical. The value of biographical inquiry is that the interviewer or biographer can gain insight into the complexity and conflicts that may be in either the leader or in the context that the leader faces.

Biographical inquiry is never quite clear and neat, as natural science might like to imply about leadership. Biographies record the dilemmas and messiness that often challenge leaders. From Burns's accumulated body of knowledge he developed a structured approach to moral leadership, one he considered foundational. In addition, one of his major contributions was the distinction between transforming leadership and transactional leadership. Leaders interacted with and influenced (exerted power with) followers in very different ways within the two frameworks.

Within Burns's framework, learning to lead draws on the study of leaders, and one avenue for studying leaders is through biographical inquiry. Biographical inquiry is rooted in the interview as a rich means of communication. For Kempster (2009), a key element in the learning process is the narrative of senior leaders. The narrative is in essence the story of the career, life and development of the successful leader. Hence, the follower, or the learner, must choose wisely which leaders from whom to learn.

Wise learners choose who to follow and who *not* to follow. Even poor leadership can be a good teacher for the wise follower, as we see in the case of John Goolsby further on, and similar with Anne Mulcahy's storytelling as chief executive officer (CEO) and chairperson of Xerox which was autobiographical as well as visionary, enabling her followers to understand her as well as her vision for the company. They could play constructive roles in the dramatic turnaround of this iconic brand (McDaniel and Mulcahy, 2016).

While John Goolsby had a vision for a leadership academy for undergraduate students at his alma mater, the task force charged with framing the academy sought input from nearly 30 executives and leaders. Conducting interviews with these men and women enabled the task force to explore the experienced thinking of leaders on their personal development, what experiences were important for them, and what content would be valuable to young men and women as they began their own leadership development.

Mack et al. (2011) found that the interpersonal dimension of leadership development was central. In addition, good leadership was seen to have a positive impact on the health and wellbeing of leaders and followers alike (Macik-Frey et al., 2009). A number of the executives interviewed, including John Goolsby, now share their own leadership journeys in an autobiographical format with the students.

AN AUTOBIOGRAPHICAL CASE: JOHN GOOLSBY

John Goolsby leads a seminar for Goolsby Scholars using an autobiographical history of his own development as a leader. While John had a strong educational foundation in accounting, he did not develop as a leader academically but rather through experience and the study of good (and bad) examples around him, with encouragement and feedback from mentors. John forged a signature brand of leadership that emphasized the central importance of ethics, character and personal integrity (Goolsby et al., 2010; Quick and Goolsby, 2013). As he shares his story with generations of Goolsby Scholars, new learning occurs for both the storyteller and the learner. Among the traits that Goolsby distilled from experience that define a strong leader are healthy self-confidence, strong character, uncompromising ethical standards, humility and vision, and the ability to identify and develop these strengths in others.

His development did not proceed from a guiding principle, nor were there life-changing events that defined it. One thing he instinctively realized early in his career was the importance of mentors. In retrospect, he understands how important the influence of strong, caring, principled mentors was in shaping him as a leader (Goolsby et al., 2010).

His first job offered great experience through an executive training program with a large international corporation. His second job was in a Big 8 firm, and that is where the importance of ethics became so clear. This firm knew the importance of ethics and strong mentoring, ensuring that every member of the firm shared its core values. Examples of ethical behavior abounded in this environment, embedded in the firm's culture.

His third job was in a company whose culture contrasted sharply with the Big 8 firm on the ethical dimension. The new company's culture condoned ethical gaps as long as the organizational unit was performing well financially. John learned great basics in his first job, the value of ethical standards in his second, and the problems with ethical lapses in his third. These formative experiences developed him to be ready for what became the opportunity of a lifetime.

John made his final career move to join Summa Corp., the principal company of the estate of Howard R. Hughes, who had recently died. The estate administrator was looking for someone he could trust completely and who had impeccable ethics and integrity. A person, who knew both the administrator and John, saw an excellent fit. After a grueling interview process, the administrator hired John as the estate's vice president of real estate. In the process of accepting the offer and moving to company headquarters in Las Vegas, John was careful in the way he left his business partner and former investors. Ethics and personal integrity had now become key principles in his development.

While initially overwhelmed, John quickly realized that his years of development had prepared him for the job. Certainly, the leadership and ethics lessons learned at several places along the way, as well as the diverse nature of businesses in which he had been involved and the individuals from whom he had learned so much, had all contributed to his feeling totally prepared for his new venture.

It would be hard to overstate the difficult position the estate administrator found himself in when John agreed to accept that appointment. Hughes had died without leaving a will and, unlike the myth of Howard Hughes, considered among the world's wealthiest individuals, many of the estate's operating companies were virtually insolvent at the time of his death. The administrator believed that proper use of the real estate assets was the future of the estate companies and the key to unlocking the considerable values that he believed existed.

The Hughes estate was finally resolved and value created from its assets, but one of the best lessons John learned was watching the administrator handle his responsibilities with the utmost integrity and in the fairest possible way, without regard to the absence of a will. The administrator demonstrated great skill in getting the disparate groups to support a plan to protect the estate from those he knew wanted a piece of it. Many claimed to be named in various false wills, while certain members of the management group sought opportunities for self-enrichment by aggrandizing their business units and themselves.

John and the estate administrator changed the entire culture of the organization over time. Estate companies were reorganized, underperforming assets and management were gradually weeded out. Liquidity issues required selling some non-strategic assets that were successful and for which a market existed – allowing their sale. Most of the remaining real-estate assets were prepared for development on a realistic timetable recognizing governmental market and financial force constraints. The administrator got the result he had always sought, which was to get the assets into a form that could be monetized so the individual heirs could make their own decisions about their interest in the estate.

The process took approximately 20 years after Hughes's death and culminated in merging the company (by now essentially a real-estate company, of which John was president and CEO for eight years) with another public company. John stayed on for several years to ensure a smooth transition. Because it was a tax-free transaction, those heirs who wanted to continue to own an interest in the real-estate assets could retain their shares in a public company while deferring the income taxes on their gains. Those who wanted to sell their stock could do so and pay the taxes. The resolution was good for the heirs as well as company employees, most of whom stayed with the acquiring company.

FACILITATING STUDENT LEARNING

John Goolsby's autobiographical presentation, along with those of other executives, is one platform for students to learn about leadership from a leader who has distilled wisdom from experience and, looking back, can see both failure and success. This process exposes students to the leader revealing his process and content while opening himself to questions. Students may wonder if John ever formally reported or complained to upper management about bad leaders. Or they may ask how the estate administrator and John changed the company culture. What specifically did they do? How did they do it? What were the effects on people in the company? Were people hurt? How did they ensure fair treatment of everyone? The learning experience does not end with the biography but with the questions that students pose.

BIOGRAPHICAL INQUIRY THROUGH INTERVIEWS

While autobiographical presentation is one way to learn from biographical inquiry, the interview is another means of building a biographical case while learning in the process. Joplin (1993) exemplifies nicely the use of the interview for biographical inquiry to learn about developing effective leadership from a member of a U.S. president's cabinet.

Henry Cisneros was secretary of housing and urban development during President Bill Clinton's first administration (1993–7). Joplin was curious about Cisneros's story, given his statement that mentors were not required to develop one's leadership skills and style. That brief comment in a public address prompted Joplin to seek out and better understand Cisneros. In the interview, Cisneros focused on the importance of studying history and biography, and choosing role models, which he distinguished from mentors.

George Marshall was one figure of import for Cisneros because of the former's life as a soldier, statesman and knightly gentleman. Brooks (2015) explores Marshall's road to character through the process of self-mastery. For Brooks, good character is at the heart of great leadership. Joplin (1993) also explored the positive impact that Elliott Richardson had on Cisneros during the latter's service as a White House fellow. From his days in the Texas A&M Corps of Cadets through a West Point conference and his service as a White House fellow, Cisneros crafted his own leadership narrative and style through biographical inquiry and the study of role models.

Students are encouraged to seek their own roles models. Brooks (2015) includes Frances Perkins, Dwight David Eisenhower and Dorothy Day, in addition to George Marshall, as studies in great leadership character. Florence Nightingale, who transformed public health and the use of statistics in addition to nursing, and Winston Churchill, who teamed with Franklin D. Roosevelt to defeat the tyranny of Adolph Hitler, and others provide exemplary models for study. Contemporary leaders such as Sheikh Hasina Wajed, the prime minister of Bangladesh, and Justin Trudeau, the prime minister of Canada, are aiming to transform the world with new thinking. Goolsby Scholars with roots in other countries are encouraged to consider leaders within their cultures, including Japan, Colombia, Vietnam, Mexico, China and Spain.

Rebecca Chopp, the first woman president of Colgate University, was instrumental in reinforcing John Goolsby's ethical leadership dimension (Quick et al., 2008, pp.13–14). A theologian by education, Chopp developed her leadership capacities first as provost of Emory University, where she took on a $1 billion budget. Rather than learn accounting, one of her wise executive advisers encouraged her to take a course in emotional intelligence. The learning was transformative. After resounding success at Colgate, Chopp went on to be president of Swarthmore for five years and is now chancellor of the University of Denver.

Goolsby interviews are based on this biographical method of inquiry with role models chosen by the students. Goolsby Scholars are challenged to seek interviews with accomplished leaders in a wide range of business and civic life. Examples:

- civic life: Judge L. Clifford Davis, pioneering civil rights litigator in Tarrant County, Texas; the mayors of Arlington (Dr. Robert Cluck), Fort Worth (Betsy Price) and Dallas (Mike Rawlings); and U.S. Congressman Joe Barton (R-TX);
- business: to include chief executives, chief financial officers, chief marketing officers and chief HR officers;
- the military: primarily senior and flag-ranked officers;
- education: a University of Texas System regent, a president of the University of Texas at Arlington, and David Gergen at Harvard's John F. Kennedy School of Government;
- sport and athletics: Jon Daniels, president and general manager of the Texas Rangers.

The backdrop for the interview is Roethlisberger and Dickson's (1939) nonintrusive interview method. Developed during the Hawthorne Studies, it is a more structured framework than the approach originally crafted.

GOOLSBY INTERVIEW PROTOCOL

The guidelines given to the Goolsby Scholars for conducting their interviews provide a structured protocol as a framework, but they are not to be followed rigidly or methodically. The protocol provided by the faculty provides guidelines for each student team to develop its own parameters and questions. The template with major domains of leadership to inquire into, with suggested questions, is a starting point.

The coaching guidance leading into the interview is to encourage the interviewee to tell his or her story. Executives have provided feedback to students and faculty over the years on select aspects of the content and the process of the interviews. Interviews are best when students practice the art of active and empathetic listening. Their first task is to understand, not to judge. The best interviews may well have the fewest questions. The interviews are more than information gathering, they are exercises in understanding the depth and range of the interviewee's leadership experience. The outline:

1. General background and leadership development:

   a. How did this leader get to her or his current position?
   b. How did the leader develop a personal leadership style?
   c. What critical events or relationships have shaped the leader?

2. Leader's leadership style:

   a. How would you describe this person's leadership style and personality based on course materials used as templates?
   b. Do you think they are transactional, transformational, autocratic, and so on?
   c. What is the leader's style of communication?

3. Leader's leadership perspective:

   a. Describe the leader's philosophy of leadership.
   b. Does he or she subscribe more to a born or a taught approach?

4. Critical skills of a leader:

   a. What does the leader consider to be her or his most important skills?
   b. Are there essential characteristics that leaders must possess?

5. Personal observations:

    a. Conclude the written report with your personal summary.
    b. Was the interview experience helpful . . . stressful . . . exciting?
    c. What takeaway lessons stimulated your own development?

INTERVIEW WITH DAN DIPERT

For two college undergraduate students to ask a well-known community leader and philanthropist to sit down for an interview can be daunting, provoking some anxiety. What if he says no? What if he is too busy? What if he does not believe in your capabilities because you are just a college student? These are among the performance concerns experienced in advance of a request for Dan Dipert, former CEO of Dipert Travel & Transportation, Ltd., to be interviewed about his journey to becoming a great leader and his reflections on what he has achieved.

Before choosing an interview subject, students must consider the range of possibilities and what it is they want to learn. They need to look inward to their own aspirations and identify a leader who will inspire them. For some, a leader who is well known is important, but someone whose story is not widely publicized may be equally meaningful. By emphasizing the latter, the one learning to lead can explore new information and engage in the deeper process of discovery.

Nikki met Mr. Dipert in late April 2015 at a community event at the University of Texas at Arlington. Mr. Dipert and his wife, Linda, founded the event, which was becoming a tradition at the university. As a first impression, he seemed to love to interact with students. He was friendly, welcoming and warm. Mrs. Dipert was inviting and gracious, and together they made the rounds, making sure they spoke with almost all of the students there and that everyone felt comfortable. Mr. Dipert gave every indication of being a strong, engaged leader who genuinely cares about the people around him.

Pre-interview Preparation

Before meeting with Mr. Dipert, the two-person team – Nikki and Keri – experienced some of the anxiety associated with performance events, especially theatrical. A great interview is both theater and art, and never routine. Mr. Dipert seemed inviting, but a leadership interview is much more than a social exchange. For the inexperienced college student inter-viewer, the key uncertainty is whether the outcome will be gain or loss.

Nikki requested the interview by email, and the electronic exchanges were positive. Mr. Dipert offered to meet anywhere they would like, which gave them significant discretionary latitude. They chose his office because of the professional nature of the setting and the respect shown to the interviewee about his space and stature. (An intriguing question might be the effects on the interview had the setting been different, even in a venue where Mr. Dipert's stature was unknown.) He also was open to when to meet, which showed his understanding of the demands on student time. This communicated his real interest in being interviewed and willingness to assist those seeking to learn about leadership.

Mr. Dipert and his wife have donated a generous amount to the university, and Nikki and Keri wanted to know why, especially since this is not his alma mater. And how did he start a travel company? What did he do to assure its success? Around Arlington, most of the tour/coach buses have the large "Dan Dipert" written across them, and Keri and Nikki were very intrigued by how this came about.

Interviewee's Background and Development

Biographical inquiry requires an appreciation of the interviewee's history and development. Keri and Nikki explored Dan Dipert's background to better appreciate his development. Mr. Dipert grew up in Arkansas and, he said, had a "tough childhood," perhaps compounded by a learning disability. He never felt like he was as good as the other kids and could tell he lacked in certain areas. But he learned to compensate by doing other things. He told us that he felt like a leader as he learned how to make up for those early losses. He never wanted to use them as excuses. He received some of his early teachings about leadership from his father, who was a World War II veteran.

Dan Dipert grew up in a small town where it was not easy to go unnoticed. The town watched his every move, and he knew everything would get back to his dad. This aspect of his childhood molded him to be able to lead in the public eye. He enrolled in the University of Arkansas and decided he wanted to be a minister. He transferred to a Baptist school in Arkansas and graduated there, then started working at a church in Little Rock as a youth minister. He was later called to the Dallas–Fort Worth area where he again worked as a youth minister.

At 32 years old, Mr. Dipert took over a small travel agency – not a promising profession in the 1970s, but he knew it was time for a change. After purchasing the agency, he branched into other businesses such as real estate and insurance. Soon he decided that he liked the travel business. He started to see major growth as older people were retiring and going on more vacations. He would market packages to groups of senior citizens and started seeing major success. A few years ago, Mr. Dipert sold his company to his daughter and son. Now his travel agency, Dan Dipert Travel & Transportation, Ltd., is owned within the family.

Mr. Dipert made it clear in the interview that he would not be where he is today if not for the risks he took to become a better leader. This was another key lesson from the interview. For example, he arranged a bank loan in the 1970s and was not sure if he would be able to pay it back. It took courage and confidence to be that daring during that time. His mind was set on becoming a strong entrepreneur and having a long-term goal. Without a doubt, Mr. Dipert's leadership skills developed as he became more familiar with his business and worked toward his long-term goals. After acquiring many small businesses and employing many people, Mr. Dipert was able to strengthen his relationships with his workers, thus further improving his leadership ability.

Keri's Personal Observations

When we sat down and started to talk to Mr. Dipert, I immediately felt at ease. I felt like I was not in front of a very successful chief executive officer and established entrepreneur. He was a very laid-back person. When he told us he had a background working as a youth minister, I began to understand why he was such an easygoing person around students. I was very inspired by his story.

I do not have a master plan, which is a source of some uncertainty and discomfort. Mr. Dipert helped me realize that just because I do not know exactly what I want to do in life does not mean that I will not be successful. Through his story, I could see a pathway to success even if it is not clear right now what that pathway is. He taught me that successful leaders are not always sure where they will end up, but they always focus on excelling and using their abilities in whatever they do.

Mr. Dipert taught me that it is good to take risks. If you never take risks, then you will never know the outcome. I also learned that your support team is vital in your growth as a leader. This reinforced the experience we had when we hosted Dr. Uhl-Bien as a Goolsby Distinguished Visiting Professor. All of us had to work together in teams, encouraging and challenging each other, and supporting each other's efforts. In Mr. Dipert's case, he credited a lot of his success to having his wife by his side.

Nikki's Personal Observations

During the interview Mr. Dipert showed up early and was very approachable. The environment of the interview was much more relaxed than I thought it would be. As the interview progressed, I began to notice several of his great traits as a leader. I was captivated by his story but also the content of his message. I will name a few traits that really stood out.

First, he was very focused on long-term goals. This led me to think about my own goals and inspired me to change. I decided to set a bar for myself to overcome every year. Mr. Dipert made it clear that as a student it is necessary that you understand what you eventually want your life to be. I need to be more mindful of that.

Another beautiful trait that I learned from my interview with Mr. Dipert: it is crucial that you understand your own strengths. This led me to consider the feedback that we were getting with the self-assessment exercises in class and the specific strengths that an assessment pointed out. For me, the MBTI pointed out my extroversion. But Mr. Dipert pointed out that, as a leader, you must know your weakness and breaking point. The self-assessment process in class helps me to understand better my own limits.

Without understanding your limitations, you are not an efficient leader because you have not experienced fear and failure. Mr. Dipert made it clear that a leader learns best from mistakes and that mistakes are usually ripple effects of one's weaknesses. Without really taking risks, a leader is not competent because there was no lesson learned to look back on and evaluate. From the interview, I really understood the power of taking risks and evaluating to become a better version of yourself. It is important that you be content with your leadership skills and believe in your strengths and understand your weaknesses.

REFLECTIONS ON CHOICE, CONTENT AND PROCESS

Choosing leaders to study and to interview is important. Goolsby Scholars spend time and energy reflecting on who would be good candidates from whom they can learn. Listening to themselves in the process of narrowing the choices is important. Intuition and the psychology of the interviewer are key elements in that process, just as other forms of biographical inquiry are key in leadership.

Choosing a subject to interview is a matter of reflection and response. Students are encouraged to consider their hopes, their interests, their dreams, and then scan their environments and beyond for those who excite their passions. A great interviewee for one person would not be a good interviewee for another. For the black man, choosing a judge who did pioneering civil rights litigation is an inspired choice for an interviewee. For the student interested in making a difference in the community, a powerful mayor can offer rich insights. For the business student with a desire for riches, a successful entrepreneur may be the best interviewee. Choosing the right interviewee is key.

Interviews can lead to breakthroughs and new insights. In exploring what stressed senior leaders and how they coped during the 1980s, a key discovery was made during the content analysis of the interview transcripts (Quick et al., 1987). The interviewers failed to find confirmation of preconceived notions about preventive stress management but stumbled on the central role of secure interpersonal relationships in adulthood in buffering life's stresses, for both men and women (Nelson et al., 1989). In addition, several inspiring stories of exceptional leadership during crises were uncovered and later explored (Cooper et al., 2006). Hence, biographical inquiry and well-executed interviews may lead to unpredictable outcomes and valuable insights.

Keri and Nikki shared some of their surprises during their interview with Dan Dipert, but first they prepared with a structure to develop content and a biographical profile. Developing the biographical content is essential in order to understand the person. However, once the loose structure for the interview is built, the interviewer needs to be open to the process. That is precisely what Keri and Nikki did. They were open, ready and available to hear the story the interviewee had to tell. They were prepared to be surprised and to be inspired in ways that neither anticipated.

A complementary aspect that biographical interviews offer for leadership learning is the profound new insights revealed for the interviewee. As interviewees tell their story and reflect on their own journeys, it is very possible that they, too, will have surprise insights that they have not thought about before telling the interviewer. When one executive was asked what it was like to grow up in a racially segregated society, it dawned on him that he had not really thought about that. His response was to simply tell the truth and talk about how, while segregated during the week, his friends met on a common field many Saturdays to play football with a team of black guys. He wondered why we all could not just do that – play together. Good biographical interviews open both the interviewer and the interviewee to new insights, new reflections and new learning.

KEY TIPS

- Seek out leaders to interview who inspire, interest and excite you.
- Be self-aware during the biographical process: what can you learn about you?

- Be prepared for your biographical inquiry, but be open for the unexpected.
- Trust yourself and your teammates as much as you trust the interviewee.

REFERENCES

Avolio, B.J. and B. Bass (1991), *The Full-Range of Leadership Development*, Binghamton, NY: Center for Leadership Studies.

Boyatzis, R.E., D. Goleman and K.S. Rhee (2000), "Clustering competence in emotional intelligence," in R. Bar-On and J.D.A. Parker (eds), *The Handbook of Emotional Intelligence*, San Francisco: Jossey-Bass.

Boyatzis, R.E. and A. McKee (2005), *Resonant Leadership*, Boston, MA: Harvard Business School Press.

Brooks, D. (2015), *The Road to Character*, New York: Random House.

Burns, J. Mac. (1978), *Leadership*, New York, NY: Harper & Row.

Cooper, C.L., J.C. Quick, J.D. Quick and J.H. Gavin (2006), "Strength of character: exceptional leadership in a crisis," in R. Burke and C.L. Cooper (eds), *Inspiring Leaders*, London: Routledge, Taylor & Francis, pp.272–95.

Goolsby, J.L., D.A. Mack and J.C. Quick (2010), "Winning by staying in bounds: good outcomes from positive ethics," *Organizational Dynamics*, **39**(3), 248–57.

Joplin, J.R. (1993), "Developing effective leadership: an interview with Henry Cisneros, Secretary, U.S. Department of Housing and Urban Development," *Academy of Management Executive*, **7**(2), 84–92.

Joplin, J.W., D.L. Nelson and J. Quick (1999), "Attachment behavior and health: relationships at work and home," *Journal of Organizational Behavior*, **20**(6), 783.

Jung, C.G. (1923), *Psychological Types*, New York: Harcourt and Brace.

Kempster, S. (2009), *How Managers Have Learnt to Lead: Exploring the Development of Leadership Practice*, Basingstoke: Palgrave Macmillan.

Macik-Frey, M., J.C. Quick, P. Shinoda, D.A. Mack, D.A. Gray, N. Keller and C.L. Cooper (2009), "Leadership from a positive health perspective," in A.M. Rossi, J.C. Quick and P.L. Perrewé (eds), *Stress and Quality of Working Life: The Positive and the Negative*, Greenwich, CT: Information Age, pp.95–121.

Mack, D.A., M. Macik-Frey, J.C. Quick, D.A. Gray, P. Shinoda, C.L. Cooper and N. Keller (2011), "Early interdependent attachments: the power of a secure base," in S.E. Murphy and R.J. Reichard (eds) *Early Development and Leadership: Building the Next Generation of Leaders*, New York and London: Routledge, pp.135–58.

McClelland, D.C. and D.H. Burnham ([1976] 2003), "Power is the great motivator," *Harvard Business Review*, January, 1–10 [Originally published in *Harvard Business Review* in 1976].

McDaniel, S.H. and A.M. Mulcahy (2016), "Leadership lessons through challenging times" (interactive session), Denver, CO: American Psychological Association, 5 August.

Nelson, D.L. and J.C. Quick (2013), "Leadership and followership," *Organizational Behavior: Science, the Real World, and You*, 8th edn, Macon, OH: South-Western/Cengage, pp.430–63.

Nelson, D.L., J.C. Quick and J.D. Quick (1989), "Corporate warfare: preventing combat stress and battle fatigue," *Organizational Dynamics*, **18**(1), 65–79.

Quick, J.C., C.L. Cooper, J.H. Gavin and J.D. Quick (2008), *Managing Executive Health: Personal and Corporate Strategies for Sustained Success*, Cambridge, UK: University of Cambridge Press.

Quick, J.C. and J.L. Goolsby (2013), "Integrity first: ethics for leaders and followers," *Organizational Dynamics*, **42**(1), 1–7.

Quick, J.C., D.L. Nelson and J.D. Quick (1987), "Successful executives: how independent?," *Academy of Management Executive*, **1**(2), 139–45.

Roethlisberger, F.J. and W.J. Dickson (1939), *Management and the Worker: An Account of a Research Program Conducted by the Western Electric Company, Hawthorne Works, Chicago*, Cambridge, MA: Harvard University Press.

Schutz, W.C. (1958), *FIRO: A Three Dimensional Theory of Interpersonal Behavior*, New York: Holt, Rinehart and Winston.

6. Leadership development using the poetic voice of care ethics

Andrew Armitage

PURPOSE

The use of poetry to explore the ethics of care in leadership development programmes is an approach that introduces participants to an alternative way of engaging with and exploring organizational issues, conflicts and decision-making processes. This approach is novel in several aspects. First, it uses an ethical perspective that is founded within relationships between people, both proximate and distant, something that is often overlooked in leadership development programmes. Second, it introduces the use of poetry to explore would-be leaders' relationships with other people, and how they operate and negotiate the 'ways of knowing' their roles. Third, it uses reflexive dialogic groups where would-be leaders can express themselves through the poetic voice within a 'safe place' to enable participants to gain a more 'connective sense' of self with their working environment and the everyday realities of their organizations.

UNDERPINNING RESEARCH

It can be argued that business ethics aims to determine the fundamental purpose and moral direction of an organization, being the rules or standards that govern organizational decisions. Business ethics can be equated with a sense of 'right' and 'wrong' articulated, for example, via a code of ethics conduct that governs an individual's behaviour, and that governs standards of organizational and professional conduct expected of employees. Sorrell (1998, p.15) has noted: 'Business ethics continues to have a marginal status in both the theory and the practice of a commercial organisation.' This has prompted some to suggest that there has been a lack of ethical organizational analysis (Stewart, 2007), and for Woodall and Douglas (2000, p.116) to note: 'Training and development activities are perhaps the area of HRD policy and practice that is least likely to come under ethical scrutiny, as they are invariably presented as intrinsically "good activities"'. As Friedman (1970) stated: 'the only entities who can have responsibilities are individuals [. . .] A business cannot have responsibilities. So the question is, do corporate executives, provided they stay within the law, have responsibilities in their business activities other than to make as much money for their stockholders as possible? And my answer to that is, no, they do not.' However, Peter Drucker (1981) advocated that the ultimate responsibility of company directors is not to harm, and businesses should adopt the principles of corporate social responsibility (CSR) where a business acts as a responsible citizen to the communities in which it operates, even at the cost of profits or other goals. Business ethics has traditionally followed the normative ethical theories of deontology or the more often called duty ethics, Utilitarianism, which is often characterized by consequential ethics, the ethics of justice and the ethics of character (please see Chapter 2 for a related discussion). However, Gilligan (1982) views these approaches as being set within a contractual ethical framework of rules and the regulation of behaviour that guides human relationships and behaviour, rather than being founded first and foremost within human relationships, which are self-determined and regulated as individuals grow together through emotional responses to their interactions. The foregoing has resonance with George (2000) who argues that leadership is an emotionally laden process entwined within socially constructed influences and process where the leader's mood can affect group and team dynamics, and where: 'Physical proximity between leaders and employees isn't always possible. But mental or emotional proximity is essential' (Groysberg and Slind, 2012, p.4).

Lipman-Blumen (2004) has explored the leader–follower relationship where the leader abuses their power to the detriment of those they are leading. She noted that a deep psychology is at play, suggesting that leaders need to feel safe and special in their community. Carson et al. (2007) claim that when individuals are given 'voice' this facilitates shared leadership by engendering a common direction and positive interpersonal support. When teams focus on a shared purpose, a greater sense of meaning and motivation for team members is given, thus leading them to 'speak up' and providing leadership to the team and responding to the leadership of others. As Carson et al. (2007) suggest, a common purpose is reinforced within a supportive climate whereby team members are recognized and supported and have more propensity to cooperate, share responsibility and commit to collective goals.

The foregoing suggests that leadership is underpinned by personal relationships, which are underpinned by trust, dignity, honesty, fairness and the rights of others – essential features within the perspective of an ethics of care that respects the beliefs and values of others. These characteristics are embedded within leadership behaviour or what might be called 'lived values' that imbue trust to those whom a leader is responsible to and has a caring responsibility for. An ethics of care therefore concerns the nature of relationships between leaders and followers, whereby leaders influence and affect followers' lives either negatively or positively. The type of influence is a function of the leader's moral character and behaviour, due to the fact that leaders are deemed to have more power, for example, interpersonal and/or formal hierarchical, and by implication they have a greater responsibility to impact on their followers (Yukl, 2012) – leaders need to respect their followers and treat those in their care with dignity, as individuals who have their own distinctive identities. Furthermore, leaders also play a central role in developing and enacting organizational values, and their personal values determine what kind of ethical climate will develop in an organization, as such ethical leadership is concerned not only with employees, but also customers, suppliers, local communities (proximate as well those at a distance) and shareholders (Daft, 2011). This suggests that there is moral significance in the fundamental elements of relationships and dependencies in ethical leadership, seeking to maintain relationships by contextualizing and promoting the wellbeing of leaders (care givers) and those in their care (care receivers) within a network of social relations. Milton Mayeroff (1972) in his classic *On Caring* argued that caring is where an individual allows 'the other' to grow: you are not using that person to satisfy your own needs, you are helping them to progress in some way. Caring is a process and a way of relating to another person. In a caring relationship, the carer focuses attention in a selfless way on the person being cared for, whereby the carer also grows and gets closer to realizing their own potential and to 'self-actualize'.

Mayeroff (1972) describes caring as consisting of several ingredients: knowing, where we understand the other's needs and to respond properly; alternating rhythms that entails focusing on the detail, at others in the wider picture, watching and seeking feedback on actions/inactions; patience, whereby the other is allowed to grow in their own time and in their own way; honesty, where you are being open to oneself and to others, seeing others as they really are and yourself as you really are; trust involves trusting the other to grow in their own time and in their own way; humility, where we learn from others and from our own mistakes; hope should be based on present and realistic possibilities, as any relationship is a journey into the unknown – we need to know the world of others in order to get a sense of what life is like for them, what they are striving to be, and what they require in order to grow (for example, empathy).

Mayeroff's ideas of care have been developed by care ethicists, who have also emphasized the centrality that relationships have an emotional import (see, for example, Jaggar, 2004; 2014). An ethics of care provides a moral epistemological alternative to other normative ethical frameworks, stressing the sensitivity to multiple considerations within a given context and 'cultivating the traits of character and of relationships that sustain caring, and promoting the reflexive dialogue that corrects and enriches the perspective of any one individual' (Held, 2006, p.20). As such, the ethics of care is found within the process of reflexive dialogue that empowers its participants to freely express themselves. For example, the characteristics evolved from a feminist moral theory that today enjoy robust intellectual exploration, principally evolving from critical feminist writings during the 1980s and 1990s. These foreground responsibilities first and foremost in ethical decision making rather than justice and rights, as do traditional ethical theories, the latter being based within a contractual relationship between people rather than personal relationships.

Carol Gilligan (1982), who is regarded as a main proponent in the development of the ethics of care, posits the notion that the self is the main object of concern; the second is to establish connections and participate in social life, as in directing one's thoughts to others. In this way one recognizes one's own needs and those with whom one has relationships, thus engendering responsibilities to the self as well as to others in deciding as to what is the right action. Gilligan does not suggest that care ethics and responsibility are to be regarded as replacing impartiality, rather she advocates that the mature responsible person involves them in a complex interaction of reflexive dialogue between the concerns of impartiality and those of the personal relationships of care (see, for example, Blum, 1988). She is adamant that ethics is concerned with being 'good' and is not about what 'good' is, thus ethics is not concerned with individuals, but rather relationships. Another proponent of the ethics of care is Nel Noddings (2003), who takes the position that traditional moral theories are not the correct place to commence from, these being 'legalistic' relationships when calling as they do for justice-based resolutions to ethical dilemmas. Noddings defends a caring position as being a universal attitude that is imbued within all humans. Self-interest is not denied by Noddings – we affirm our own interest by affirming other's needs. Noddings argues that moral dilemmas are relational, not a monologue, where those involved in moral dilemmas and decision making reach a consensus. Noddings advocates the use of reflexive dialogue to promote a responsible attitude when engaging with others in order to converse about situations, feelings and outcomes. Heller (1990) also supports this view, offering what she terms orientative principles of care that reject principled-based ethics as not having a proper regard for another person's vulnerability or having a regard for another person's autonomy, morality or suffering.

DESIGN

The workshop exercise set out below uses reflexive dialogue to build upon the foregoing literature concerning the ethics of care by using poetry to explore how leaders cope with, react to and resolve their everyday experiences. Cunliffe (2004) notes that reflexivity is where students and the teacher are engaged in a process where their roles are more equal and where: 'critically reflexive practice embraces subjective understandings of reality as a basis for thinking more critically about the assumptions, values, and actions on others.' According to Cunliffe (2004, p.407), reflexive practice is therefore important to management education, because 'it helps us understand how we constitute our realities and identities in relational ways, and where we can develop more collaborative and responsive ways of managing organizations'. Reflexive dialogical conversations can be of several types and take different directions. There are conversations we have with ourselves, and conversations that we have with others. These are interlaced with our past and present experiences, future expectations, hopes and ambitions. These are further layered with those conversations that are hidden, and have remained silent, or hold untold secrets. Conversations are built within our personal connections and relationships with ourselves and others – at their core they require trust, honesty and reciprocity between people, where we and others are listened to. Reflexive dialogical is a space where we, and others, can come together in mutual respect. As David Whyte (1996, p.115) notes: 'The voice emerges from the body as a representation of our inner word. It carries our experiences from the past, our hopes and fears for the future.' These characteristics are essential for a workshop that uses poetry as its mode of engagement, given also that this is not an exercise of how to write 'good' poetry, or an evaluation of what makes good poetry; rather its focus is what poetry can bring to, and inform, those who have leadership roles within their organizations.

However, this exercise also is interactive. Whilst those taking part in the workshop are invited to bring poems to share within their reflexive dialogue groups of their experiences of ethical leadership, or being subjected to another's ethical or toxic leadership style, those attending are also encouraged to bring personal artefacts as a means to locate and contextualize their poetic storytelling. For example, objects from the workplace and/or personal possessions to explore how, and to what extent, ethical leadership and the organization are juxtaposed and intertwined. The intention is to make this 'real' and meaningful to those sharing their poems with other participants. This aspect has a strong connection with Chapter 9 in this volume on using artefacts in leadership development, and I encourage a cross-read of these two chapters.

Pre-workshop Planning Activities

Participants are to be briefed in advance of the workshop. Experience suggests that a two-week pre-planning period is sufficient to allow those taking part to have the time to think about a set of tasks prior to them attending the workshop. They are provided with pre-information that asks them to think about ethical leadership using poems. They are given four options to choose from – this allows those attending the workshop, and who are new to poetry, the confidence to engage in this form of organizational storytelling.

Option 1   Some may be closet organizational poets and may have written their own leadership poetry. Ask them to bring this to the reflexive dialogue groups to share and deconstruct with participants.

Option 2   Participants can select their own leadership poem, which they bring to the workshop to deconstruct with participants in their reflexive dialogue group. The following are some useful web sources to take inspiration from:

- Leadership Tools at http://www.leadership-tools.com/leadership-poem.html
- Everyman Edict at http://www.everymanedict.com/poetry-leadership.htm
- Tweetspeak Poetry at http://www.tweetspeakpoetry.com/

Option 3   Participants are given suggested leadership poems by the facilitator, which they bring to the workshop to deconstruct with participants in their reflexive dialogue group.

The following are examples of my leadership poems that I use in order to show how the issues of care ethics can be explored. The first poem is called 'To Bear the Soul'. This poem speaks directly to those who are in leadership positions, dealing with a personal crisis of one of the members of their team. This is what I call a 'listening' poem – it addresses the issue of compassion, empathy and sympathy. Questions raised could be: how do you deal with personal crisis in the workplace? How do you manage work

and personal relationships? Should the leader put to one side their status
of power in situations of those undergoing personal trauma? How can
you as a leader help a colleague undergoing times of stress? How can we
improve and enhance our relationships in the workplace?

> He was unravelling,
> bearing his soul,
> Trembling like a child,
> out of control,
> He sat bended back to confess,
> Ready to pray for my forgiveness,
> Listless slumped in front of me,
> Me his mentor, me his leader,
> His life unfolding – pleading,
> Waiting for me to react,
> To gather the facts,
> Did he have personal issues?
> Some trauma out of the blue,
> It's true I could rant and rave,
> Drive him to an early grave,
> Pour on scorn to shower,
> Or exert my petty power,
> See only an object in front of me,
> Show distain – choose not to see,
> Dehumanize his humanity,
> To appease my vanity,
> Take revenge – rage,
> Take centre stage,
> But no!
> I had to find out more,
> To connect,
> To empathize, grow wise
> to reprise my curiosity,
> Bring calm and luminosity,
> Shine a light on this dark place,
> To seek truth and not debase,
> Stretch out my hand of hope,
> Not pre-judge or reproach,
> Search for truth in conversation,
> The generation of mutual trust,
> I must be a bridge over troubled waters,
> Like a parent to their sons and daughters,
> To see him for who he is,
> To see him for what he is,
> Not as a means to an end,
> Touch his broken spirit to mend,
> I must look in the mirror and reflect,
> And from my eyes remove the fleck,
> That blinds and imprisons my humility –
> For I was once he in need of my sympathy.

The second poem, 'The journey', is a short poem and describes how a leader can offer a hand of friendship to those they are responsible to in the workplace. This poem strikes a non-instrumental tone of empathy and oneness. It is a poem that might also be seen as attempting to transcend contractual working relationships, trying as it does to establish a relationship of human unity and care. Questions raised by this poem might be: is it possible for a leader to be responsible to those they lead beyond contractual working relationships? How can we as leaders develop our interpersonal relationships to a human level? Should leaders 'touch the inner circles of our minds'? And if so how should we do this?

Let me take your hand and let us
travel together,
Like souls entwined, like sister,
like brother

Let me take the burden of all your
trouble and woes,
On this winding jagged path that
we both chose

Let me be your counsel,
Your eyes and ears,
Give you comfort through darkest
hours and fears

Let me give you protection; be a refuge
of compassion,
On this journey let us share our desires
and life mission

Let us touch the inner circles
of our minds,
Lend each sweet succour when
truth we find

Option 4   Some participants might be prepared to 'have a go' to write their own leadership poetry. They can write their poetry in any style they wish. Some common poem types are:

- The rhyming couplet: simple rhyming of adjacent lines.
- The Shakespearian sonnet: 14 lines, three-stanza rhyming structure – ab, ab; cd, cd; ef, ef; gg.
- The free style: does not have to rhyme or follow any set rhyming pattern. This consists of non-metrical, non-rhyming lines that closely

follow the natural rhythms of speech. A regular pattern of sound or rhythm may emerge in free-verse lines, but the poet does not adhere to a metrical plan in their composition.

- The haiku: three lines, 5–7–5 syllable structure.
- Tanka: five lines, 5–7–5–7–7 syllable structure.

When writing a poem participants are asked to keep in mind the following:

- Know your purpose: why are you writing a poem; what do you want it to do?
- Pick a subject: you do not have to pick a stereotypical poetry topic such as nature, animals, love, or some sort of darker topic. Poems can be written about any topic whatsoever.
- Choose a pattern: you might choose to use free-verse rhyming couplets, or an epic poetry style. It is better to let the words flow with the style than to return later and try to fit your already-written ideas into a totally new scheme.
- Avoid clichés: these are sayings that have been overused, such as 'busy as a bee', or 'blind as a bat'.
- Use imagery: paint with your words and use concrete words that appeal to the senses. Abstract words cannot give the reader a good picture of what you are trying to say.
- Use similes and metaphors: similes compare two things, such as 'you are sweet as honey' and usually use the word 'like' or 'as'. Metaphors state that one thing is another thing, such as 'organization' as 'brain', or 'organization' as 'psychic prison' (after Gareth Morgan, 1997). Things being compared in a metaphor have at least one thing in common but are very different in other ways.
- Alliterations: the occurrence of the same letter or sound at the beginning of adjacent or closely connected words.
- Stanza: a division of a poem (like a paragraph in a story).
- Rhyme: correspondence of sound between words or the endings of words, especially when these are used at the ends of lines of poetry.
- Metre: like the rhythm in a piece of music, the metre is an underlying structure. I call this the 'bounce' of a poem.
- Remember: poems do not have to rhyme. If a poem is too much like a nursery rhyme, it can distract from the poem's purpose.

Participants are asked to think of a situation of their own where they perhaps should have been more conscious of taking account of relationships in their leadership roles. They are then asked to create a 200- to 300-word account of some suggested situations, as follows (or one of their own choosing):

- The ethical leader: what are the requirements for an ethical leader? Who or what do they have responsibilities towards? Have you or a leader you know displayed toxic leadership behaviour – for example, bullying, underhand point scoring and organizational politicking? What are your feelings about this? How does this leader react to you? How do you react to them? What is your relationship with them?

- Ethical vision and mission: do you have an organizational vision or value statement based on the ethics of care? What are the points it tries to get across to those who work in the organization? Does it ring true in practice, or is it a fantasy? If you have access to your vision or mission statement can you rewrite this as an ethics of care poem? If you don't have access to your vision or mission statement can you write your own as you perceive it being practised in your own organization?

- Leadership and power: this is often determined by positional authority; the higher in the hierarchy, the more power and authority people have. What are the reporting structures? Can you describe this within a poem that focuses upon the ethics of care?

- Organizational culture: can you define yours? Do you live it? Do you reject it? How do you respond to it? Has it changed over time – for better or for worse? What organizational cultural obstacles have you encountered in your organization? To what extent does it uphold the ethics of care?

- The leadership speech: what type of speech would you give to your board or members of staff? Tell us your narrative in the form of a poem. If you have given a speech, do you have the text you wrote? Do you have a favourite speech given by a business leader, a political or cultural leader? Could you rewrite this as a poem?

- Leadership and organizational crisis: have you experienced crisis in your organization or one that you have worked for? How did you cope? How did you and/or your colleagues feel? What caused it? How did the organization respond to it? Who took the flack? How were relationships handled? Were people inside and outside the organization taken care of?

- Leadership and organizational conflict: organizational conflict can take place out of sight behind the closed doors of the boardroom, but its consequences invariably impact those who work in the organization. How could you handle this using an ethics of care? What relationships have to be taken account of? Do you only have responsibility to your immediate colleagues or does this extend to distant relationships either inside or outside the organization?

Participants are then asked them to pick out the verbs, adverbs and adjectives they have used from their 200 to 300 word accounts. These are written down in no particular order before asking them to think of other words they may or may not have used to rhyme with them (I always use rhyme as a starting point as this is what the received wisdom of poetry writing is and it helps put participants at ease). Having done this 'staged' poetic writing process I then ask participants to construct a poem of 100 to 150 words about their chosen situation.

Workshop Activity

The reflexive dialogue groups ideally should not consist of more than four to six people. This allows everyone to speak and give feedback on each other's poems and/or reflections on the poems they have selected to read. Larger groups tend to drown out those who are more introspective or hesitant to present their poems, the consequence being that their 'voice' can be lost in the discussions. It is advisable that these are peer-to-peer reflexive dialogue groups. If they are a mix of senior and junior participants this introduces power relationships between 'the boss' and 'us'. Authentic reflexive dialogue groups are those that avoid such tensions, allowing conversation in a safe space. It also engenders an ethos of inclusivity whereby poetry can be accessed at different ability and confidence levels. It means that participants have something to 'bring to the party' within their reflexive dialogue groups; the intention is to share organizational stories in a safe environment, and to open up further questions for discussion, self-reflection and learning. For example:

- What does the poem you have written/read mean to you?
- Does it take account of other people's vulnerability?
- Does it express feelings of sympathy, love or respect to another person?
- Does it respond to another person's needs?
- Does it consider saving the face of another person?
- Does it manipulate others?

This can then be followed up with some more general questions concerning the use of poetry to explore ethical care and leadership, for example:

- Is poetry a legitimate way to explore care ethics in leadership practice?
- How can we deal with our own and others' unspoken needs and relationships, whether real or imagined?

- Can poetry be used as a means to change our own leadership approaches and styles when dealing with relationships with other people?

Facilitators conducting reflexive dialogue groups do not actually lead but rather remain in the background, thereby helping the group to take responsibility for itself and where individuals can 'problematize' their issues; their role is to listen and take notes, which are to be collated and presented back to each group at the conclusion of the workshop as a means to offer self-development and learning of their leadership roles. Any notes become the property of the reflexive dialogue groups, whereupon they can decide as to how they will share this amongst each other, or otherwise. As such, this is a democratic process of engagement that follows the characteristics of reflexive dialogue group work. The workshop can be summarized by asking participants to reflect upon the following questions to stimulate further discussion:

- As leaders, how well do we demonstrate that we care for others?
- As leaders, in what settings are we not currently demonstrating ethics of care?
- As leaders, how will we help our leaders to know what caring leadership looks like?
- As leaders, how will we incorporate the concept of care ethics into our leadership development?

REFLECTIONS

The language of care when attached to leadership does not 'ring true' for many traditionally held views of what an organization should be conceived as – this being formed within the value system of capitalist profit motives, and the maximization of shareholder value. The ethics of care goes beyond mere fiduciary duty. When care ethics 'comes onto the scene' this can be seen as a threat and challenge to the 'hard' veneer of contemporary organizations. This is further exacerbated by the use of poetry as the vehicle for people to express their inner concerns and emotions within (even) the private space of reflexive dialogue groups. I have used poetry with a variety of groups. However, it has to be stressed that those attending these workshops should be selected carefully, due to the obvious issues that some have around engaging with poetry, and to a lesser extent the content and subject matter of the ethics of care. Notwithstanding, some are still reticent to use this mode of engagement, often citing 'when the chips are down' that they cannot write poetry, or they perhaps hide behind a 'veil of resistance' whereby they will try to justify to themselves that 'poetry (after all) is not for me'. This is to be expected; when the word poetry is uttered this signals that any pretence of a hard outer core surrounding their character will be shattered as they divulge the inner workings of their consciousness; poetry can open up a chasm to expose the vulnerabilities of the human psyche. I have found that by doing the pre-workshop activity this can provide a good gauge or filter to determine who might be receptive to this mode of organizational engagement – it is important that those who attend the workshop do so voluntarily and with an open mind. I would advise that one hour should be allocated for the pre-workshop activity. Whilst the production of poetry is the ultimate goal for some participants, I have also found that asking participants to bring in a favourite poem is a very useful 'way in' to the poetic process. The actual workshop itself can last from two to three hours depending on the number attending and the preparation that participants have done prior to them attending.

Facilitating the workshops also needs to be handled with care and sensitivity – it also requires the facilitator to be reflexive in their practice. The production of poetry can open up 'the unknown thought', exposing as it does the emotional baggage that an individual carries with them – this is especially the case with ethical leadership as this points the finger directly back towards the author and the contents of their poem. Facilitators need to 'plan ahead' in order to head off any potential issues of sensitivity and/ or situations where participants might 'go too far'. This is central for the development of trust between facilitator and participants, as Schiuma (2012, p.145) notes: 'in order to guarantee the production of positive benefits for the organisation, artists and business people have to shape a mutual trustful relationship'. This again pushes home the point that a pre-workshop meeting can be beneficial and even essential to the success of using poetry as a means to explore ethical leadership and the subject matter of this chapter – the ethics of care.

As noted previously, the introduction of this can be alien to many, being an oft unheard approach to organizational ethics. This is where, again, the pre-workshop activity can prove useful to allow the facilitator to take the cultural temperature of the organization. It is often the case that the language of ethics and the ethics of care are wrapped up in organizational speak – for example, within an organization's code of conduct. I have found the pre-workshop exercises to be of benefit in the introduction of the ethics of care, without mentioning this in a direct manner.

KEY TIPS

Ensure you meet participants before the workshop, either individually or as a group to explain the pre-workshop activities and answer any concerns and questions they might have about the workshop. This is also a good opportunity for the facilitator to allay any fears about producing and using poetry. It is always a good idea to tell participants that poetry is a journey of exploration that allows us to see things in a different way. It is more about the journey rather than the end product; there are no certainties, only different ways of seeing how care ethics can be enacted within leadership.

REFERENCES

Blum, L. (1988), 'Gilligan and Kohlberg: implications for moral theory', *Ethics*, **98**(3), 472–91.

Carson, J.B., P.E. Tesluk and J.A. Marrone (2007), 'Shared leadership in team: an investigation of antecedent conditions and performance', *Academy of Management Journal*, **50**, 1217–34.

Cunliffe, A. (2004) 'On becoming a critically reflexive practitioner', *Journal of Management Education*, **28**(4), 407–26.

Daft, R.L. (2011), *The Leadership Experience*, 5th edn, Manson, OH: Thomson Western.

Drucker, P. (1981) 'What is business ethics?' *The Public Interest*, **63**(Spring), 18–36.

Friedman, M. (1970), 'The social responsibility of business is to increase its profits', *New York Times Magazine*, 13 September.

George, J. (2000), 'Human relations, emotions and leadership: the role of emotional intelligence', *Human Relations*, **53**, 1027–55.

Gilligan, C. (1982), *In a Different Voice*, Cambridge, Mass.: Harvard University Press.

Groysberg, B. and M. Slind (2012), 'Leadership in conversation: how to improve employee engagement in today's flatter, more networked organizations', *Harvard Business Review*, **90**(6), 76–84.

Held, V. (2006), *The Ethics of Care: Personal, Political, and Global*, Oxford: Oxford University Press.

Heller, A. (1990), *A Philosophy of Morals*, Oxford: Blackwell.

Jaggar, A. (2004), 'Feminist politics and epistemology: the standpoint of women', in Sandra Harding (ed.), *The Feminist Standpoint Theory Reader: Intellectual and Political Controversies*, London: Routledge, pp.55–66.

Jaggar, A. (2014), *Gender and Global Justice*, Cambridge, UK and Malden, Mass.: Polity.

Mayeroff, M. (1972), *On Caring*, New York: Harper.

Morgan, G. (1997), *Images of Organizations*, London: Sage.

Noddings, N. (2003), *Caring: A Feminine Approach to Ethics and Moral Education*, California: University of California Press.

Sorrell, T. (1998), 'Beyond the fringe? The strange state of business ethics', in M. Parker (ed.), *Ethics and Organisation*, London: Sage.

Stewart, J. (2007), *The Ethics of HRD: Critical Human Resource Development*, London: Prentice Hall.
Whyte, D. (1996), *The House of the Belonging*, Langley, WA: Many River Publishing.
Woodall, J. and D. Douglas (2000), 'Winning hearts and minds: ethical issues in human resource development', in D. Winstanley and J. Woodall (eds), *Ethical Issues in Contemporary Human Resource Management*, Basingstoke: Macmillan Business.
Yukl, G.A. (2012), *Leadership in Organizations*, 8th edn, Harlow: Pearson Publications.

7. Using Greek mythology in leadership development: the role of archetypes for self-reflection

Doris Schedlitzki, Carol Jarvis and Janice MacInnes

INTRODUCTION

Deep, critical self-reflection is not easy (Reynolds, 1999). It requires time, space, courage and careful support and is often very difficult to achieve in the context of busy, demanding organizational lives where we are expected to be confident, strong decision makers in the here and now. Yet, critical self-reflection on the past, present and future is crucial as it enables us to step back and evaluate our own and other's actions and decisions in the context of our own and other's needs, aims and values. The development of skills for self-reflection seems therefore an important task for organizations and we will – in what follows – suggest one way in which this could be achieved.

This chapter will evaluate the usefulness of working with Greek mythology to enhance self-reflection through the discussion of an example of how the characteristics of Greek gods and goddesses have been used in a classroom-based executive education setting to encourage critical self-reflection and engender deep conversations on notions such as leadership, followership, power and gender. Drawing on Gherardi's (2004) view of myth as the most fundamental form of narrative knowledge, connecting the past, present and future of humanity, we link throughout to existing contributions on the use of mythology in leadership development (for example, Hatch et al., 2005; Schedlitzki et al., 2015), reflecting specifically on the role and usefulness of archetypes offered through mythology within management education and leadership learning. Of particular interest here is how cultural memory is embedded in and transmitted through myths and how the archetypal characters of myths are still relevant and applicable today (Schedlitzki et al., 2015). It is through the use of the metaphorical language of these archetypes that participants in leadership development may be able to see the complex and often paradoxical nature of human characteristics and behaviour, enabling a safe space for deep, critical self-reflection and identity work. Lessons from the use of these archetypes will be shared and particular attention paid to the ways in which they help to highlight the dualistic nature of personal strengths and weaknesses within working relationships and changing organizational contexts. Based on the experience presented here, it seems that working with archetypal characters from Greek mythology enables participants to challenge existing norms of good and bad leadership, for example, by allowing them to explore how certain characteristics usually associated with strong/weak or good/bad leadership may have quite the opposite effect in different organizational contexts and in interaction with other colleagues.

The chapter will conclude with reflections on the efficacy of the workshop and show how, for some participants, working with Greek mythology in this setting has opened up new ways of seeing and evaluating leadership and helped them to reassess existing relationships at work. It will also highlight that other participants have found it more difficult to embed this learning in their day-to-day practice. Finally, we reflect on how to deal with the range of emotional reactions of participants that may be triggered by this process of critical self-reflection.

USING GREEK MYTHOLOGY IN THE CLASSROOM

Inspired by a mutual interest in mythology, storytelling and leadership development, we have developed a dialogic technique that combines these three elements within a three-hour workshop in order to make space in a supportive learning environment for deep, critical reflection on the self and on interactions with others in the workplace. In this section our main focus is on our engagement with archetypes from Greek mythology during the first half of the workshop (for details on storytelling see Schedlitzki et al., 2015). In the last two sections of the chapter we reflect further on the intended and experienced outcomes and lessons learned.

The workshop is usually limited to a maximum of 16 participants and starts with a detailed introduction, outlining the structure of the workshop, intended learning outcomes and situating these within the wider literature on leadership development. This includes careful, detailed contracting to ensure that participants are focused on the aims and intended learning outcomes of the workshop, and are aware of the possible emotional impact that critical self-reflection may engender and the need to be mindful of this when giving feedback and/or discussing aspects of this self-reflection as a group. We further stress the conditions of confidentiality applying to information shared in order to ensure a safe learning space that encourages honesty and trust. The intended learning outcomes communicated during this introduction are:

- encourage self-reflection and self-awareness through the use of archetypal characters from Greek mythology;
- provide and maintain a safe environment to explore and act out possible work scenarios that help to confront perceptions and attitudes within the self as well as towards others and from others; and
- explore implications for our understanding of leadership in changing and complex contexts.

Introducing Arts-based Methods and Greek Gods and Goddesses as Archetypes

The initial phase of contracting is then followed by an introduction of the archetypal nature and attributes of Greek gods and goddesses, through a set of PowerPoint slides, where we also connect to existing literature on the use of arts-based approaches and mythology in leadership development. We first provide an overview on recent developments within leadership development and the benefits of taking an arts-based approach (for example, Cunliffe, 2009; Purg and Sutherland, 2010; Taylor and Ladkin, 2009) to enable bodily experience or 'sensory perceptions of the world and the thoughts and feelings that spring from them' (George and Ladkin, 2008, p.78). We highlight that the use of arts-based methods – such as an engagement with Greek mythology – in leadership development particularly aims to encourage deep, critical self-reflection and to explore alternative perspectives on organizational life (Schedlitzki et al., 2015).

We then introduce the idea of archetypes as *typical examples of certain behaviours and characteristics* and myths as *cultural memory* transmitted from one generation to another through stories and, as such, universal in their existence and application in modern-day life (Hatch et al., 2005). We explain to participants that working with archetypal characters from Greek mythology will allow them to engage in critical self-reflection through the metaphorical language of Greek gods and goddesses and to become aware of existing assumptions on leadership roles and relationships within the safe learning environment of the classroom (Schedlitzki et al., 2015). We draw on Schedlitzki et al. (2015, p.417), who argue that 'it is the archetypical nature of the characters in Greek Mythology that make them in their metaphorical, symbolic format highly transferrable to current day situations'. They propose that 'an archetype provides a model or prototype for recognising and acknowledging an aspect of our deep existence' (Hatch et al., 2005, p.75). We also make reference to Spence (1994), who stresses that engagement with this archetypal nature of the characters in myths may enable access to what Taylor and Ladkin (2009) call the 'essence of a concept' due to their continuing relevance across the millennia and into today's organizations and societies. In the context of leadership development, this access to 'deep existence' and the 'essence of a concept' through identification with the complex constructs of the Greek gods and goddesses helps to illuminate different aspects of the self and therefore encourage critical reflection on taken-for-granted assumptions about organizational roles and relationships. Drawing on Gadamer's (1986) work, Schedlitzki et al. (2015) argue that the metaphorical language of Greek gods and goddesses allows us to explore the paradoxical, contradictory nature of their characteristics by highlighting both similarity and difference, the ordinary and extraordinary, the good and the bad in individuals and organizational reality. This bears potentially significant insights for a more nuanced understanding of leadership practice and relationships at work.

We conclude this introduction by quoting Schedlitzki et al. (2015, p.417), who argue that 'an exploration of the contradictory nature of the Greek gods and goddesses can provide insight into ways of accommodating, rather than seeking to resolve, the paradox that Stacey (2000, 2010) suggests is an important leadership characteristic in complex organizational environments. Unlike the rationally driven nature of trait theories of leadership, the use of Greek mythology in leadership development therefore aids a multi-faceted self-reflection through personal identification with the virtues and vices of the ancient complex constructs of the Greek gods and goddesses.

Working with Greek Gods and Goddesses

In the next part of the workshop, participants are split into small groups of four to six and are given a set of laminated cards, where each card features the name, image and archetypal behaviours and attributes of a particular Greek god or goddess (Figure 7.1).

These card sets usually cover a pre-selected range of up to ten gods and goddesses that are deemed to be of relevance to organizations and that cover a range of different characteristics, such as 'innovative, risk taking' (Hermes), 'creative' (Apollo), 'strategic thinking' (Athena), 'competitive' (Ares), 'caring' (Demeter) and 'global vision' (Zeus) (Schedlitzki et al., 2015, p.420). This pre-selection can be further tailored to particular group and/or organizational needs. We give participants at least 30 minutes to look through the card sets and think about their attributes and how they

Figure 7.1   Workshop card for Heracles (front and back)

personally feel they relate to them. At this stage participants usually ask follow-up questions about Greek mythology and the particular gods and goddesses they face, requiring facilitators to have a good level of knowledge in this area in order to give participants enough background information and enable them to think deeply about these archetypal characters. We again stress at this point the dualistic nature and flexible meanings of these archetypes as a means to exploring aspects of self, others and interactions of different archetypal behaviours and attributes at work. The intention here is for participants to consider how a specific behaviour, attribute or characteristic can have multiple meanings, ethical implications and indeed be equally seen as a strength and weakness, depending on the work context and interaction with others. In relation to management and leadership, this opens up new avenues for participants to consider and reconsider what they see as good/bad and effective/weak and how there can be no definite answer or one model-fits-all solution to organizational complexities.

Participants are encouraged to choose specific gods or goddesses that they feel close to and/or see mirrored in colleagues they work with, and then to engage – over the next 90 minutes – in a small group discussion based on their selection. This usually quickly leads to vivid conversations where participants not only explain why they have chosen particular gods and goddesses and how these relate to themselves and others they work with, but also start to discuss 'tensions, synergies and paradoxes within roles and relationships at work' (Schedlitzki et al., 2015, p.420). Facilitators sometimes need to stimulate these conversations further and/or ask questions to enable participants to extend their discussions and reflect further on underlying assumptions held by participants about roles, relationships and wider issues such as leadership, followership, power and gender at work. Again, the focus of these conversations – like the selection of gods and goddesses – can be changed to focus on specific challenges in the workplace that facilitators would like the participants to reflect on in relation to themselves and work colleagues. A quick whole-group discussion on emergent themes from the smaller group conversations then completes this first half of the workshop.

The remainder of the full workshop builds on these critical reflections and introduces the method of storytelling as a means of engaging participants in the processes of re-storying existing narratives and envisaging alternative futures (for a full description see Schedlitzki et al., 2015). Back in their small groups, participants are given a specific narrative – ideally closely linked to challenges they are currently facing at work – and asked to re-story the narrative, including their chosen Greek gods and goddesses, and to enact this new story as part of the workshop. This allows participants not only to explore their chosen archetypes in action and interaction but to also challenge themselves to envisage different plotlines – for example reframing tragedies as comedies – and multiple endings to a given narrative. This then deepens their reflections on the ambiguity and nature of roles, relationships and processes at work and vividly demonstrates how individuals differ in their sense making and reactions to different situations. The improvised enactment of the stories and subsequent group reflections on the role of the archetypes in this helps to engage participants in further critical reflections on the socially constructed nature of organizational life – an aspect of the workshop that is more fully illuminated by Schedlitzki et al. (2015).

LESSONS LEARNED

In order to draw out lessons on the usefulness of our workshop – and thereby Greek mythology – for self-reflection in leadership development, we present here a thematic analysis of participant and facilitator feedback gathered post-workshop delivery to three groups: a group of 23 full-time postgraduate students, a second group of five managers from different backgrounds and a third group of eight NHS-based managers. The groups varied considerably in age, work and managerial experience. The majority of the 23 postgraduate students had less than five years' work experience and were aged 25 to 40 years. Several nationalities were present in this group, including British, Indian, Vietnamese, Greek, Polish and Dutch. The two groups of managers, in contrast, were all in full-time employment and had at least eight years' work experience, and were aged 30 to 60 years. Feedback was sought from each participant across the three groups and we draw here particularly on the themes that emerged from qualitative answers to a questionnaire handed out to participants at the end of the workshop and from focus groups that participants were invited to attend at two and six months after the event. We end this section with our own brief post-delivery reflections as facilitators.

The qualitative responses to the questionnaire handed out at the end of the workshop reveals that the most useful aspect of the workshop was participants' engagement with the Greek gods for individual analysis, reflection and exploration of others and self at work. One of the managers from group two commented on plans to use the Greek gods and goddesses allegory to work on understanding each subordinate better. Another manager from this group suggested repeating this workshop for subordinates. They further reported that they had learned to look at ideas from different perspectives, which helped them then to understand other people and personalities and to empathize with them. One of the key suggestions for improvement from these questionnaires was to include stories and real examples of Greek gods and their application in the preparation phase of the workshop or as pre-reading. With a view to how the learning from this workshop could help participants in their current and future leadership positions, some responded that the Greek mythology element would enable them to help their team to 'think about their own identity and the relationship with others in work groups'. The workshop as such was stated to have inspired them to use more innovative and creative methods for personal development in their work context. Whilst most of the participants referred in their answers to the impact of the workshop in relation to greater levels of self-reflection and ability to see others as complex human beings and therefore appreciating different perspectives, two participants took a more strategic approach to the content of the workshop. They suggested that understanding the different characteristics of their subordinates would now help them to assess people's strengths and weaknesses better and hence assign them where they 'fit best' within the work group.

Due to the low number of participants from group two and three taking part in a focus group, we largely focus here on themes emerging from the focus groups conducted with group one. The strongest theme here was in relation to the ease with which participants felt that they could engage with the Greek gods and goddesses archetypes and how closely linked these were to their own work situation. Participants felt that working with these archetypes had helped them to understand roles and relationships further and in relation to their own identity. It seemed to have also generated a wealth of questions about themselves, who they are and could be, and how they relate to others at work. Indeed some participants continued to ponder these questions after the workshop. It was recognized, particularly by one of the managers, that change is difficult and as such responses showed some scepticism as to the long-term impact of this workshop. Some participants from group one further raised criticism around lack of time available during the workshop and that more time was needed to explore their own identities as leaders, group identity, use of metaphor and stories as such. Reviewing further some of the original questionnaire items during these focus groups showed that everyone still agreed on the usefulness of Greek mythology in helping them to become more aware of their strengths and weaknesses. The two managers also responded – when asked what they recalled most distinctly from the workshop – that it was the cards with their images and characteristics of Greek gods and goddesses, and the values and emotions that these cards had evoked in the participants.

For us as facilitators, the most striking theme running through all deliveries was the great affinity that participants showed towards the archetypal characteristics of specific Greek gods and goddesses. We were not prepared for the emotionally laden engagement of some participants with these archetypes, who at times proclaimed that this medium had allowed them to voice their true or preferred self. These dynamics were particularly complex when participants knew each other well and made judgements or provided unconstructive feedback as a result. On one occasion, a participant was openly challenged in her depiction of herself by a close colleague who exclaimed 'this is a joke . . . this is nothing like you'. Managing and containing these emotions was hence an unexpected but crucial part of our role as facilitators and we did not always have enough time within the workshop setting to respond to and deal adequately with these complexities. It further reinforced the need for careful contracting at the start of the workshop, including setting expectations and rules around confidentiality and giving constructive feedback. For us, this stresses the importance of recognizing Taylor and Ladkin's (2009) warning that art-based methods that engage the participants in creative projects and deep self-reflection can entail possible problems and complexities. Yet, as difficult as managing the emotions was during the workshop, it seems to be this emotional engagement that has had a lasting impact on participants. When we have talked to participants since, they have quickly recalled the workshop, the cards and their learning from it and usually make reference within this to the emotions they had experienced. We also found it fascinating that the cards triggered complex and at times very personal and emotional small-group discussions about toxic leadership, power and politics, gender, hierarchy, ethics, culture and followership. Only in very few cases did the cards and the associated archetypes not resonate with participants, and in those rare cases significantly inhibited their learning from the workshop. Yet, as facilitators, it required often some effort on our behalf to create and maintain a safe learning environment where participants felt comfortable and confident to engage in critical self-reflection and reflection on roles and relationships at work. This highlights, for us, the important role of skilled facilitators, time and space in supporting critical self-reflection within leadership development programmes.

DISCUSSION AND CONCLUSION

Our workshop was primarily aiming to enable the revelation of inner thoughts and feelings through the engagement with Greek mythology and storytelling, projecting them onto the archetypal characters of Greek gods and goddesses (Taylor and Ladkin, 2009). The process of analysis and identification with specific gods and goddesses further aimed to enable greater self-awareness, critical self-reflection and exploration of the social construction of roles, processes and relationships in organizations. From the questionnaire and focus group responses we can certainly deduce that the workshop was very successful for most participants in terms of enabling self-reflection and also in having a lasting impact on their understanding and questioning of different aspects of selves, initially stimulated through analysis and choice of Greek gods and goddesses in the session. For some participants, this had also enabled them to reassess existing relationships and understanding of leadership at work, whereas others were more critical in their assessment of their ability to change as a consequence of this workshop.

Also, facilitators noticed that discussions during the workshops enabled participants – particularly in groups two and three – to reflect on wider historical, societal developments; issues of ethics and morality in organizations; historical and cultural roots of leadership in organizations; and considerations of how roles, relationships and interactions at work affect our understanding of what makes good/bad and effective/weak leadership. Although we did not probe for this learning in the questionnaires and focus groups, it could be argued that this workshop has started to make participants aware of the taken-for-granted, historically and culturally rooted assumptions on the role of leader, follower and relationships in organizations. Yet, we would also suggest the need for a follow-up workshop to deepen this learning by focusing specifically on critical self-reflection in relation to the Greek gods archetype in order to help participants to move further away from an essentialist view of leadership.

Participants' feedback also highlighted the emotional impact of this aesthetic workshop on the participants' recollection (memory) of the workshop over a two- to six-month time period, and its learning outcomes leading to a lasting learning experience. Eight participants referred to 'learning in a fun, different way', linking positive emotions to the experiences in the session and their learning from it. This is in line with existing findings by Hatch et al. (2005) and Gabriel and Connell (2010) regarding 'the emotional engagement of the audience and the storytellers with a told or enacted story' (Schedlitzki et al., 2015, p.424).

Some of the process-related issues emerging from the data set are the participants' perception of lack of time and a perceived need for further introduction to relevant background literatures as part of the workshop. Whilst the time issue is one that can more easily be resolved through a lengthening of the time span of the workshop or a follow-up workshop, it seems that the second issue is one of greater significance yet also difficult to resolve. Where should the workshop start: with theory and wider literature or with the individual and group experience to reach deep learning? To what extent may a wider literature review at the start of the workshop shift the focus from the experiential and participant focus to a theoretical one? What are the implications for the emotional experience and its link to learning?

KEY THEMES

We can draw several key themes from this evaluation that support the benefits of aesthetic approaches to leadership development in general and Greek mythology more specifically. There is clear evidence that the workshop fostered critical self-reflection through its engagement with the archetypal characteristics of the Greek gods and goddesses. It enabled participants to reflect deeply on themselves and their relationship with others at work and as such offered support in their ongoing process of becoming a leader in their work context. Participants have through this aesthetic workshop been able to start challenging essentialist views of leadership (Cunliffe, 2009; George and Ladkin, 2008) and develop their ability to engage with the idea of different aspects of selves through the lens of Greek gods and goddesses' virtues and vices. It had therefore some – albeit limited – positive impact on participants' ability to explore the paradoxical nature of these characteristics and to challenge the binary nature of taken-for-granted assumptions about what makes good/bad or effective/weak leadership. Finally, the influence of this aesthetics leadership development workshop on participants' memory is noteworthy, and the emotional experience of working with Greek gods and goddesses cards and images – to reflect on the self – helped the workshop to have a lasting impact on them and their leadership practice.

REFERENCES

Cunliffe, A. (2009), 'The philosopher leader: on relationalism, ethics and reflexivity – a critical perspective to teaching leadership', *Management Learning*, **40**(1), 87–101.

Gabriel, Y. and N.A.D. Connell (2010), 'Co-creating stories: collaborative experiments in storytelling', *Management Learning*, **41**(5), 507–23.

Gadamer, H.-G. (1986), *The Relevance of the Beautiful and Other Essays*, Cambridge: Cambridge University Press.

George, A. and D. Ladkin (2008), 'The aesthetics of leadership development', in Kim Turnbull-James and James Collins (eds), *Leadership Learning: Knowledge into Action*, Basingstoke: Palgrave Macmillan, pp.77–92.

Gherardi, S. (2004), 'Knowing as desire: Dante's Ulysses at the end of the known world', in Yannis Gabriel (ed.), *Myths, Stories and Organisations: Premodern Narratives For Our Times*, Oxford: Oxford University Press, pp.32–48.

Hatch, M.-J., M. Kostera and A. Kozminski (2005), *The Three Faces of Leadership: Manager, Artist, Priest*, Oxford: Blackwell Publishing.

Purg, D. and I. Sutherland (2010), 'Arts-based leadership development at the IEDC-Bled School of Management', *Business Leadership Review*, **8**(4), 1–7.

Reynolds, M. (1999), 'Grasping the nettle: possibilities and pitfalls of a critical management pedagogy', *British Journal of Management*, **19**, 171–84.

Schedlitzki, D., C. Jarvis and J. MacInnes (2015), 'Leadership development: a place for storytelling and Greek mythology', *Management Learning*, **46**(4), 412–26.

Spence, L. (1994), *Introduction to Mythology*, London: Senate.

Stacey, R. (2000), *Strategic Management and Organisational Dynamics: The Challenge of Complexity*, 3rd edn, Harlow: Pearson Education.

Stacey, R. (2010), *Complexity and Organizational Reality: Uncertainty and the Need to Rethink Management After the Collapse of Investment Capitalism*, London: Routledge.

Taylor, S. and D. Ladkin (2009), 'Understanding arts-based methods in managerial development', *Academy of Management Learning and Education*, **8**(1), 55–69.

FURTHER READING

Edwards, G.P., C. Elliott, M. Iszatt-White and D. Schedlitzki (2013), 'Critical and alternative approaches to leadership learning and development', *Management Learning*, **44**(1), 3–10.

Ford, J. and N. Harding (2007), 'Move over management: we are all leaders now', *Management Learning*, **38**(5), 475–93.

Guillet de Monthoux, P. (2004), *The Art Firm: Aesthetic Management and Metaphysical Marketing*, Stanford, CA: Stanford University Press.

Hancock, P. and M. Tyler (2008), 'It's all too beautiful: emotion and organization in the aesthetic economy', in S. Fineman (ed.), *The Emotional Organization: Passions and Power*, Malden, MA: Blackwell Publishing, pp.202–16.

Hansen, H. and R. Bathurst (2011), 'Aesthetics and leadership', in A. Bryman, D. Collinson, K. Grint, B. Jackson and M. Uhl-Bien (eds), *The Sage Handbook of Leadership*, London: Sage, pp.255–66.

Nicholson, H. and B. Carroll (2013), 'Identity undoing and power relations in leadership development', *Human Relations*, **66**(9), 1225–48.

Petriglieri, G. (2011), 'Identity workspaces for leadership development', in S. Snook, N. Nohria and R. Khurana (eds), *The Handbook for Teaching Leadership*, Thousand Oaks, CA: Sage, pp.295–312.

Sinclair, A. (2011), 'Being leaders: identities and identity work in leadership', in A. Bryman, D. Collinson, K. Grint, B. Jackson and M. Uhl-Bien (eds), *The Sage Handbook of Leadership*, London: Sage, pp.508–17.

Snook, S., H. Ibarra and L. Ramo (2010), 'Identity-based leader development', in N. Nohria and R. Khurana (eds), *Handbook of Leadership Theory and Practice*, Boston, Mass.: Harvard Business Press, pp.657–78.

8. 'Tents': constructing a narrative of leadership learning

Steve Kempster

NATURALISTIC LEADERSHIP LEARNING

It is generally accepted that leadership is learned through lived experiences throughout our life course. Earliest work in this area was Burgoyne and Hodgson (1983) who illuminated how everyday workplace experiences developed tacit learning of managing and leading. At about the same time Davies and Easterby-Smith (1984) gave detail of how the variety of contexts greatly extended this tacit learning. In the United States, colleagues provided a typology of three influences common in a manager's lived experience: line experiences (prominent early career activities of leading); notable others; and hardships (McCall et al., 1988; McCall, 2004). Following this work Cox and Cooper (1989) added insight on the influence of childhood experiences, while Bennis and Thomas (2002) offered the notion of a 'crucible' in which experiences are forged, and Avolio and Luthans (2006) gave attention to critical 'trigger events' within such crucibles. Janson (2008) has usefully captured this range of influences in her notion of leadership formative experiences. In my research I have given prominence to notable others as foundationally formative to the development of implicit theories of leadership, from which other experiences appear to refine leadership learning – processes of observational learning being most instructive (Kempster, 2006, 2009a, 2009b; Kempster and Parry, 2013). So it is almost without doubt that lived experience is the key to understanding leadership learning at the level of everyday practice. Attention to practice and how this has been learned is central to and arguably fundamental to enhance leadership development effectiveness.

However, here is the rub. Whilst we know that this is so very important it is also so hard to access, and therefore so difficult to change. The cumulative outcome of countless and repetitive learning prompts from observing and participating with numerous people in many contexts is the *tacit* that cannot be expressed. In my earlier work it became apparent through interviewing senior managers that most were unable to explore in any depth their experiences and relate these in a meaningful and organized fashion to their everyday practice.

I have recalled elsewhere (2009a) of reflecting on a television chat show and how the presenter was able to move people through their biographies with ease, unpicking in depth moments of interest. 'In the spirit of good science I experimented on myself. I created a timeline going from my earliest memories to current influences' (2009a, p.110). The excitement I felt doing this was eclipsed by the emergent findings. I was able to recall moments that surprised me. I was able to organize my thinking about leadership learning. In essence, and with great naivety at that moment, I was gaining an insight into how a narrative can reveal so much for an author in real time as it becomes constructed.

With narrative inquiry as my new bedtime companion I discovered some wonderful gems with regard to underscoring the theory of my experience. First, that we are all able to construct narratives as part of our everyday social interactions (Goffman, 1969). A narrative is not demanding on us to shape in terms of its flow and structure; further it operates at a low level of consciousness and, as Wengraf (2001) helpfully highlights, it is through narrative that respondents tend to limit self-censorship. Second, there are prominent features that people employ to construct the narratives that give a sense of scaffolding to the meaning being offered in the stories. For example, Gabriel (2000) suggests that prominent in narratives are four sociopoetic modes: epic, tragic, comic and romantic (Gabriel, 2000). As authors of stories we create, or consume, we use these common archetypes. Third, narratives are able to draw on many cultural aspects that form the detail of that tacit awareness that normally cannot be expressed; it gives an insightful nuanced depth that interview questions cannot reveal. Fourth, the narrative can be easily expressed to another person yet that ease also makes it so very difficult to meander from 'truth' – a respondent sense of truth (Lawler, 2002) – where 'we are the most avid listener and fiercest critic [who] hears all our stories [. . .] We live, move and have our own being marinated in our own stories' (Sims, 2003, pp.1196, 1199).

So producing a narrative is straightforward. It provides the opportunity of deep access to tacit awareness and an ability to construct an organized account of our sense of being and knowing. In the context of leadership learning it can point to the sense of identity we associate with leadership and a glimpse of our practice of leading. In recent research I have illustrated this relationship of being and knowing, of identity and practice, as a process of becoming captured in an 'emplotted' narrative (Kempster and Stewart, 2010). The research examined the first three months of a senior manager learning to become a chief operating officer. Amongst a number of aspects was the importance of a narrative identity (Ezzy, 1998).

The senior manager was [re]writing his story – informed from his past, captured in the activities of the present with a keen eye on the future. Timeline explorations provide a story of how someone has 'become', in terms of their leadership learning journey. Mischel (2004) suggests the notion of signatories as elements of this becoming. The timeline brings to the fore 'signatories' in the form of feelings, expectations and beliefs associated with the memory recall of people and past events (Kempster, 2009a, p.64).

Stories that inform a sense of the person we are in the roles we perform are thus a central concern. With regard to leadership it is arguably most central. For example, authenticity is the present zeitgeist of the leadership development industry. Shamir and Eilam have asserted that 'the construction of a life-story is a major element in the development of authentic leaders' (2005, p.395). However, without an approach to help leaders understand and construct a coherent understanding of their life story how can such development occur? Simply asking them about the roots of their authenticity is highly unlikely to be productive.

Finally, the creation of a timeline and the narrative that emerges requires a process of writing. This seems overwhelmingly axiomatic. But here's the powerful thing. Writing is more than a process of capturing what has been thought. As Richardson (2000) has suggested, writing is a process of inquiry. As we write we think, reflect, construct, sense-make and reconstruct in an ongoing manner. Going beyond the writing and recounting the text to others is similarly a process of inquiry. The same iterative process of thinking, reflecting, constructing, sense making and reconstructing occurs again.

This, then, is the case for the necessity to reveal leadership learning through a timeline process. It enables recall through the use of narrative. I now turn to a design by which this has been undertaken.

THE TENTS' DESIGN

I recall a very cold and dryish January day in Hertfordshire, UK – although snow flurries were in the air. I was using the tents with our partner Ashridge on a leadership development programme for senior managers of further education colleges. The previous day (before I arrived) had been an introduction to reflective practice and explorations of using action learning sets. The group didn't know me yet but the stories of the tents had percolated from one cohort to another. This group was ready for me and had plans to change the day! Following the introductions and purposes of the day 'to examine the development of leadership practice through lived experience' I reached for my envelopes to hand out to people and nodded

to my colleague to bring in the tents. I began to explain what we were about
to do when the group seized the moment – a form of distributed leadership, I guess. A coordinated and most eloquent argument unfolded that
people were most keen to engage in the process but not go outside. They
would find a quiet place in the wonderful building that is Ashridge. Mobile
phones would be switched off. It was agreed that metaphoric tents would
become the process and, in pairs, people disappeared with their envelopes.

It was such a different process than the tried and tested approach –
although it was a success in terms of the '*happy sheets*' that constituted the
feedback. The managers felt they had learned much about themselves and
added that the choice not to go out into the snow was good. In many ways
it was, as we avoided health and safety concerns that might have been most
real. Yet the difference to the previous groups and the subsequent groups
was palpable. There seems to be no substitute for sitting alone, in a context
that is very different, for a period of time that is deeply unusual, to think
about one thing only – lived experience of leadership.

I give emphasis here to the importance of 'trusting the process' and that
the process includes context. My compromising led to compromising of
the desired outcome. The cold context may have created an exceptional
moment. The intensity of sitting in the tent 'surviving' may have led to
explorations and reflections that would be lasting in terms of personal
insight and impact to practice. I and they will never know. What we did
learn is that the coffee and shortbread biscuits served up while sitting
by log fires are most enjoyable and not necessarily conducive to critical
reflection!

So to the process. I have served up already that the 'tents' is situated
in the context of a workshop focusing on leadership practice. I have not
undertaken the tents with anyone other than practising managers. The
foundation of drawing on a timeline quantum of leader–follower relationships appears to necessitate this.

The pedagogy of the workshops has been oriented to giving emphasis
to engendering reflexive dialogue (Cunliffe, 2001); for managers to explore
aspects of their everyday practice in dialogue with other managers, facilitated and sometimes provoked through the use of theory (Ramsey, 2011).
In this way, theory on leadership and leadership learning follows the tents
experience, rather than informs and directs the process. The use of the tents
does strongly reflect a pedagogic commitment to the primacy of reflection
and exploration to understand and enhance practice. Although I shall
return to this point in the final part of the chapter when I reflect on the
process and its challenges, the emphasis here is to highlight two connected
antecedent influences: first, a practice-centric pedagogic approach steeped
in experiential adventures to leadership development over many years that

led to the creation of the tents; and second, the research informed under-standing of leadership learning that required a method to allow for the tacit practice-based knowledge to be surfaced.

Two further aspects are important to enabling the tents process to be successful. First is a consideration on the nature and composition of the group. Do they have symmetry between themselves? Do the groups have similar quantum of leadership experiences? Is there congruence on roles and levels of responsibility? Aspects of diversity have not been salient thus far. That is not to say it is not significant in terms of exploring lived expe-rience. Rather, considerations for addressing aspects of diversity have not been evident. Unrelated to this aspect, I hope, is the second consideration of the levels of trust between people in the cohort. Part of the tents process requires a conversation with a partner that explores personal insights – asking questions and encouraging examination. By its nature personal and sensitive incidents sit within the timeline and become the central focus of the conversations. Trust is therefore essential. As a minimum the tents process is never the first thing we do. If it is in the first workshop, and it typically is, then it would follow a set of activities that seek to establish relationships, boundaries and confidences. Typically pairs are formed by mutual selection. During the outset of the process we overtly seek to enhance the sense of bond between the pair through a shared activity of finding the tent locations and building the tents.

Some of the programmes we have delivered the tents within have been single company, some within the same sector and some as an open pro-gramme. The aspects of trust and symmetry are just as relevant to all three. The aspects of trust seem less acute on open programmes than single company, where there is understandably much more at stake. For example, the tents process could examine notable people from the organizational context; disclosure may therefore be potentially censored or opaque in detail.

As you can tell from the 'Ashridge tale' I have not added a third consid-eration of the weather .

After the pairs of managers have been created, each manager is given a fisherman's tent – a simple design with two poles, a large opening and no flysheet. Additionally a map is given that shows where the tent is to be pitched; and after a brief conversation with their partner they realize the tents are close enough to each other. Not so near that they can easily shout to each other, but sufficiently close that they can get attention from the other. Rations are also given out in terms of a bottle of water and some chocolate and/or fruit. Finally they are handed an envelope with instruc-tions on the front not to open until they are seated in their respective tent. Prior to them all leaving, a verbal briefing is given to kindly follow the instructions in the envelope, a health and safety comment (relevant to the particular context) and assurance that we would be passing by from time to time to check all is okay.

The journey to the locations is a central aspect to the process. Map reading, excitable conversation, sometimes airing irritations and negativity, creates a strengthening of the pair in terms of a trusting relationship, with both going through the same thing and able to rely mutually on the other. This becomes reinforced with the process of pitching the tent. For some it is easy and for others a process of much hilarity; but it is done together. It creates a sense of building shelter, protection, a sanctuary from the weather and for some a metaphoric sanctuary from the pressures and demands of their lives. In essence, the common experience provides a bonding that is drawn on later when confidences are required.

Once the tents are up and the managers are safely out of the wind and rain (or the sun) excitedly the envelopes are opened, which read:

Leadership Learning

You are in a field, in a tent with a bottle of water and some chocolate and hopefully alone! What I would like you to do is concentrate only on leadership and address these three questions:

- *What do you think leadership is?*
- *How do you approach leading?*
- *What has shaped your thinking and approach to leadership?*

To address these questions please do the following:

Think about how you would define leadership and write this down. Draw a line and create a timeline which you will populate with memories on leadership. These could go as far back as childhood and probably would incorporate organisational experiences. As you recall these memories try to capture them onto the timeline and then go back and work your way through the detail and clarify what is the meaning of these memories. Don't rush this – you have 90 minutes. Conclude with listing how your thinking shapes your approach to leading. The list might reflect advice you would give about leading in your organisation or another context. For example 'be in control and be seen to be in control'. Look at the list and see if you can determine whether the points can be connected to your memories.

> *You should only be able to see one other person and that person will be both your interviewer and your interviewee. Please do not contact them until you have been alone for 90 minutes. After 90 minutes make contact and meet with them at one of your tents. Interview each other in detail for at least 45 minutes each.*
>
> *Start with the person's definition of leadership and then work your way through the timeline, in detail exploring what the person means – ask questions and ensure you clarify things as you proceed. At the end, talk through the rules of thumb on how to lead and see how they relate to the experiences. Then switch roles and repeat the process above – make sure you capture critical issues emerging from both interviews as this will be useful in the afternoon's discussion.*
>
> *Enjoy and soak up the sun!! I hope you can take advantage of this rare quiet time to concentrate on just one issue. As with everything – the more you put in to this the more you will get out of it. Good luck.*
> *Steve*
>
> *Source:*   Kempster, 2009a, pp.115–16.

The first time the exercise was piloted was with an executive MBA cohort. We had an odd number and therefore needed one of us to make up the complement of pairs. No 'family hold back here' – I asked the EMBA manager if I could join him. I recall sitting in my tent waiting for my new 'buddy' to grab my attention, through waving, to send messages via sign language about who would go to the other's tent at the end of the 90 minutes. It was agreed, I think, that he would host me.

With that out of the way I wondered whether I would gain anything from doing the exercise. I had designed it with a sense of what I expected to occur. Also I had tried out the process of leadership learning time-lines a few years earlier. All seemed very pedestrian as I went through the questions – most notable was the prominence of my grandfather. He had been a dispatch rider in the First World War, running messages back and forth from the commanders to the front line. He told me once that he delivered the final draft of the peace treaty to the Germans. You can imagine the impact this would have on a young lad. We both watched football together, chopped wood, and he shared many stories. When I was 25 minutes into the exercise I looked up and a hare was close to me, about 10m away. I was clearly in his (possibly her) backyard. I'd never seen a wild hare before. We stared at each other. It seemed quite a long time, then he darted off and was out of sight. I imagined he was watching me.

I daydreamed and drifted back to World War One, my grandfather and the contrast with my father. I thought deeply about the different relationships and some disappointments. But for the first time I began to see that the disappointments were centred with me and not with my father. My romanticized view of my grandfather as role model had distorted so many things. I recalled incidents with my father and I was struck deeply with how much he had shaped me that I had not realized. I reflected on this for a long time, when I realized my 'buddy' was trying to catch my eye with wild rotations of his arms. So rather than wondering what I might do in the 90 minutes, it was for me too short.

Sitting cozily in this one-person tent we both went through our timelines, with him going first. On my recounting I was struck for a second time. The telling of the narrative changed the narrative. As I spoke new aspects emerged, insights of depth to the recall. Many a time my 'buddy' prompted this extra or changing detail through his questions and desire for clarification on context and relationships. I could be much mistaken but I am sure he had not done this before; but he was so capable of teasing out more and more. The reciprocal process engendered for us a strong commitment in learning about the other's narrative. Aligned to this was the tacit skill of participating in co-constructing a narrative, when to listen, when to ask questions, when to recap to summarize understanding and nudge forward for the next bit of the story. Again, our 45 minutes each flew by in what seemed like a moment.

The process of taking the tents down and walking back is more than a logistical issue. It is a most natural movement from close and intimate reflective sharing to more ritualized and factual conversation of engaging with practical and physical endeavours. How does the tent come down? Will it go in the bag? Perhaps we'll get just as lost getting back as coming here. Do you think we'll be the last back?

With all back at the workshop (and that is more of a hassle than it might seem!) the approach we have taken is to suggest that the conversations in the tents should not be shared openly with all. Rather we move to exploring commonalities of influences on leadership learning and connections of experience with how leadership is practised. This concluding session is typically brief – perhaps 30–40 minutes. There is a palpable sense of exhaustion, and often much hunger. Lunch is important. It forms a most desirable time out; a moment for conversation on the process, out of earshot of anyone other than the person you wish to speak to.

The depth of material unearthed from the tents becomes a central resource for the remainder of the workshop. For example, exploring aspects of authenticity, ethics, contingency and situational leadership, managers offer forward critical incidents from their experiences to examine and apply respective theories. At a moment the class can split into small groups. We do not introduce prepared case studies. These are in abundance in the group from the timelines. People do offer these forward. The commonality of the tents experience creates a strong feeling of trust and comfort to share. Managers have had time to decide what they wish to share and the reciprocal sharing reinforces the sense of being part of a community. There is normally quite a special atmosphere in the 'classroom'. In this respect the Ashridge situation was very different – more a process of getting through the remainder of the workshop all on good terms without revealing too much; and there was not much to reveal . . . still the food was good.

REFLECTIONS

We have used the 'tents' for many cohorts (perhaps over 200 managers at the time of writing), and it has been used for many years by Warwick Business School and other colleagues in their own consultancy. It is not always undertaken in a tent. Sometimes it is whatever space is available. Sometimes the 90 minutes is cut back. However, as expressed through the Ashridge tale, cutting back on time and not giving good attention to context and the process of 'buddying up' to generate a safe trusting context has been shown to be problematic to the process – not fundamental issues that undermine the design, but this does require very careful consideration and managing. Understandably there is much pressure on crowded timetables to cover many curriculum aspects. The notion of sitting in a tent for 90 minutes and up to another 90 minutes in reflexive dialogue seems to some very inefficient. The legacy of testimonials from managers has greatly helped us to argue the case.

We draw here on the review of the 'tents' by MacKay (2012), who examined the processes of reflection of participating managers. She suggests that 'leadership practice is shaped by not simply the practices seen and learnt at work, nor through replicating behaviours from those who we admire or detest, but [also] within a complex dynamic of personal, contextual and socially [derived] influences (2012, p.392). MacKay provides for us some helpful participant quotes:

● On experiences:

> *'I hadn't considered the impact of family life, school etc. but solely on the experience of work. I had without realizing only considered my leadership journey in relation to work at the exclusion of life outside this.'*

'The significance of my personal life was a revelation.'
'I have always been clear that my previous manager had a huge influ-ence on my leadership style, but I have not thought beyond that.'
(Mackay, 2012, p.398)

- On emotions:

  'I was surprised by the emotions that came up with the quiet reflection.
  As I delved more deeply into my past, pride rose [to] the surface [and]
  I began to think about the things I am most proud of but pangs of con-science also struck as a I reflected on things that I have not got right!'
  'This was one of the most intense learning experiences of my life and
  helped me to locate the source of my values and beliefs about leader-ship within significant stages in my life.' (MacKay, 2012, p.401)

- Leadership stories:

  'I do have a leadership story to tell.'
  'It allows me to organize the jigsaw pieces of my experience.'
  'Sharing stories showed difference [but] there were startling similari-ties in how we established ourselves in leadership positions.' (MacKay,
  2012, pp.401–2)

- On doing the tents:

  'Chinese whispers were rife from previous groups [such as] repenting in
  tents with a stranger.'
  'My initial cynicism of the activity was replaced by the later under-standing of the value of the activity. However my real understand-ing and development came later, after the event.' (MacKay, 2012,
  pp. 404–5)

So in protecting the time needed the testimonials help provide an evidence base. Complementary to this is the research evidence of how managers learn to lead and the great difficulty managers have in surfacing the tacit learning that shapes their daily leadership practice. We also speak of the necessity to create a pedagogy that has an emergent curriculum formed out of the experiences derived from undertaking the tents, which enables examination of practice.

Yet we need to be cautious of the impact of the experience. For example, MacKay highlights a comment from one manager on the sharing of stories that 'during the time we spent together interviewing each other both of us became emotional' (2012, p.401). The 'tents' is rarely a neutral process. It therefore requires careful consideration of why it is being used. The delineation of examining only leadership learning does help bracket out personal journeys into bigger 'what if' questions of life course. Further, the time out of 90 minutes with the range of questions/tasks to be undertaken limits far-reaching meanderings beyond leadership. Finally, the movement of telling the leadership learning story appears to bring cohesion rather than fragmentation to someone's reflections. The loose ends become tidied up through organizing a coherent narrative that is told in a short time with little preparation.

It is necessary to make the 'tents' central to the workshop and not a bolt on, a piece of entertainment or an isolated event. The investment that participants put into the process requires empathetic appreciation and utilization – not an expectation on people to expose their emotional selves as the potential raw emotion has been tidied away with packing up the tents and walking back to the workshop. Rather the pedagogy draws on the recall of incidents, episodes and role models as material to apply theory to and draw out insights on their leadership practice going forward. To this end it is imperative to design the inclusion of 'tents' early enough so that it can be usefully used; but also if there are any remaining 'raw aspects' these can be made sense of and tidied up prior to leaving the workshop.

The central focus on leadership practice throughout is key, with no temptation to move on to other related 'life' aspects. We give orientation in the workshops to the notion of leader becoming (Kempster, 2009a, pp.64–5). The sense is that past experiences continually inform the present; yet the present has a continual eye on the aspirational sense of what the person wishes to become (see Ibarra, 1999, and her argument for provisional selves). In this way we use the workshop to focus on the development of leadership practice, with the tents experience providing an insight into the past that impacts on the present. At the same time the discussions are future orientated: knowing what you know now, what does this mean going forward? Interconnected with leader becoming is the notion of narrative identity. The 'tents' allow a manager to form a rich sense of their narrative identity (Ezzy, 1998) related to leadership. I described at the beginning of this chapter that narrative identity is a combination of past, current and future aspirational identity. Commonly in our assessments related to a 'tents' workshop we ask for the manager-students to reflect forward with regard to their narrative identity – to consider the influence they hope to have on others' timelines (those in the leader–follower relationship) to shape the next generation in the ongoing process of others' leader becoming.

Finally, to the research still to be done. There is so much that we have not understood with regard to naturalistic leadership learning. In some ways the inaccessibility of leadership learning is metaphorically like the exploration of dark matter. (The term originally suggested by Fritz Zwicky in 1937 for matter that is suggested to provide an explanation that accounts for discrepancies between measurements of the visible estimated mass in the universe and the total mass theorized as necessary to explain why the galaxies do not collapse into themselves. Dark matter is argued to constitute approximately 80 per cent of the matter in the universe, while the visible matter makes up only 20 per cent: see Freeman and McNamara, 2006). Scientists appear to have found evidence of this dark matter. In (not so) similar ways the field of leadership learning recognizes the significant influence of naturalistic learning events on emergent leadership practice. It is the 80 per cent that shapes everyday activity. It is the big unresearched and undertheorized aspect of leadership studies. The 'tents' exercise has much potential to become our 'metaphoric' laboratory. If every time the tents exercise was undertaken leadership developers became partners in this research project we would gain considerable insight. Being watchful not to intrude and damage the process MacKay (2012) has given an example of such illustrative insight.

Additionally, we do need to travel with managers on their journeys of leader becoming – a longitudinal research approach to gain insight into the impact of the 'tents' and how people's sense of their narrative identity remains salient (or not); and to what extent it has impact on their everyday leadership practice. Too often the leadership development industry falls short on understanding the impact of interventions. At the same time there is such a need to demonstrate impact; impact for developers, researchers, clients and managers, but also a contribution to society to get a glimpse of this important dark matter of leadership learning. I guess, though, that funding may be less abundant than it was for the Cern project!

KEY TIPS

- Book good weather . . . !
- Place the tents exercise near the front of a workshop . . . but not at the front.
- Design the pedagogy of the workshop around the exercise . . . not as bolt on – and allow for an emergent curriculum.
- Develop trusting pairs – allowing people to select is important.
- Use the walk and the set-up of the tents as part of the process – it is tempting to let others set them up.

● If you short-change the process you will probably short-change the participants . . . so trust the process.

REFERENCES

Avolio, B.A. and F. Luthans (2006), *The High Impact Leader: Moments Matter in Accelerating Authentic Leadership Development*, New York: McGraw Hill.

Bennis, W.G. and R.G. Thomas (2002), 'Crucibles of leadership', *Harvard Business Review*, **80**(9), 39–46.

Burgoyne, J.G. and V.E. Hodgson (1983), 'Natural learning and managerial action: a phenomenological study in the field setting', *Journal of Management Studies*, **20**(3), 387–99.

Cox, C.J. and C.L. Cooper (1989), 'The making of the British CEO: childhood, work experience, personality and management style', *The Academy of Management Executive*, **3**(3), 241–5.

Cunliffe, A. (2001), 'Reflexive dialogical practice in management learning', *Management Learning*, **33**(1), 35–61.

Davies, J. and M. Easterby-Smith (1984), 'Learning and developing from managerial work experience', *Journal of Management Studies*, **21**(2), 169–83.

Ezzy, D. (1998), 'Theorizing narrative identity: symbolic interactionism and hermeneutics', *Sociological Quarterly*, **39**(2), 239–52.

Freeman, K. and G. McNamara (2006), *In Search of Dark Matter*, Berlin: Springer Science & Business Media.

Gabriel, Y. (2000), *Storytelling in Organisations: Facts, Fictions and Fantasies*, Oxford: Oxford University Press.

Goffman, E. (1969), *The Presentation of Self in Everyday Life*, London: Penguin Press.

Ibarra, H. (1999), 'Provisional selves: experimenting with image and identity in professional adaptation', *Administrative Science Quarterly*, **44**(4), 764–92.

Janson, A. (2008), 'Extracting leadership knowledge from formative experiences', *Leadership*, **4**(1), 73–94.

Kempster, S. (2006), 'Leadership learning through lived experience: a process of apprenticeship?', *Journal of Management and Organization*, **12**, 4–22.

Kempster, S. (2009a), *How Managers Have Learnt to Lead: Exploring the Development of Leadership Practice*, Basingstoke: Palgrave Macmillan.

Kempster, S. (2009b), 'Observing the invisible: examining the role of observational learning in the development of leadership practice', *Journal of Management Development*, **28**(5), 439–56.

Kempster, S. and K. Parry (2013), 'Exploring observational learning in leadership development for managers', *Journal of Management Development*, **33**(3), 164–81.

Kempster, S. and J. Stewart (2010), 'Becoming a leader: a co-produced autoethnographic exploration of situated learning of leadership practice', *Management Learning*, **41**(2), 205–19.

Lawler, S. (2002), 'Narrative in social research', in T. May (ed.), *Qualitative Research in Action*, London: Sage.

Luthans, F. and B. Avolio (2003), 'Authentic leadership: a positive development approach', in K.S. Cameron, J.E. Dutton and R.E. Quinn (eds), *Positive Organizational Scholarship*, San Francisco, CA: Berrett-Koehler, pp.241–58.

MacKay, F. (2012), '"I don't have to be like my principal": learning to lead in the post-compulsory sector', *Educational Management Administration and Leadership*, **40**(3), 392–409.

McCall, M.W. (2004), 'Leadership development through experience', *Academy of Management Executive*, **18**, 127–30.

McCall, M.W., M.M. Lombardo and A. Morrison (1988), *The Lessons of Experience*, Lexington, MA: Lexington.

Mischel, W. (2004), 'Toward an integrative science of the person', *Annual Review of Psychology*, **55**, 1–22.

Ramsey, C. (2011), 'Provocative theory and a scholarship of practice', *Management Learning*, **42**(5), 469–83.

Richardson, L. (2000), 'Writing: a method of inquiry', in N. Denzin and Y. Lincoln (eds), *Handbook of Qualitative Research*, 2nd edn, London: Sage, pp.923–48.

Shamir, B. and G. Eilam (2005), 'What's your story?: A life-stories approach to authentic leadership development', *The Leadership Quarterly*, **16**, 395–417.

Sims, D. (2003), 'Between the millstones: a narrative account of the vulnerability of middle managers' storying', *Human Relations*, **56**, 1195–211.

Wengraf, T. (2001), *Qualitative Research Interviewing*, London: Sage.

PART III

Artefact-based approaches

Artefact-based approaches

9. Leadership artefacts: a process of storytelling within newly formed groups

Emma Watton and Philippa Chapman

PURPOSE

The aim of the activity is to encourage participants to share stories associated with personal artefacts brought along to an academic (or other) programme. We have found this to be particularly helpful to use at the start of a programme, with groups who have not worked together in the past, and have used it to great effect with private-sector organizations in a university setting. The chapter will outline the background and theory to the use of artefacts, directions on how to run the activity, its potential benefits for participants and programme leaders, some examples of artefacts in use and our tips for ensuring the activity is a success.

UNDERPINNING RESEARCH

Background

This activity combines the use of an artefact or object with the leadership story behind it. Pahl and Rowsell (2012) comment on the use of objects, observing that they are 'linked to timescales and are also tied to particular places and spaces', and that created 'spaces can be intercultural and transnational, and can cross linguistic and cultural boundaries' (2012, p.266). This description resonates with our experiences of using artefacts in the classroom.

The leadership artefacts activity takes advantage of the natural affinity people have for storytelling, an oral tradition found in every society and one that, for many people, has been a part of life since an early age. Alexander Mackenzie, programme director of storytelling at Cranfield School of Management, observed in 2012 that 'a good leader is a good storyteller'.

What Do We Mean by Artefacts?

An artefact is defined as being an object that is made by a human being; typically one with cultural or historical interest. An artefact is durable, public and materially present (Kafai, 2006). Sometimes an artefact can be a naturalistic object.

Pattison (2007) describes the significance of the numerous, yet frequently overlooked, humble artefacts found in the everyday world, which are so often almost invisible when compared to 'high-art' objects such as paintings, drawings and sculptures. Despite being less common and not typically used or accessible as everyday objects these art objects attract a disproportionate depth of examination and recognition. Pattison proposes methods that draw on the relationships we have with, and the sense making that can be gained through, more humble artefacts.

The use of artefacts in education has a rich history. A learning artefact is created by learners during their course and is used to help make knowledge visible. The use of the term 'cognitive artefact' is used when the object created is a represented idea or concept. This type of artefact is helpful to convey feelings, memories or experiences and aims to develop cognitive ability. The activity described in this chapter combines the idea of a learning artefact, making the learners' knowledge visible, and a cognitive artefact, helping to convey feelings, memories and experiences. We could perhaps refer to it as a cognitive, learning artefact. Artefacts are valuable ways for people to link important events and memories that they can construct stories around. Different types of artefacts include the use of letters (Clandinin and Connelly, 2004) and other chapters in this book explore the use of finger puppets, collage and films.

What Do We Mean by Storytelling?

Storytelling is gaining popularity in a higher education context, with several studies demonstrating the use of storytelling as a reflective and learning process (Clandinin and Connelly, 1998; McDrury and Alterio, 2003; Moon, 2010). Storytelling is extensively used in some areas of professional practice, most widely in nursing and teacher education (McDrury and Alterio, 2003; Moon and Fowler, 2008).

For human beings the ability to tell, and an interest in telling and listening to stories, dates back thousands of years and is one of the earliest experiences of childhood. According to McEwan and Egan (1995, p.viii) 'a narrative, and that particular form of narrative that we call a story, deals in facts or ideas or theories or even dreams, fears and hopes, [. . .] from the perspective of someone's life and in the context of someone's emotions'.

Brody et al. (1991) espouse the ability of storytelling to connect thoughts with feelings.

The coupling of artefacts and storytelling is an underresearched area. Whilst some studies have been undertaken in anthropology (Hoskins, 1998), creative arts (Gauntlett, 2007) and theology (Pattison, 2007). We have not been able to identify any studies from a management education context. Combining personal artefacts and storytelling allows programme participants to select an artefact that has meaning for them and then for them to choose which parts of their story to tell. Hoskins (1998) used biographical objects to study the Kodi society in Eastern Indonesia. She described the process of narrative creation through objects as being 'significant because of the ways they are remembered, hoarded, or used as objects of fantasy and desire. They are used to reify characteristics of personhood that must then be narratively organized into an identity' (Hoskins, 1998, p.24). Hoskins (1998, p.198) summarized this process as a 'metaphor for the self'.

USE OF THE ACTIVITY

The artefacts activity has been used predominately in programmes focusing on responsible leadership and sustainability in major part because artefacts connect so strongly to participants' sense of purpose and place. As such it works so very well for us exploring responsible leadership which is the central theme of most of our programmes (Pless, 2007). Whilst we feel the activity resonates with these core themes the activity works equally well in other settings.

Within our programmes the use of storytelling, or the creation of a narrative to help learners organize their lived experience in meaningful ways, is a central element. For Clandinin and Connelly (2004, p.xxvi) 'experience is the stories people live. People live stories, and in the telling of these stories, reaffirm them, modify them, and create new ones. Stories lived and told educate the self and others'. Sharing stories about practice is an established approach for teaching and a recognized tool for developing reflective and critical thinking (McDrury and Alterio, 2003). We have found that the storytelling activity is frequently and most naturally followed by a process of reflection.

Tomkins (2009) describes this approach as 'active learning' or a series of staged activities, fundamental to the module design, which enable learners to reflect upon aspects of their personal and professional development and, ideally, to create future actions in order to develop and apply these new insights.

The leadership artefacts activity connects storytelling with the use of artefacts. In a management education context the use of artefacts has been shown to enable learners to use a more creative space to reflect upon prior experiences (Ward and Shortt, 2013).

The activity is conducted within a group, very often at the start of a programme when participants have come together for the first time. It is used to help learners to get to know one another and, in addition, to get to know the programme tutors. Each person, including the tutor/s, brings to the programme an artefact that has personal leadership significance, and passes around this artefact among the participants whilst telling the story of the object and its personal meaning.

Hornyak et al. (2007) describe learners undertaking this type of activity as 'intentional learners'. The learners are able to adjust quickly to different environments, to assimilate knowledge from a variety of sources and to develop lifelong learning skills. Similarly, Raelin (2000) identifies the value of reflection from a work-based learning perspective, which affords group participants an opportunity to share and discuss issues and then identify potential solutions. Raelin (2000) expands on the broader skills, such as confidence building and team working, which peer-group activity helps to foster. The skills and reflective learning associated with this activity align well with notions of action learning; indeed this activity could be used with a new group being inducted into action learning. Pedlar (2011) describes the practice of action learning in the following terms: 'what we do, we can also learn from – if we reflect on our actions and their outcomes' (2011, p.xxii).

The use of this activity with a newly formed group enables trust to be developed amongst the tutors and the programme participants. Luhmann's (1979) description of interpersonal trust as a key element in personal and work relationships, and in providing the foundations for developing new knowledge and experience, is helpful in this context. The opportunity to build interpersonal trust is significant for learners on the residential module and also during the remaining programme of study.

Further to trust development the artefacts activity helps learners to undertake a process of sense making with regard to their leadership learning. For example, one student brought along a sailing throw line as an example of the rules of an organization, the need for communication, knowledge of use of the equipment and the ability to save lives. Kempster (2006) argues that this process is more than an expansion of 'learning by doing' or experiential learning, as it encompasses tacit aspects of observation and participation in a variety of contexts. The design of the programmes, and the activity itself, creates a safe space and time for learners to offer insights of this experience. Importantly, in a leadership context, these activities are valuable for learners in underpinning the value of studying leadership itself. Jackson and Parry (2011) describe this as doing, seeing, talking and reading, and, in some cases, writing about leadership, which, as a method, helps learners to understand what good leadership looks like situated in their own experiences.

Activity theory is a useful lens to apply to this activity. Developed over a period of time by Yrjö Engeström, activity theory promotes the use of artefacts as 'object-oriented and cultural formation that has its own structure' (Engeström, 2005, p.20). A process of a shared understanding through the use of an artefact by a community can enable social transformation by individuals through a mediated activity (Engeström, 1999). Typically for Engeström this process takes place over an extended period of time. The activity itself is a moment in time during the module; the programme can be seen as an extended period of time for the community of learners to undergo a process of social transformation.

In summary, then, through this activity there is an emphasis on reflection, personal belief and peer-to-peer learning. Ciulla's (1998) pioneering work on ethical leadership alludes to the significance of these design principles, which include the importance of reflection and introspection and the establishment of a shared values base to build upon. Maak and Pless (2006) describe the need to focus on relationships and the daily difficulty that a leader may face in balancing conflicting values and ethical dilemmas. This activity is useful in helping individuals and groups to start exploring these little-discussed areas.

DESIGN

How is the Exercise Run?

The artefacts or 'leadership objects' exercise is flexible, takes approximately one hour, and is ideally run with small groups of between three and six participants, with groups sitting at tables set out in a café style. It is typically used as an ice-breaker activity during an intensive residential week and is an ideal activity to do on the first day as part of a getting-to-know-one-another exercise. With smaller group sizes, for example up to 15, and if time permits, the exercise can be run in one large group.

Delegates are asked, in advance of the programme, to bring with them an artefact. The details should be included with the programme joining instructions, for example:

Please bring with you a small object that holds personal leadership significance and be prepared to talk about your artefact and its significance during the first day of the course. Your object might be an award, a photograph, a certificate, a family keepsake or a poem – or something completely different.

We often combine this activity with a pre-coursework 'leadership timeline' exercise, as described by Steve Kempster in Chapter 8. The selection of the object prompts learners to give thought to their leadership lived experience in advance of the residential module week.

At the start of the activity a member(s) of faculty shares the artefact they have brought in order to help demonstrate the activity and what the participants will then go on to do in their own group. The added benefit of this is that programme participants also learn a little bit about the tutor(s) on the programme. The brief we have found to be effective is then as follows:

In your table group, take it in turns to each spend 10 minutes talking about:

- *why you chose your object*
- *what particular leadership significance it holds for you*

Pass your object around your group so everyone can see and feel it, and be prepared to ask questions of each other in order to gain a deeper understanding of the leadership significance of the object and to begin to get to know its owner a little better.

The questioning by story listeners is almost as important as the storytelling; it is very often through the questions that story tellers develop the story, evaluate their feelings and reflect more on what occurred, therefore enabling them to start to make sense of the situation (McDrury and Alterio, 2003). Care is needed so that story listeners, when asking questions, do not take over from the story teller by recounting their own experiences or anecdotes.

Our personal artefacts are described and illustrated here by way of examples:

Figure 9.1 Emma's map (left) and Phil's bike (right)

Emma's map:

> *My object is a 1971 copy of an Ordnance Survey map of Land's End in Cornwall, the most south-western tip of England. It's where I grew up and where I had some of my early leadership experiences as a young girl. The map is a vintage edition and is about the same age as I am. It also holds significance for me through previous generations of my family as my grandfather was a cartographer who worked for the Ordnance Survey. Further, my father, who was a Scout leader, made sure I joined the Scouts for a term in order to learn how to navigate and use a map and compass to find my way around. In fact, now, the first thing I do when I find myself in a new place is to buy a map so I can get my bearings.*
>
> *One of my first leadership experiences took place in St Buryan, not far from Land's End, when I went on an expedition for my Duke of Edinburgh award scheme. Six or seven of us had to each take turns at navigating and leading the group for a day. This was a valuable and interesting exercise for a 15-year-old.*
>
> *Also on the map is The Lizard and, in particular, Bass Point. This spot was also the setting for an incident that features large in my family's leadership history as it was where, in 1913, a sea clipper ship heading back from the West Indies and captained by my great uncle*

was shipwrecked. My great uncle had given the order to raise the sails in an attempt to outrun a storm brewing in the Bay of Biscay, and he was almost successful with this tactic but the storm caught up with them as they approached Falmouth Harbour and they were pushed onto the rocks at Bass Point. Everyone survived and my great uncle was the last man off the ship, but the shipping company didn't recognize his heroism and demoted him for the loss of the ship and the cargo! He's still a great leader to me, though.

So this map holds many significant memories for me; whenever I look at the map and the place names I can remember the stories that took place and the people involved.

Phil's bike:

As well as having the obvious sustainability links, I chose this object because of an incident in which sustainability met leadership for me on the bike.

The event was a fundraising bike ride from London to Paris. A large group of women (made up of smaller groups all raising money for their own preferred cause) set off from London at the same time. Our little group of six was raising money for an organization based in Wolverhampton in the West Midlands of the UK, which supports victims of domestic violence. Our team was of very varied bike fitness and experience and, as quite a keen cyclist, I somehow unofficially became the appointed leader. One thing that became very apparent to me very early on in the trip was how competitive some of these women were! It seemed that a lot of people were determined to ride as fast as they could to prove themselves, even if they had entered the event, like we had, as a team supporting the same organization. I thought this was a bit strange because for me the important thing was that we all stayed together if possible, and that we all got to Paris, had a great time and raised a good deal of money too – all of which we did. And the fabulous outcome of this was that, when it came to the final dinner in Paris, two of the three awards presented during the evening came to our team, one of them for best team spirit! And if I link this to my timeline, I'm aware that at times in my cycling past I have operated like the competitive women on that trip. In retrospect, I realized that for the first time in

> *my cycling life I had been employing the leadership skills and strategies that I've used in my professional life for many years.*
>
> *This got me thinking about the bike itself as a great metaphor for leadership, so before I finish I'd just like to share a few of those thoughts with you too:*
>
> - *You need balance to ride a bike, and you can only actually balance on a bike if you keep moving!*
> - *You need to have a pretty good idea where you're going – in other words you need direction, and the front and the back wheels need to be in alignment to make smooth progress.*
> - *You need to work hard to get up the hills, but when you get to the top of them you get a good view down the hill, and it gets easier for a while (although you still have to take care going down the hills that you don't gather too much speed and come to grief on the way down).*
> - *If you can work together with other people also on bikes (to use the Tour de France terminology, working as a peloton), then you can move much more quickly and efficiently, but you have to be really aware of the people around you, and work with them not against them! It's very impressive when it works well and terrifying when it doesn't!*

These are the stories behind our artefacts and the leadership significance we place upon them; our illustration above is how we introduce them during our programmes. The objects themselves are of little monetary value, yet they are highly prized possessions to us personally because of the memories and emotional attachment we have imbued in them. We hope these examples help to demonstrate why artefacts and storytelling are an evocative learning tool on leadership development programmes.

REFLECTIONS

This activity is a good way of getting people to open up about themselves in a very personal way, which, typically, would not happen so early in a programme. Many of the stories convey personal values or leadership rules of thumb that are significant to the individual and their view of the world. Through the use of oral storytelling, the story teller and the story listener are able to make sense of, and gain new insights into, their leadership practice and lived experience. We glimpse aspects of an individual that would perhaps otherwise be closed off – significant insights shared between relative strangers and a set of rich and meaningful experiences that have contributed to the process of them becoming a leader. An additional benefit of using an exercise like this early on in a programme is that those who are perhaps more introverted, and therefore find the whole experience of joining a large group daunting, can arrive feeling prepared in advance and comfortable in the choice of their artefact. Added to this, the fact that there is only a requirement of communicating with one or two other individuals makes this a highly accessible route into the more challenging aspects of the programme to come. The nature of the activity generally lends itself to people choosing an artefact and story that has a positive outcome. Whincup (2004), in his work on objects, indicates that these 'generally encapsulate the best of people's reflections about themselves' (2004, p.81). McDrury and Alterio (2003), in their work on learning through storytelling, comment that the stories that appeal to us connect with 'a situation [that] excites, upsets or intrigues us' (2003, p.47). From our experience these insights into the benefit of combining the use of artefacts and storytelling makes the activity accessible for all learners. The activity helpfully demonstrates many of the key skills that leadership development programmes often seek to address such as reflective and critical thinking, observation, confidence and trust building, and communication skills. Further, by its positive and collaborative nature it helps the group to operate more effectively at an early stage in the module and the programme overall.

Through the two examples illustrated in this chapter we have shared some of our own insights. By sharing the stories associated with the map, we learn about Emma's family and her early life, and her earliest memory of leadership. We sense the pride she still feels about the role that her father, grandfather and great uncle have played in her leadership identity.

Similarly, Phil's bike story gives us an insight into what 'makes her tick', what is important to her and something of her leadership journey from 'then' to 'now'. The bike serves as a memory for a significant experience Phil had, both physically and intellectually, and she shares how this event has helped her to better understand both leadership and sustainability.

Bolden in his integrated framework for leadership development (2006) describes, at an individual level, the need for an individual to consider 'who am I and why am I here' within a context of 'occupation, personality and life experience' and to view these factors through 'motivations, aims and ambitions, personal identity and needs analysis'. Through the artefacts activity and story sharing, peers are able to capture this foundation and are enabled to then move on to linking this to their organizational position and the ongoing development of themselves as leaders.

BOX 9.1   COMMENTS FROM LEARNERS

'It demonstrates both our differences and our similarities.'
'It demonstrates similarities in leadership journeys, challenges and insights despite different backgrounds.'
'Most objects were life/personality defining, not only about leadership.'
'I learnt and got more insight/new perspective into: what is leadership? Leadership versus management; [it was] anecdotal so easier to remember.'
'It broadened my horizons listening to others, especially hearing the story from Annie regarding the gourd.'
'I felt relief that other people had the same ethos, understanding and reason to be here.'

Crossan et al. (2013) also cite the use of symbols or objects as part of a process on a business programme to help participants introduce themselves at the start of the programme. Selecting a symbol or object that 'signifies who they are' helps to explore core concepts of 'virtue, character strengths, values and so forth' (2013, p.298).

We would like to share some of the comments from learners who have participated in this activity (Box 9.1), which we feel demonstrate how the activity has been helpful in the forming of new relationships, in increasing peer understanding and in sense making about different backgrounds and leadership journeys.

We hope that by telling the story of our experience through this chapter you may wish to develop or adapt your own version of the leadership artefacts activity to use in other leadership development programmes – or perhaps to consider which personally significant object you would choose and what your story about that artefact would be.

KEY TIPS

- Be prepared for one or two members of the group to have forgotten to bring an artefact with them. Reassure them that this is okay and that during the demonstration they will have time to think of an object that they 'would have brought' and to describe this or draw a picture of it.
- Give the groups a nudge to move on every 10 minutes (adjust to suit group sizes and time available for the activity) so that time is equally distributed. This may need a bit of extra management if there are different-sized groups as a result of overall numbers.

- Become engaged in some of the discussions that are going on and try to get a sense of some of the more unusual objects/stories.
- Set up an artefacts table. At the end of the exercise invite everyone, including staff, to place their artefacts on the table with a name label. This means that with large groups people can see the different artefacts that they might not have heard about during the activity, and if there is one they are intrigued by they can talk to that person during the week.
- Take a photo of the artefacts table, this can be shared after the week as a reminder of the artefacts and the stories of the people who shared them.

VARIATIONS ON THE ACTIVITY

Once you are familiar with the basic premise of the activity we are sure you will come up with your own variations on it. We offer a few ideas below to get you started:

- Variant 1. Provide participants with images on cards or a selection of objects and ask them to choose an object that resonates with them before asking them to articulate the meaning they associate with their chosen image/object.
- Variant 2. Ask people to work in pairs to tell the story relating to their artefact. People then introduce one another and tell the story of the artefact for their partner.
- Variant 3. Run the artefact exercise towards the end of the programme once participants have grown more familiar with one another. They can then add their thoughts on the artefact and weave their story around their experience of spending time with fellow learners on the programme. New insights for both the story tellers and the story listeners are often provided.
- Variant 4. Ask people to bring in a work artefact as opposed to a personal artefact.

REFERENCES

Bolden, R. (2006), 'Leadership development in context', Leadership South West Research Report 3, University of Exeter, accessed 20 June 2017 at http://business-school.exeter.ac.uk/documents/discussion_papers/cls/LSW-report-3.pdf.
Brody, C., C. Witherell, K. McDonald and R. Lundblad (1991), 'Story and voice

in the education of professionals', in C. Witherell and N. Noddings (eds), *Stories Lives Tell: Narrative and Dialogue in Education*, New York: Teachers College Press.

Ciulla, J.B. (1998), *Ethics: The Heart of Leadership*, London: Westport, CT.

Clandinin, D.J. and F.M. Connelly (1998), 'Stories to live by: narrative understandings of school reform', *Curriculum Inquiry*, **28**(2) 149–64.

Clandinin, D.J. and F.M. Connelly (2004), *Narrative Inquiry: Experience and Story in Qualitative Research*, San Francisco: Jossey-Bass.

Crossan, M., D. Mazutis, G. Seijts and J. Gandz (2013), 'Developing leadership character in business programs', *Academy of Management Learning & Education*, **12**(2), p.285.

Engeström, Y. (1999), 'Innovative learning in work teams: analysing cycles of knowledge creation in practice', in Y. Engeström et al. (eds), *Perspectives on Activity Theory*, Cambridge, Cambridge University Press, pp.377–406.

Engeström, Y. (2005), *Developmental Work Research – Expanding Activity Theory in Practice*, Berlin: Lehmanns Media GmbH.

Gauntlett, D. (2007), *Creative Explorations: New Approaches to Identities and Audiences*, Abingdon: Routledge.

Hornyak, M.J., S.G. Green and K.A. Heppard (2007), 'Implementing experiential learning: it's not rocket science', in M. Reynolds and R. Vince (eds), *The Handbook of Experiential Learning and Management Education*, Oxford: Oxford University Press, pp.137–52.

Hoskins, J. (1998), *Biographical Objects: How Things Tell the Stories of People's Lives*, New York: Routledge.

Jackson, B. and K. Parry (2011), *A Very Short, Fairly Interesting and Reasonably Cheap Book About Studying Leadership*, 2nd edn, London: Sage.

Kafai, Y.B. (2006), 'Constructionism', in R. Keith Sawyer (ed.), *The Cambridge Handbook of the Learning Sciences*, Cambridge: Cambridge University Press, pp.35–46.

Kempster, S. (2006), 'Leadership learning through lived experience', *Journal of Management & Organization*, **12**(1), 4–22.

Luhmann, N. (1979), *Trust and, Power: Two Works*, New York, NY: Wiley.

Maak, T. and N.M. Pless (2006), *Responsible Leadership*, Oxon: Routledge.

Mackenzie, A. (2012), 'Storytelling is at the heart of leadership', Cranfield School of Management 'Pause for Thought' digital article, accessed 21 July 2016 at http://www.som.cranfield.ac.uk/som/dinamic-content/media/Praxis/Storytelling%20is%20at%20the%20heart%20of%20leadership.pdf.

McDrury, J. and M. Alterio (2003), *Learning Through Storytelling in Higher Education*, London: Kogan Page.

McEwan, H. and K. Egan (1995), *Narrative in Teaching, Learning, and Research*, New York: Teachers College, Columbia University.

Moon, J. (2010), *Using Story: In Higher Education and Professional Development*, Abingdon: Routledge.

Moon, J. and D. Fowler (2008), '"There is a story to be told . . ." A framework for the conception of story in higher education and professional development', *Nurse Education Today*, **28**, 232–9.

Pahl, K. and J. Rowsell (2012), 'Artifactual literacies', in J. Larson and J. Marsh (eds), *The SAGE Handbook of Early Childhood Literacy*, London: Sage, pp. 263–78.

Pattison, S. (2007), *Seeing Things: Deepening Relations with Visual Artefacts*, London: SCM Press.

Pedlar, M. (2011), *Action Learning in Practice*, 4th edn, Farnham: Gower.

Pless, N.M. (2007), *Understanding Responsible Leadership: Role Identity and Motivational Drivers*, *Journal of Business Ethics*, **74**, pp. 437–56.

Raelin, J.A. (2000), *Work Based Learning: The New Frontier of Management Development*, New Jersey: Prentice Hall.

Tomkins, A. (2009), 'Learning and teaching guides: developing skills in critical reflection through mentoring stories', Higher Education Academy Network for Hospitality, Leisure, Sport and Tourism, accessed 14 December 2014 at http://www.heacademy.ac.uk/resources.

Ward, J. and H. Shortt (2013), 'Evaluation in management education: a visual approach to drawing out emotion in student learning', *Management Learning*, **44**(5), 435–52.

Whincup, T. (2004), 'Imagining the intangible', in C. Knowles and P. Sweetman (eds), *Picturing the Social Landscape: Visual Methods and the Sociological Imagination*, London: Routledge, pp. 79–92.

10. Leadership development through videography

Jon Billsberry* and Carolyn P. Egri

PURPOSE

The goals of this chapter are to first explain the theoretical underpinnings of videography as a tool for leadership development, second describe how videography sessions can be conducted in a manner that allows the reader to develop and deliver such teaching sessions themselves, and third discuss the lessons from multiple experiences with this approach for leadership development.

UNDERPINNING RESEARCH

We use videography to support a social construction approach to leadership development (Billsberry, 2013). In its simplest terms, the social construction approach to leadership holds that leadership is – like love, beauty, admiration and hate – 'in the eye of the beholder'. This means leadership is not a quality of leaders. Instead, it is a perception of observers; people who see the actions of leaders and for whom these actions equate to leadership. Their perceptions, and the alignment of what they see with their implicit or lay theories of leadership, determine who is regarded as a leader and who is not.

Videography is a valuable tool in the social construction leadership developer's repertoire because the film director's job of having an audience accept that a character is a leader is analogous to people's efforts to be seen as a leader. People have to manipulate their behaviour, language, appearance, surroundings and such like to influence how people see them – and the same is true for film directors trying to make one of their characters appear as a leader to the audience. Working with film to learn leadership has many benefits compared to other pedagogies (for example role plays, simulations, case studies). Specifically, the filmmaking process mimics many real-life perceptual processes, and utilizes actors who take direction.

The end result can be viewed and analysed multiple times for in-depth reflection and learning. When people view the same film, the different ways people 'read' the film highlights differences in individuals' perceptions, interpretations and implicit theories. Moreover, videography is new, fun, engaging and memorable for most students. But first we need to explain the underpinning theory, the social construction to leadership and implicit theories of leadership, and define videography.

The Social Construction of Leadership

The approach to leadership labelled as social construction (Billsberry, 2009; Fairhurst and Grant, 2010; Grint and Jackson, 2010; Meindl, 1995; Sjostrand et al., 2001) refutes traditional notions of leadership as a quality of leaders' traits (for example, Judge et al., 2002), behavioural skills (Kouzes and Posner, 2012; Mumford et al., 2007) or adaptability to contexts (Hersey et al., 1979; Heifetz et al., 2009). Instead, the social construction perspective argues that leadership is an attribution by others who observe and perceive actions as leadership according to their own implicit theories of leadership (Harvey, 2006; Pearce, 1995). These perceptions are not wholly independent and particular to the individual observer; there are powerful voices, social conventions and discussions that shape how people's observations are interpreted. Hence, the 'social' in social construction.

Interest in this approach to leadership has grown as scholars begin to appreciate the fundamental nature of the theory. When a group of eminent leadership scholars were summoned by James MacGregor Burns in the early 2000s to search for a 'general theory of leadership', ideas associated with social construction came to the fore. Harvey (2006) captures the conclusions of scholars looking for answers to two questions: (1) 'in the human condition, what makes leadership necessary?' and (2) 'what makes leadership possible?' (p. 39). They explored philosophy, evolutionary psychology, anthropology, history, political science, sociology, ethics and religious studies. They concluded that in the cruel and competitive world that humans evolved in, people realized it was a world of inequality where people had differing knowledge, skills and abilities. Some people had better ideas than others and these ideas were evaluated by self-interest, for example, improved hunting, scavenging or safety. People with these better ideas were the ones accorded the nomenclature of 'leader'.

Harvey's (2006) analysis is fundamental in helping students understand the concept of leadership. By going back to the roots of the word, it becomes clear that 'leader' and 'leadership' are words developed by humans to describe phenomena they observed. Unfortunately, 'leadership' happens to be a word that tricks us. Other words used to describe emotional responses to external stimuli – such as love, beauty, admiration and hate – do not contain an object in their construction, thereby allowing people to apply this emotion to a wide range of things without mistakenly thinking their emotion is a component of the thing being observed. In that the word 'leadership' contains the word 'leader', it suggests to the user that leadership is about leaders rather than observers. Harvey's (2006) analysis helps centre the concept as something integral to observers, a particular way of evaluating people, and thereby integrates implicit, or lay, theories (see for example, Schyns et al., 2011; Shondrick et al., 2010) into the social construction approach to leadership.

Once people have observed behaviour they process, analyse and interpret their perceptions. Is what they have just seen leadership? To do this, they must compare their observations with their own theories of leadership. Implicit leadership theories are largely held tacitly (Schyns et al., 2011) and so this comparison is conducted intuitively. Interestingly, this approach promotes implicit theories of leadership over other leadership theories because implicit theories of leadership affect behaviour, whereas leader-centred theories provide critical insight, but do not directly influence actions. Indeed, people's implicit theories of leadership shape what people do when wanting to be seen as a leader. And this is the common mistake that our students admit to. The first big 'a-ha' learning moment is when they realize that their own implicit theories of leadership are biasing them. Then they understand that if they want to be seen as leaders, they have to be observed doing things that other people regard as leadership – not doing the things that they think is leadership, which was their original thinking.

After theory relating to the social construction of leadership and implicit theories of leadership, the next knowledge domain that students are taught relates to observation, perception and interpretation as psychological processes. These topics feature in most psychology and organizational behaviour courses and need little elaboration. The topics our students find most useful in understanding how leadership perceptions are shaped are the perceptual biases such as fundamental attribution error and self-serving bias, attention and distraction, selective perception, gestalt psychology (especially closure) and framing.

Videography

Kempster (2009) argues that it is almost beyond debate that leadership is learned interpersonally through observation, participation and enactment. As such, videography (defined as 'filmmaking that captures moving images on electronic media') makes an ideal tool for leadership development as it involves interpersonal leadership of and participation with fellow film-makers and acting talent; keen observation and manipulation of human behaviour to create strong depictions of leadership for the audience; and the enactment of leadership behaviour. Moreover, videographic methods deny the definitive learning outcome of 'making someone a leader', as inherent in the approach is the notion of 'multiple readings of films' and a sense of engagement with a process of discovery. Instead, videography gives participants an opportunity to explore and express their leadership as part of their own leadership journey. Videography is particularly powerful because the intense and creative journey, and the ability to play and replay the artefacts, foster retention of ideas, experiences and lessons.

In its strictest terms, videography is defined as the capture of moving images on electronic media, thereby distinguishing it from filmmaking, which is the capture of moving images on celluloid or other physical film stock. However, in common parlance and in how we use the term, videography has come to mean non-professional filmmaking working within a digital world. In this chapter, we use the term videography for any activity in which students produce a video in digital form. We are limiting our discussion to student activities, but an obvious extension is the production of your own video artefacts for inclusion in your teaching.

Videography has many advantages as a teaching technique. Amongst the most important are that it is very involving, and gives students an opportunity to explore matters of interest to them. The learning process is very memorable, and it allows students to show off their work to friends, family and colleagues. Videography assignments can be adapted to suit many topics or learning objectives. The outputs can be reviewed repeatedly for critique and reflection. Videography also develops digital literacy in students whilst teaching them about leadership. But for us, there are three main advantages. First, it allows us to bring behaviour into my classrooms. We do not want to be talking to students about theory and its application to students; we want students to see, experience, shape and influence behaviour, and experiment with the application of theory. By making films about theory and its application, students learn practical, grounded and valuable lessons about leadership. Second, the process of depicting a leader in a film is analogous to the real-world challenge of being seen as a leader. Just as a film director must manipulate a multitude of factors to convince the audience that a particular character is a leader, so a prospective leader must manipulate a similar range of factors in their own circumstances. Third, people 'read' films differently. Although people may view the same film, each person will see different things in it. This informs students about perceptual biases, their own implicit theories of leadership, and the nature of reality.

There are several limitations with videography that must be mentioned at the outset. First, we have found that a very small minority of students are strongly set against videographic activities and prefer more traditional forms of teaching. To alleviate this problem, we make it known as students are signing-up that videography will be featured and in the opening session we explain why. Second, although videography brings behaviour into the classroom, it is not necessarily the same behaviour as in other contexts. This is because the camera modifies most people's behaviour. For most people, it takes a lot of time in front of cameras before they can relax and behave naturally. Third, the video medium is one where the 'normal' and 'mundane' do not sit comfortably. Films and TV programmes emphasize drama, the unusual and the unconventional. This means that videography works particularly well when looking at the margins or boundaries of ideas, but less well when looking at 'the everyday'.

DESIGN AND REFLECTIONS

Videography is incredibly flexible and can be applied to a wide variety of tasks. To illustrate this range, we describe below four different forms of videography that we use in our leadership courses.

Leadership Short Films

The social construction of leadership is most vivid when we fully integrate videography and leadership development and use videography as an analogy for leadership development. We do this in a week-long intensive activity that utilizes professional filmmaking equipment, professional actors and professional filmmakers to support the students (see Box 10.1).

The first five days run for about 12 hours each. The first day is dedicated to theory on the social construction of leadership, perception and filmmaking. The second day is dedicated to writing an original script and other pre-production work such as sourcing props and scouting locations. Filming happens on the third and fourth days. The fifth day, usually the longest by far, is dedicated to editing and post-production. On the sixth day, we view the films, discuss them and draw lessons.

Devoting an entire week – a very long week – to the task of making a film about leadership might be seen as indulgent if it were not that every element of the challenge addresses the practical manipulation of leadership perceptions. Students must make two versions of the same film using the same screenplay. Without changing the script, the words spoken or the order of scenes, they must change the perceptions of the audience towards

BOX 10.1   INSTRUCTIONS FOR A SHORT FILM USING PROFESSIONAL EQUIPMENT AND ACTORS

Part 1: The Screenplay

Each pair or group of three will agree on an idea for a short film, write the screenplay and do all the pre-production work, including the development of storyboards, before shooting (Wednesday and Thursday) and editing (Friday) the short film. The short film must be a new idea, not a remake of an existing film, and the film should be complete with a beginning, middle and end, not just a few scenes from something longer.

The 'twist' in this original film is that you are to produce two versions of the film using the same screenplay. In one version of the film, none of the characters are to be depicted as leaders. In the other version, one of the characters should be subtly manipulated (without altering the screenplay) so that he or she comes across to the audience as a leader. The goal, and higher marks, will go to groups where the manipulations are subtle, perhaps involving small changes of camera angle, lighting, tone of voice, inflection, emotion, alterations to costume, positioning, and so forth. Both versions of the short film should work as complete films, with the only difference being the portrayal of one character as a leader, or not.

The same screenplay must be used for both versions of your film; that is, the content of the dialogue must be the same in both versions, and the scenes and order of scenes must also be identical.

You have complete freedom to create whatever film you want. The only limitations are that you do not include any nudity, do not include anything that will be physically dangerous to shoot, and that you do not include any material that is subject to copyright (for example, commercial music). Please also remember that there are practical constraints given the time, location and budget realities.

This part of the assignment is worth 20 per cent of your total marks for the unit. These marks are divided evenly (as in 2 x 10 marks) between the two components that must be submitted for this assignment:

1. Your screenplay.
2. A 1,000-word essay describing, explaining and justifying the manipulations you intend to make in order to influence the audience's perceptions of leadership.

Part 1: screenplay

Write a screenplay for your original leadership film. The screenplay can be as long or as short as you want, as long as filming and post-production can be completed within the allotted time. The screenplay should be written in an industry-standard format.

Marks will be allocated against four criteria:

1. Engagement – the creation of a rich and believable story within which relevant course theories are subtly embedded and/or which that lends itself to multiple leadership interpretations by the audience.

2. Creativity – the extent to which you have developed a high-quality, new and innovative screenplay for your short film.
3. Ambitious practicality – the extent to which the screenplay is simultaneously ambitious and realistic.
4. Format – the degree to which you use the format outlined in the BBC's guidance.

Guidance on the format of a screenplay can be found on our unit website. The BBC wrote this file on how to format a film screenplay and these guidelines will be used as the template against which marks for format will be assessed.

Part 2: Essay

You should submit an essay (1,000 words maximum) in which you describe, explain and justify the manipulations you intend to make in the two versions of your film in order to influence the leadership perceptions of the audience.
Marks will be allocated against three criteria:

1. Application of theory to the task of depicting, or not depicting, behaviours in a leading character that are perceived as leadership (or not).
2. Ingenuity (as in the cleverness, originality and subtlety of your proposed manipulations).
3. The strength of your argument in persuading the reader that your proposed manipulations will be effective in influencing perceptions.

Part 2: The Film

In this part of the assignment, your main goal is the production of an original short film. (Description of film copied from Part 1 instructions.)

Assessment   The assignment carries 60 per cent of the total marks for the unit. Marks will be allocated thus:
Leader and No Leader films (60 per cent):

1. Overall quality, ambition and entertainment offered by the two films (30 marks).
2. Effectiveness of the perceptual manipulations (15 marks).
3. Subtlety, creativeness, ingenuity of the perceptual manipulations (15 marks).

Note: The remaining 20 per cent comes from an additional exegetical assignment submitted several weeks later.

one of their characters. In one version, the character must be viewed as a leader, but not in the other version. This means that every time the students point a camera or microphone, every time they set up a scene, and every time they give instructions to their actors, they have to think about the impact on the audience's leadership perceptions. Amongst other things, they can shape the way words are spoken, the emotions on display, costumes, make-up, props, camera angles and positions, lighting and shadows, set backgrounds, accompanying music and sound effects.

For this activity, we supply the equipment needed to make professional-quality videos.[1] This includes 'prosumer' Canon XA10/20/30 cameras capable of outstanding 1080p HD pictures, both full manual and full automatic control, phantom power and, crucially and most importantly, XLR audio input. For sound recording, there are microphones on boom poles, shotgun microphones and lavalier microphones. With all these, the audio is recorded on to the video file so that worries about synchronization are eliminated. We also supply professional tripods, dollies, LED lights, gel packs and lots of spare batteries. We levy a surcharge of AUD $750 to each student.[2] This money is used to hire professional actors (approximate ratio of one-to-one with students) and a couple of professional filmmakers to help with production and editing; and to pay for evening meals and some replacement costs. With this surcharge and the one-off grant from the university, the unit is financially self-sustaining.

The films that students have produced can be viewed on my Vimeo channel (https://vimeo.com/user19041673). Any assessment of the films' quality is subjective, but many exhibit professional elements and some have been judged sufficiently strong to be screened at film festivals. To assess the effectiveness of the activity, we reflect below on the three different ways in which it focuses on leadership.

One interesting aspect of this activity is students' choice of topic. Whereas the leadership literature traditionally focuses on the big issues of the day and the prominent leaders, these films have centred on things that matter to students. There is a strong domestic quality to many. Topics have included theft, honesty, abortion, pregnancy, heart attack at work, bereavement, immigration, racism, corporate ethics, cults, foreign students, domestic violence and adultery. We advise students to stay away from 'boredroom dramas' as these make very dull films, although some management students find this advice difficult. We occasionally throw in a theme, usually a film genre such as science fiction, silent movies or film noir, which helps to focus the undecided. Interestingly, these genre films more often deal with the type of global leadership issues we are more accustomed to seeing in leadership teaching. Giving students a free choice seems an important element of this activity as it allows them to explore topics that matter to them, thereby increasing their attachment to the project.

On a related note, it is interesting how students subvert the activity. Most groups try to have a 'twist' in their films; not just a narrative twist, but a twist with the format. For example, one group decided to use different actors in their lead role and just let the actor's personalities change the tone. Other groups have added silent scenes, or silent moments to the end of scenes, or used the same words in two completely different films (one about a foreign student coping with university life in Australia, the other about the same foreign student's recruitment as a terrorist). To pull off subversions, the students have to manipulate many changes successfully. Typical ones include changes in body language and performance, camera angles and the settings in which they shoot, particularly the accoutrements surrounding the actors.

On a filmmaking note, the first time we ran this course all of the output shared one characteristic. The 'non-leader film' featured a dramatic ending: the consequence of failed leadership. The film showing leadership, on the other hand, had a much duller ending. In subsequent courses, we mentioned this to students upfront and students found dramatic ways to end both versions of their film. Perhaps the most interesting was a film about a chap who has a heart attack at work in which his manager offers a friendly (leader) or unfriendly (non-leader) pep talk at his hospital bedside. In a comment on the worthlessness of words, both versions of the film end in the same way with the unhappy employee alone in his office waiting for his next heart attack.

In addition to creating a film about leadership and learning some film-making techniques related to the presentation of leaders, the activity is itself a leadership activity. Working in pairs or trios, students must lead effectively to deliver the film they envisage. One of the great benefits of using professional actors is that they are used to taking direction and this allows students to explore different ways of getting the result they want. Generally speaking, the most common observation after the event is that the students had to adapt their style to be more directive, but directive towards a goal that they had to communicate clearly to their actors, helpers and colleagues.

Leadership Theory and Application Videos

Videography can also be tailored to particular learning objectives, and produce memorable results. Two such video assignments are learning about leadership theory and application to practice. These activities utilize amateur videography equipment and software that are widely available and most often supplied by the students. (Amateur videography technical details and teaching support is described later in the chapter.)

Despite taking a social construction approach to leadership, we still feel it is important that students develop a critical understanding of the main leadership theories. Therefore one key challenge in leadership teaching is explaining a large number of leadership theories, and doing so without being dry or repetitive. Our solution to this age-old problem is to hand over the task to the students. We assign individuals or small groups (two or three) a theory and ask them to produce a video that explains the theory to their classmates (see Table 10.1). Not only does this bring variety to the teaching of the theories, it is an effective form of teaching as it is well established that having students teach other students is one of the most effective forms of instruction (Zajonc and Mullally, 1997). Moreover, it is a lot more interesting than listening to us for theory after theory.

In the Principles of Leadership residential course, after students have produced and discussed their theory videos, we want them to think about how this leadership theory might be applied in real circumstances. This activity has the considerable benefit of allowing students to locate the application of leadership theory to situations and issues that are important to them. It allows them to examine the complexity of leadership situations, to explore the robustness and realism of solutions, and to imagine different paths, outcomes and implications.

With small class sizes (up to 30), we show each video and after it is screened discuss the theory and then any filmmaking lessons. With larger class sizes, we ask students to post the videos to the unit website (on a securely protected intranet) and set an assignment in which they must watch other videos (usually a selection depending on the class size) and critically appraise the theories and discuss video production lessons.

Introductory Videos

Every time we set video assignments of any significant size, students will have first done an introductory video assignment. Our main objective with this form of videography is for students to learn the basics of video editing. Another objective is for students to develop an understanding of the fundamentals of videography and what can be achieved by the medium.

The introductory video assignment requires that each student create a short video (maximum five minutes) that does not contain any copyrighted material. Instructions for these introductory videos are: (1) introduce yourself to your classmates; (2) provide an explanation of what leadership means to you; (3) explain what you hope to achieve from this unit. As this is a developmental task to demonstrate learning of some basic videography skills, the assignment is assessed for 10 per cent of unit marks with one mark for completing each of ten specific requirements (such as content, formatting, transitions, timing).[3]

Students are required to post links to their introductory videos in the unit website. They are also asked to view all the other students' videos and

Table 10.1   Instructions for video creation

	Leadership Theory Explanation Video Instructions	Application of Leadership Video Instructions
Goal	Your goal is to create a short video that explains an assigned leadership theory or issue to your classmates.	Your goal is to create a video that informs your classmates about leadership theories and their application. Videos will contain three elements: ● A dramatic re-creation of an incident where leadership was required, but missing. ● A critical analysis of the incident applying one or more leadership theories. ● A second dramatic re-creation of the same incident, but this time with the leadership theory or theories discussed in Part 2 (see Box 10.1) applied to it.
Marking criteria	● Effectiveness of your video in explaining the theory to the audience. ● Clarity, depth and richness of your explanations. ● Your ability to 'bring the theory alive' and engage the audience. ● Ambition and creativity of your video. ● Level of professionalism in the production of your video.	● Clarity, depth and richness of your critical analysis of the incident. ● How well you apply theory in the second dramatic re-creation. ● Your ability to 'bring the subject alive' and engage the audience. ● Ambition and creativity of your video. ● Level of professionalism in the production of your video.
Video Length	10 minutes maximum	10 to 20 minutes
Parameters	● You should assume that your audience is intelligent, but unaware of leadership or leadership theories. Hence, the video needs to be informative, persuasive and entertaining. ● You have complete freedom to do whatever you wish in your video as long as you act within the laws of the land and no harm comes to any living being. ● Your video must not contain any copyrighted material whatsoever. ● Please ensure that anyone appearing in your video has signed a video release form.*	

* The video release form not only teaches students about best practice in filmmaking, it ensures that all participants have given their permission to be in the film and protects students if someone 'rips' their video from the unit's secure intranet and puts it on the internet. Even material shown on secure university intranets that prevent downloads can be ripped with screen recorder software.

record a substantial and meaningful comment about what they learned from each video. Not only does this create a lot of discussion about the art of videography, it also creates a positive teaching climate where students learn how to give and receive feedback and, of course, they get to know each other. Students comment that when they meet for the first time, it is like reuniting with friends rather than the typically mildly stressful start of a new unit.

Learning Amateur Videography Basics

In recent years, none of our students have complained about not having access to video cameras and many have experience uploading videos to the internet. Indeed, it is common for students to want to use their own cameras and equipment (including smartphones, action cameras and drones). Even so, at residential schools and during intensive presentations of leadership units, we supply students with amateur-level equipment so that all students are on a level playing field. The type of equipment provided is a high-definition (HD) camcorder with an external microphone socket, a shotgun microphone that sits on top of the camera, a lavalier microphone and a tripod. There are also a few dollies and LED lights around, and usually a green screen is set up.

A much greater worry is about editing software. Many students are unaware that their computers probably have free video-editing software on them. Macs have iMovie, and we encourage Mac users to download the free 30-day trial of Final Cut Pro X, which is even easier to use. Students with PCs should have MovieMaker on their machines.[4] While good enough for basic video editing, students report that this software is more cumbersome to use than the alternatives. Hence, we recommend that they download Adobe Premiere Pro CC or try Lightworks (free trials are available). There is also (relatively) easy-to-use animation software that make comic-strip-style cartoons and lip-sync avatars speaking students' words that produce professional-looking animated clips (for example, www.reallusion.com/crazytalk), and websites that allow students to create their own material (for example, www.videoscribe.co; www.goanimate.com; www.wideo.com).

In the past, we permitted the use of a limited amount of copyrighted material (such as clips from feature films) in the leadership theory and introductory video assignments. The enduring problem with this approach is copyright infringement (Champoux and Billsberry, 2012), but in most territories, if the finished products remain within the confines of the classroom and its controlled intranet, such use is permissible.[5] However, do check your own institution's interpretation of copyright law relating to students' video work.

To alleviate students' initial trepidation about the technology, we teach some basic filmmaking skills through video and face-to-face workshops, and in-class lectures. We also direct them to various sources of help, and have a discussion zone on the unit website to answer questions. After discussing the need to attune to the audience, we present '10 Top Tips', which focus on a few key elements:

1. You can 'say' much less on video than you think in the time. What are your key messages?
2. Video is a visual medium. Whenever possible, 'Show don't tell'.
3. Sound is more important than image.
4. Position the camera for the best shot, not because it is convenient or comfortable.
5. When you want to close in or pull out of a subject, move the camera, don't zoom.
6. Use a tripod or other solution to support the camera when possible.
7. To avoid distraction, to create the tone you want, and to plant subliminal messages, really think about your backgrounds.
8. Narrative over images and footage works well, but don't overuse. Avoid talking heads with no supporting visuals.
9. Amplify actions, behaviour, gestures, appearances and so on, but not to the point of absurdity.
10. Credit/acknowledge all your sources. (Note: we don't include credits in the time budget for the film, which means that students can credit people appropriately.)

Last but not least, we always advise students to do some test shoots to check everything is working properly, especially the microphone. The most common problem is getting footage from cameras into the software, so students should check that they can import the test footage into their video-editing software.

CONCLUSION

These videography activities range from leadership development learning from videography, to videography in service to leadership as an instructional technique. Many of our students experience all or most of these activities as they are delivered in two separate and unconnected units. By the end, they are digitally literate and able to create their own videos and to project themselves effectively as leaders. With the rare exception, students have developed more creative and imaginative videos than we would have thought possible.

Leadership insights and skills that students learn through videography endure long after the course ends. We receive reports from about half of my graduates telling us they have created their own video material and found this skill useful at work. More importantly, they tell us they have retained the notion of leadership being 'in the eye of the beholder'. In fact, they tell us they cannot shake the idea that every time they hear someone talking about leaders and leadership, they realize the person is talking about themselves. And along with this, they realize that to be seen as a leader, they must be seen doing the things that other people think is leadership.

KEY TIPS

- Within your overarching learning objective, give students as much freedom and latitude as possible so that their films matter to them.
- Set tasks that requires students to think about the perceptions of the audience.
- Make student groups as small as possible for team assignments.
- Ensure that all films are screened and discussed by students.
- Sound is much more important than vision. Invest in sound equipment.
- Have all students edit their videos on the same configuration of computer and software. The 30-day free trial of Final Cut Pro X on iMacs is highly recommended.
- Encourage originality, creativity and adventure – even when it is risky. Tell students that there are more marks for heroic failure than for the mundane. And then mark accordingly.

NOTES

* The Chapter is written from the perspective of Jon Billsberry and his videography teaching experiences.
1. A university grant for course enhancement funded the purchase of six sets of this equipment.
2. This surcharge is permitted under Australian rules if there is a non-surcharge alternative way of achieving the unit outcomes. We offer an alternative version of the unit without the surcharge, in which students make their films over a whole trimester without the help of professional actors.
3. Components are: (1) a title near the beginning of the video; (2) at least two transitions sensibly placed somewhere in the video to signify a significant switch of the viewers' attention; (3) credits that acknowledge the contributions of everyone who has helped in the making of your video, somewhere towards the end of the video; (4) your appearance on screen for at least 20 per cent and no more than 80 per cent of the video's length; (5) at least 30 seconds during which there are multiple layers of sound; (6) at least 30 seconds

of narration (for example, where the voice the audience hears does not appear to come from anyone on screen); (7) a creative element that is more elaborate and engaging than a person speaking directly to a camera; (8) an introduction of yourself; (9) an explanation of what leadership means to you; (10) an explanation of what you hope to achieve from this unit.

4. Although Microsoft does not supply MovieMaker with Windows 10, it can be downloaded free from their website.
5. See Promoting Fair Use in OnLine Video for an unofficial US interpretation of legal issues associated with the use of copyrighted materials: http://fairusetube.org/guide-to-youtube-removals/3-deciding-if-video-is-fair-use.

REFERENCES

Billsberry, J. (2009), 'The social construction of leadership education', *Journal of Leadership Education*, **8**(2), 1–9.

Billsberry, J. (2013), 'Teaching leadership from a social constructionist perspective', *Journal of Management & Organization*, **19**(6), 679–88.

Champoux, J.E. and J. Billsberry (2012), 'Using moving images in management education: technology, formats, delivery and copyright', in J. Billsberry, J. Charlesworth and P. Leonard (eds), *Moving Images: Effective Teaching with Film and Television in Management*, Charleston, NC: Information Age Publishing, pp.149–58.

Fairhurst, G.T. and D. Grant (2010), 'The social construction of leadership: a sailing guide', *Management Communication Quarterly*, **24**(2), 171–210.

Grint, K. and B. Jackson (2010), 'Toward "socially constructive" social constructions of leadership', *Management Communication Quarterly*, **24**(2), 348–55.

Harvey, M. (2006), 'Leadership and the human condition', in G.R. Goethals and G.L.J. Sorenson (eds), *The Quest for a General Theory of Leadership*, Cheltenham: Edward Elgar, pp.39–45.

Heifetz, R.A., A. Grashow and M. Linsky (2009), *The Practice of Adaptive Leadership: Tools and Tactics for Changing Your Organization and the World*, Boston, MA: Harvard Business Press.

Hersey, P., K.H. Blanchard and W.E. Natemeyer (1979), 'Situational leadership, perception, and the impact of power', *Group & Organization Management*, **4**(4), 418–28.

Judge, T.A., J.E. Bono, R. Ilies and M.W. Gerhardt (2002), 'Personality and leadership: a qualitative and quantitative review', *Journal of Applied Psychology*, **87**(4), 765–80.

Kempster, S. (2009), *How Managers Have Learnt to Lead: Exploring the Development of Leadership Practice*, New York: Springer.

Kouzes, J.M. and B.Z. Posner (2012), *The Leadership Challenge: How to Make Extraordinary Things Happen in Organizations*, 5th edn, San Francisco, CA: Jossey-Bass.

Meindl, J.R. (1995), 'The romance of leadership as a follower-centric theory: a social constructionist approach', *The Leadership Quarterly*, **6**(3), 329–41.

Mumford, T.V., M.A. Campion and F.P. Morgeson (2007), 'The leadership skills strataplex: leadership skill requirements across organizational levels', *The Leadership Quarterly*, **18**(2), 154–66.

Pearce, W.B. (1995), 'A sailing guide for social constructionists', in W. Leeds-Hurwitz (ed.), *Social Approaches to Communication*, New York: Guilford, pp.88–113.

Schyns, B., T. Kiefer, R. Kerschreiter and A. Tymon (2011), 'Teaching implicit leadership theories to develop leaders and leadership: how and why it can make a difference', *Academy of Management Learning & Education*, **10**(3), 397–408.

Shondrick, S.J., J.E. Dinh and R.G. Lord (2010), 'Developments in implicit leadership theory and cognitive science: applications to improving measurement and understanding alternatives to hierarchical leadership', *The Leadership Quarterly*, **21**(6), 959–78.

Sjostrand, S.E., J. Sandberg and M. Tyrstrup (eds) (2001), *Invisible Management: The Social Construction of Leadership*, London: Thompson Learning.

Zajonc, R.B. and P.R. Mullally (1997), 'Reconciling conflicting effects', *American Psychologist*, **52**(7), 685–99.

11. Use of multi-ethnic, contemporary and historical finger puppets

Arthur F. Turner

PURPOSE

The salient use of puppets touches upon many theoretical ideas, both ancient and modern, however this chapter will seek to look at the underpinning theory that helps to explain their uses and impact. Two different but complementary theories are key here. First, Vygotsky (1981) highlights the way in which objects help, in humans, to mediate cognitive ideas. Second, that knowledge transfer occurs through translation acting as 'mediating actors' (Rovik, 2016). The puppets seem to do this in leadership development. Descriptions of practice plus feedback from two recent delegates will help to tie in the theory with practice and alert the reader to the possibilities of using finger puppets in many different leadership development opportunities. The puppets are an adjunct to learning, used in circumstances during learning opportunities where feedback, reflection or another's point of view are required to more deeply examine an area of learning. Once the puppets are introduced many different interactions have been observed. This physical introduction of a puppet moves delegates from a position of observing only surface variations to those changes of a deeper structural nature, variation and insight (Kempster et al., 2014). This change allows the delegates to become more adept at engaging in the inherently difficult task of frame changing (Nelson et al., 2010).

After developing insights through some interlocking theories and related ideas in the first part of this chapter, the second part describes the various roles that the puppets have managed to 'adopt' since the start of their use in leadership development programmes in 2012. It is hoped that this description will help the designers of leadership development interventions to consider the use of all sorts of puppets and other humanoid figures in the wider circle of artefact and aesthetic approaches in this field (Sutherland, 2014; Page et al., 2013). To give depth to this insight I will focus in detail on one group as they worked with puppets in a leadership programme over a period of two days; I draw on my (and their) observations of the impact of the puppets on their learning and development.

In the final section I will reflect upon the use of puppets – pitfalls and limitations – and offer some key tips.

THEORETICAL APPROACHES – PUPPETS AS LIMINAL OBJECTS

Emergent from my own research, in the development of leadership in middle managers, was the observation as to how managers learning about leadership, particularly in the outdoors, drew on objects in their reflections, explanations and emergent ideas (Turner, 2013).

In Chapter 9 of this volume, Emma Watton and Philippa Chapman outline the case for the role of leadership artefacts in leadership development programmes, whereby participants bring into a facilitated learning event an artefact that means something personal to them. The use of puppets seems to reverse this idea, whereby an artefact – in this case a small finger puppet – can become something personal and act in the same way, eventually, as the previously chosen, more personal, artefact. Each artefact chosen or selected seems to 'store' ideas about leadership development in the same way as souvenirs act as a repository for holiday memories. For further explanation of this idea see Chapter 12: 'Seeing beyond the usual – the social photo matrix (SPM) as an experiential method of leadership development', by Wadii Serhane, Sigrid Endres and Jürgen Weibler.

Leadership development programmes can sometimes target theoretical ideas through words or written models, thus denying the physicality of human beings. Places of learning are often fixed (chairs, tables and rooms) and the main medium of transfer, speech or written word. Yet puppets can challenge that status quo by acting to translate the imparted knowledge into practical use – acting, for example, as boundary spanners. Both types of artefacts, chosen or finger puppets, produce a physical response to them that leads to philosophical views of the ways in which the body and mind link in learning opportunities (Schandorf, 2012). The puppets, with their lived characters, represent a wide range of the ways in which people engage with the world, and challenge and disrupt the way in which the delegates see their own world and the fundamental problems of leadership. In addition, the puppets promote reflexivity (Shaw, 2010) that allows the participant to think about themselves and their interactions in leadership scenarios – revealing something of the underlying influences on them.

The puppets therefore play a part in the practice of reflection on actions (Schon, 1987). This is not a one-off reflection as the puppets are with the participants across a period of time, both as an object but also as an entity. The puppet character remains in their minds as a tangible set of ideas for which there are multiple potential triggers for thoughtful and thought-provoking interaction with practice. This differs from the one-off presentation of an example of leadership, or of the behaviour of a leader, which might be more transient or lost in the moment.

Descartes's writing in the 17th century put forward the argument that the mind and body were not one unit but separate entities and from this can be conceived that the mind and body each have a different epistemology and a different ontology. Ideas inside the head or mind have no shape nor do they occupy a physical space, whereas such objects in the world – that can be felt and touched – occupy space and can therefore be 'sensed' in different ways. Therefore handling puppets enables the body and mind to be linked with the physical shape of the puppet capturing ideas with 'no shape' to retain or borrow a physical presence.

In a similar vein, a modern philosopher, David Abrams (1996, p.57) reminds us of the interwoven experiences of Aboriginal people whereby:

> [O]stensibly inanimate objects like stones or mountains are often seen to be alive [. . .] particular places and persons and powers may all be felt to participate in one another's existence, influencing each and other and being influenced in turn.

I return to Vygotsky. Drawing on his work (he was a pioneering Soviet Belarusian psychologist with a diverse interest in the fields of child development and developmental psychology), I was interested to discover whether the introduction of a tangible artefact, such as a puppet, could aid an educational internalization process, leading to the deeper processing of information imparted throughout the duration of the courses or programmes.

Vygotsky, who was keenly interested throughout his body of work in the role of mediation tools in cognitive processes, and who reinterpreted the psychological concept of internalization of knowledge, stated that:

> Internalization can be understood in one respect as 'knowing how'. For example, riding a bicycle or pouring a cup of milk are tools of the society and are initially outside and beyond the child. The mastery of these skills occurs through the activity of the child within society. A further aspect of internalization is appropriation, in which the child takes a tool and makes it his own, perhaps using it in a way unique to himself. Internalizing the use of a pencil allows the child to use it very much for his own ends rather than drawing exactly what others in society have drawn previously. (Vygotsky, 1978)

He believed that humans, standing apart from any other living creatures, have a desire to mediate their actions through artefacts, and to cause the appropriation of these mediational means, be they any one of a whole range of potential artefacts (Vygotsky, 1981).

Further to this he stated: 'the central fact about our psychology is the fact of mediation' (Vygotsky, 1982, p.166). In this instance, artefacts clearly do not serve simply to facilitate mental processes that would otherwise exist. Instead, they fundamentally transform and shape them. In these various ways historical puppets seem to act as translators and their role could be interpreted as the: 'power behind the "travel" of ideas stems not from one powerful central agent, but from the richness of interpretations that the idea triggers in each actor' (Rovik, 2016, p.291).

The puppets enable the learner to be more central to the process of learning – their own words, mediated through the puppet, encourage the articulation of challenging models and ideas. Educationalists such as Parker J. Palmer and Philippa Cordingley have been instrumental in the ideas of incorporating the learner into the process of learning. Cordingley (2010), whose research included the incorporation of tools that: 'connects abstract principles with detailed illustration and practical examples', works through artefacts connected to the workplace. Palmer, through his reverence to the world and thoughts of the students and allowing them time to articulate their thoughts, offers this explanation, which resonates in the leadership development world using historical puppets: 'with its complexities and convolutions, surprise is a constant companion: its lies just around the bend or hidden in the next valley, and though it startles us, it often brings us delight' (1998, p.112).

Lévy-Bruhl, a French philosopher who died just before the Second World War, observed that the modern logic of the Western world did not overcome the primitive logic of a less developed world. He hypothesized that there was a law of participation that he described as pre-logical. In this principle he foresaw that logic does not overcome the tendencies of our more primitive cerebral structures and processes. This amounts to a set of thought processes where a being or an object can be both itself and something else. This theory of participation helps to outline how the use of puppets works in a leadership development setting by encouraging or even precipitating representation and/or symbolization.

The idea of the puppets working with individuals links, in my mind, to the work of George Herbert Mead. Douglas Griffin (2002) cites Mead's ideas in his book *The Emergence of Leadership*, whereby an individual is not just a unit of interaction but, through learning, becomes a different individual through 'the emergence of the individual in interaction'.

The use of the puppets provides an interaction between an idea and a supposed character. They help to move an idea or concept to a wider-ranging set of interactions and mediations between the participant's growing ideas and pre-existing thoughts, through a mediating 'object-puppet'.

Lindsay Hamilton's work in a veterinary surgery highlights this growing interest in objects and their meanings. Using Hamilton's insights we may be able to track how objects '"move", "attach" and "detach" themselves to enact and magnify the dominant narratives, discourses and social relations' (Hamilton, 2013, p.272). In her conclusions she identifies this phenomenon as:

> [M]aterials not only 'move' to reflect organizational relations and values but also take on a form of meaningful agency in their own right. It has offered a different way of interpreting the 'transformative' power of cultural meaning-making by shedding light on the contested, political and sometimes even 'magical' nature of what are easily overlooked as 'mundane materials'. (2013, p.284)

Finally objects – and I am counting the historical puppets and other puppets as objects – carry meaning with them that can be observed and interpreted by individuals in an individual way and that carry for them both meaning and insight. One object can carry different meanings for different people and different times (Cannadine, 2016) – this is why, I think, puppets are useful in precipitating or stimulating a catalyst change in individuals learning about leadership.

BACKGROUND TO UTILIZING PUPPETS AS A DEVELOPMENT AID

Prior to using the finger puppets in my courses I had used a similar experiential concept where each person was given a picture card containing details and an artistic representation of an unusual or rare wild animal. Each person was asked, in a non-directed manner, to use the card to help their understanding throughout the day. It appeared to the facilitators that people were studying their cards, internalizing the information and using it to feed back to the group. Similar links to their card, as captured by the phrases 'my flying squirrel card leads me to glide more slowly across what I believe', were often heard throughout the day. This created a feeling that the use of objects with a history or background had a fundamental role to play in what Vygotsky termed as mediation. Not only are the thought processes mediated through the object but they are also changed and altered through interaction (Griffin, 2002).

The chance encounter with a finger puppet led to the discovery of a wide range of small finger puppets, produced by an American company called the Unemployed Philosophers Guild. These objects are based on a wide

Figure 11.1   A pair of puppets – ready for action

range of famous individuals and concepts, elaborately decorated with a strong likeness to the character that they portray. Attached to each puppet is a small booklet that, in a minor way, identifies some crucial facets of their character. A broad range of puppet characters occupy a diverse blend of personalities (Figure 11.1) and people, taking in mainly historical characters across a spectrum that includes race, religion and gender. The use of the puppets can symbolically represent both a different approach to a topic as well as a strong achievement or outstanding achievements.

These historical finger puppets have been bought randomly over a period of a few years and are often used spontaneously, without the course facilitator trying to manipulate the choice or combination. The puppets travel in a box, or a smaller cohort attends workshops in a bag.

I recall an earlier use of the puppets in an Institute of Leadership and

Management (ILM) Level 5 group in a Welsh Council programme and they were asked to feed back on the day's activities through a randomly selected historical finger puppet. This proved to be an interesting and engaging way of working with the group and led to some interesting observations. Some people were able to 'play' their character well, using both appropriate voices but also in assuming some of the traits of the character itself.

From the initial use of the puppets I entered into a second phase of experimental use of them, particularly in terms of seemingly random unconnected opportunities. They have now been used in several other, initially experimental, options. They have been used with additional data sheets as philosophical puppets; they have been used on programmes to behave as temporary programme mentors.

During these experimentation periods it became clear that the puppets fulfilled a joint role as mediating object in the translation of conceptual ideas into an individual's specific context and approaches. They seem to play a part in learning, as Hamilton's empirical research observed in the field, as the puppets are able to move or be moved and to detach and attach themselves to workshop delegates and themselves. This helps to shed light upon the topic or issues under discussion. For example, a puppet-mediated exercise might allow participants to see different points of view – as Hamilton observed objects might do – in creating meaningful agency. Moreover, 'puppetry' objects have semi-human agency in the form of their interpreted characteristics or historical activities, which can shed light on opinions and points of view – the puppet becoming, as Lévy-Bruhl suggests, both itself and something else and, I would add, representing another aspect of a problem or issue.

Use of the Activity

This is a description of a two-day interaction within a longer programme of four days. The description of this use of puppets gives a fine-grained view of their use.

The data was collected contemporaneously with the permission of the group and included a photographic record of the interaction of the puppets with the candidates. The analysis of the data, which included video and audio transcripts and independent observations, allowed for a more relaxed interpretation of the puppet use and helped to highlight the ways in which puppet sessions can be run.

During the first day of a four-day course covering various aspects of leadership development, delegates were shown a selection of puppets embodying various famous people and characters in history and/or fiction and were asked to select one puppet to keep with them throughout the day.

Choosing puppets and subsequently collecting them at the start of later days in the course had the overall effect of increasing the level of discussion and movement in the room.

The puppets chosen, from random, were as follows: Thomas Edison, Rosa Parkes, Julius Caesar, Andy Warhol, Alice in Wonderland, Elizabeth I and Buddha. The resource of pre-manufactured finger puppets through the Unemployed Philosophers' Guild gives a broad selection of historical figures. Most of the characters depicted are well known and would have broad exposure to most delegates, who may well start with a preconception of their character. Philosophers such as Descartes and Abrams remind us that inanimate objects can often be charged with meaning, and a new association with a puppet framed around a small booklet of facts over a few moments can begin to transform thinking. This attachment occurs at various speeds with individuals over the few days of interaction. Each puppet already has a meaning depicted by either a tangible memory in the part of the participant or by the rubric depicted on their attached information booklet. Moreover, interpretation of their character deepens as the exercise continues. In addition, the puppet also induces physical movement and many delegates place the puppet on their finger, perhaps suggesting a bridge between Descartes's separate ontology of mind and body.

Initially some delegates on the course were apprehensive about the puppets although they became used to the presence of the puppets, which became something 'tangible' to use during the day, mainly as a talking point, encouraging humour whilst suggesting novelty. Despite the fact that the puppets drew some cautious reactions amongst the delegates, there was an overall feeling of something different in this approach to learning (see Figure 11.2).

For this particular four-day programme I chose a different way of engaging with the puppets. The day began by asking delegates to select a puppet that would be 'theirs' for a whole two days within the study days. In some ways this ritual of selection reminds me of the rituals that surround liminal space and how the selection of the puppet introduces a gateway into the liminal space of learning (Meyer and Land, 2005). Liminality is an anthropological concept that notices that human activities, particularly in transition, such as puberty, are surrounded by rituals and this helps the humans in transition to learn these new roles. The rituals around the use of the puppets help to keep the participants in a zone of transition as they learn how to develop their leadership. Having to collect their puppets at the start of each course day offered an immediate yet indirect hint of what type of work was to come throughout the day. Positive feedback included that the tone of the day was set early on, partially by use of the puppets, as

Figure 11.2   Puppets as part of the fabric of learning

being out of the normal range of training courses, a fact that was considered in a positive light.

Delegates seemed to fit into one of two categories with regard to the use of their puppet. The first group seemed reticent to use their puppets, demonstrating embarrassment when selecting them and reluctance to hold them, even when being asked to use them for the purpose of that particular exercise. They appeared to use them simply, and without refinement, because they were expected to as part of the programme. This did not have a negative impact – but gradually the delegates became used to the presence of the puppets and used them as instructed. Often the participants who are more naturally inclined towards the use of the puppets were markedly more enthusiastic about their use, silently picking up the puppet during work together. However, the familiarity with the puppet emerged more strongly with their use and the initial reactions did not seem to negatively impact on their use nor the insights that they gave to the group.

The second, larger, group were fully engaged in the use of the puppets, enjoying the selection process, taking their chosen puppet with them from task to task without prompting. None of the group engaged with the puppets as far as to 'mock' dialogue with them, however they were used significantly for gesticulating, enhancing emphasis on key points, and several delegates 'looked' at things with the puppets.

Two tasks in particular required the delegates to actively use the puppets as opposed to simply having them nearby through the rest of the course. The first task set was for the delegates to research the background of their chosen puppet. This was an exercise undertaken in the context of leadership development in the wider remit of a qualification for managers and was priming the candidates for looking at the topic of leadership in a different light. The puppet characters represent a wide and diverse range of leadership over and above the theories of leadership that had been introduced during the day. The hope was that this exercise of enquiry would lead to what Hamilton (2013) described as being an object that magnified the prevailing narratives, discussions and social structures in the experience of the delegates, related to the pre-existing narrow view of leadership expressed at the beginning of the programme.

Having researched their background and history, several of the group expressed a wish that they had chosen different puppets as there was a vast amount of information available to them about the person and narrowing down discoveries and linking this to leadership development had proved difficult.

All of the delegates were confident in their presentations, however, and several enjoyed the task greatly, most notably S. with Thomas Edison; E. with Queen Elizabeth I; and S. with Buddha – each of whom had been inspired on a personal and professional level and talked with great enthusiasm, using the embodiment of the character of the puppet whilst engaging in the theoretical aspects of the leadership programme.

The task also appeared to have the effect of allowing the delegates to consider historical events through another person's eyes, many expressing empathy for 'their' person's/puppet's situation. Some of the notable thoughts relating to the delegates' research and to leadership development were:

- Delegate one's quote from Julius Caesar – 'Ask everything of your men but reward them like kings'. This resonated with the whole group and drew a lively discussion about methods of motivation.
- Delegate two's empathy with Andy Warhol, who tried to instigate novel approaches but was scorned by those around him who preferred more conventional approaches to work problems. This delegate saw himself in an artistic role, which was not always fully understood or appreciated by the team around him.
- Delegate three's uncovering of all of the less-known discoveries of Thomas Edison, how influential he was – without people necessarily

knowing exactly what he had done – made a great impact on the group. The group became strongly involved in considering whether or not they overlook skills and characteristics of people within their work teams; the pitfalls of assuming that a person is only 'useful for one purpose' and what this may do to their motivation level; and also a discussion around how to fully engage team members in order to fully realize their potential.

The second task in which delegates were asked to specifically include their puppet was during an action learning set, where they were instructed to ask at least one of their questions regarding an offered issue of seemingly excessive and not well planned change to the structure and layout of their office 'from the puppet's point of view'. These were fascinating and varied, humorous and invited much lateral thinking, and offered a significantly different 'feel' to those asked by the delegates from their own standpoints, which tended to be more (however unwittingly) leading and also more conventional.

In this instance, it would appear that the puppets become observers, offering an 'external viewpoint' coming from the delegates themselves. This appeared in several cases to allow freer speech than might have been the case had the puppets not been involved.

Questions the 'puppets' asked included:

- Queen Elizabeth I – 'Why are you running around like headless chickens?'
- Andy Warhol – 'Are you afraid to stand out from the crowd?' 'Was this change/move necessary?'

A further point was then made that the company for which the delegates' work was attempting to position itself as a sector leader for innovation, but there was an overall feeling that this was not in fact the case and that things had stagnated somewhat:

- Buddha – 'Where are you going?' 'What do you want to achieve?' 'Who are the enlightened ones?' 'What will it take to get where you're going?' 'How will you know when you've got there?'
- Rosa Parkes – 'Who will the change benefit?'

Another notable puppet/delegate parallel was between L. and Andy Warhol, with L's marketing role appearing to be particularly artistic. L. discussed how he would often put forward a more creative idea, only to have it replaced by something more in keeping with the overriding style of what 'has always been done' at the company.

As well as the puppets being an embodiment of their 'real-life persona', in several cases it was felt by the delegates as though they were at least, to some extent, an embodiment of themselves, or of their work personas. It may have been that their research of their puppets drew them into their own particular areas of interest, thus further skewing the idea that delegates' and puppets' lives contained parallels.

Pitfalls and Limitations

The use of historical puppets has been a very interesting engagement with academics, facilitators and leadership development delegates since 2010. However, they are not offered as a panacea for all approaches, clients or organizations seeking to improve and develop leadership. Facilitator confidence is essential when introducing them to a group. Indeed the use of puppets, along with the use of other artefacts, can be highly contested unless the learning is facilitated through appropriate timing and well-adjusted reflection(s).

The pitfalls and limitations can be characterized in many ways. The puppets are a soft toy, and their use, for example, for some people may not meet the expected gravitas of the leadership development investment. The puppets are expensive to import and similar puppets used in expanding options have been expensive and time-consuming to commission.

Historical puppets as described here are ideal, and other commercially available puppets can work too. Indeed I have also commissioned knitted puppets for the Welsh market, where no historical puppets exist commercially.

The use of a mixture of historical figures is very stimulating yet there are clear challenges in using certain characters with a cultural mix of delegates who sometimes have not heard of the character or who are instinctively opposed to the views or ideas represented by the puppet. Clearly religious icons or controversial figures such as Che Guevara have to be presented to groups carefully. In addition to this, the puppets alone may not carry sufficient information held on their booklet attached to their clothing and so delegates may not have sufficient awareness of their character – even a character who is superficially well known – in order to use them with enough confidence that they are 'getting it right'.

Despite the confidence of underpinning theory and my experiences thus far using the puppets, they do not have a universal role in my designs and enactment of leadership development or management training; the puppets can often lie in their box unused, waiting for an appropriate moment to be utilized. Timing is key for the group and the facilitator, because their use over four years has revealed that reactions by groups are variable and alternative exercises or approaches need to be on hand!

The underpinning theories of objects (Vygotsky, 1978) as helping humans mediate is core to the use of the puppets and in understanding how the puppets work. Using a physical object in debating and dealing with intangible ideas linked to management and leadership gives a physical shape to aid sense making and reflections; it allows us to mediate theoretical ideas. The use of puppets also allows for the participants to partner with their puppet to find their voice and express their own ideas through the liminal space of the puppet's character – quite a liberating and, for some, confidence-giving dynamic.

Objects both in pre-history (Abrams, 1996) and in a more modern political sense (see prime ministers' props, Cannadine, 2016) have a role in enabling people to find meaning in their everyday experience of the world. Historical puppets, as nuanced objects, appear to help to do the same in understanding leadership development. Reflectivity also allows the participants and the facilitator to probe more generally about the difference in people and to open out debates otherwise hidden from view. The puppets enable general discussions about leadership as well as inner discussions about each delegate's own leadership challenges. This creates a way in which Shaw (2010, p.236) suggests that 'reflexivity, on the other hand, is an explicit evaluation of the self' and allows for people in the world and objects in the world to be intimately interacting and interconnected. Use, and exposure to their use, has given rise to a broad band of applications throughout traditional approaches to leadership development. Use of questions via the puppet, overhearing fictitious conversations between puppets, allowing groups of puppets to inform debates about power and authority, for example, highlight the diversity of their use.

I think there is the potential for so much more in leadership development. Much more can be explored in the use of puppets, including working with simple outline puppets, providing detailed biographies to go with them, and expanding their aligned and complementary use into coaching, action learning and as a vehicle for giving and receiving feedback on observations of existing behaviours.

KEY TIPS

The use of the puppets is manyfold and can be used to suit many educational and practical roles within many forms of leadership development and coaching. Their use can feel idiosyncratic but they can offer the facilitator of groups and individuals an extension of the possibilities of working with people in leadership development:

- Buy or produce a collection of puppets that are contrasting in their ethnicity, gender and backgrounds and that will increase the likelihood of stimulating more comparisons, and viewing management and leadership theory and practice from different perspectives. Huge differences seem to stimulate the process and too similar appear to limit the process. Although there may be puppets that are more useful in certain circumstances (such as philosophers and ethical decision making), practice implies that all characters can register a 'view' of any leadership or management topic.
- Twenty or so individual puppets are probably enough to start to make the use of them possible. This allows the puppets to be available for use for both larger and smaller groups.
- Preparing laminated 'extension' cards can widen their appeal.
- Think about your current practice and visualize the times when puppets might help to offer a different type of approach. For example, historical finger puppets work well with exercises involving listening, questioning (such as action learning approaches) and problem solving. Opposing couples help to register a set of interesting tensions in virtually all management or leadership challenges.
- Once you have a collection then take them with you to workshops, seminars or coaching sessions in order to be able to use them spontaneously.

ACKNOWLEDGEMENTS

With thanks to Professor Steve Kempster for his help with the theoretical aspects of this chapter.

REFERENCES

Abrams D. (1996), *The Spell of the Sensuous*, New York: Vintage Books.
Cannadine D. (2016), 'Prime ministers' props: Professor Sir David Cannadine explores political fame and image by looking at how an object or prop, whether chosen deliberately or otherwise, can come to define a political leader', Radio 4, August–September.
Cordingley, P. (2010), 'Stepping stones, bridges and scaffolding; effective tools and processes for research use', paper presented at American Educational Research Association (AERA) Conference, Denver, CO, 2010.
Edwards, G., C. Elliott, M. Iszatt-White and D. Schedlitski (2013), 'Critical and alternative approaches to leadership learning and development', *Management Learning*, 44(1), 3–10.

Griffin, D. (2002), *The Emergence of Leadership – Linking Self-organization and Ethics*, London: Routledge.

Hamilton, L. (2013), 'The magic of mundane objects', *The Sociological Review*, **61**(2), 275–84.

Kempster, S., A.F. Turner, P. Heneberry, V. Stead and C. Elliott (2014), 'The "finger puppets": examining the use of artefacts to create liminal moments in management education', *Journal of Management Education*, **39**(3), 433–8.

Meyer, J.H.F. and R. Land (2005), 'Threshold concepts and troublesome knowledge (2): epistemological considerations and a conceptual framework for teaching and learning', *Higher Education*, **49**, 373–88.

Nelson, J., S.J. Zaccaro and J.L. Herman (2010), 'Strategic information provision and experiential variety as tools for developing adaptive leadership skills', *Consulting Psychology Journal: Practice and Research*, **62**(2), 131–42.

Page, M., L. Grisoni and A.F. Turner (2013), 'Dreaming fairness and re-imagining equality and diversity through participative aesthetic inquiry', *Management Learning*, **45**(5), 577–92.

Palmer, P.J. (1998), *The Courage to Teach*, San Francisco: Jossey-Bass.

Rovik, K.A. (2016), 'Knowledge transfer as translation: Reive and elements of an instrumental theory', *International Journal of Management Reviews*, **18**, 290–310.

Schandorf, M. (2012), 'There is no space: meaning and embodiment in mediated environments' [No hay espacio: significado y corporalización en entornos mediados], in J.C. Arias et al. (eds), *Codificar/Decodificar: Prácticas, espacios y temporalidades del audiovisual en internet*, Bogota: Editorial Pontificia Universidad Javeriana, pp.217–46.

Schon, D. (1987), *Educating the Reflective Practitioner*, San Francisco: Jossey-Bass.

Shaw, R.L. (2010), 'Embedding reflexivity within experiential qualitative psychology', *Qualitative Research in Psychology*, **7**(3), 233–43.

Sutherland, I. (2014), 'Art-based methods in leadership development: affording aesthetic workspaces, reflexivity and memories with momentum', *Management Learning*, **44**(1), 25.

Turner, A.F. (2013), 'Leadership development in middle managers', unpublished doctorate in business administration (D.B.A), University of South Wales.

Vygotsky, L.S. (1978), *Mind in Society*, Cambridge, MA: Harvard University Press.

12. Seeing beyond the usual: the social photo matrix (SPM) as an experiential method of leadership development

Wadii Serhane, Sigrid Endres and Jürgen Weibler

PURPOSE

As an experiential method of leadership development, the social photo matrix (SPM) aims:

- to offer a space of dynamic potential that allows an experience of polyphonic voices, snapshots and free associations in relation to ongoing leadership processes;
- to support exploration of often unseen and unrecognized facets of participants' daily leadership practice;
- to enable learning how to see already known and taken-for-granted dynamics in a different light;
- to support learning orientation toward different situations and atmospheric conditions;
- to support revitalization of important clues and keys for orientation in various dynamic organizational landscapes; and
- to enable critical integration of new thinking to move toward expanded possibilities of leadership in practice.

UNDERPINNING RESEARCH

In this section we briefly introduce three key aspects: First, the SPM's roots and key theoretical concepts, second research on the SPM's core working processes, and third the central role of photographs.

Roots and Key Theoretical Concepts

The SPM is a socioanalytical method that is rooted both in psychoanalysis and system theory. The latter approach studies the characteristics and dynamics of complex (social) systems, and focuses on how the components interact in the production of emerging phenomena at the systemic level (as in the behavior of the system as a whole). Psychoanalysis seeks to understand the hidden and "beneath the surface" aspects of (often repressed) unconscious psychological and behavioral dynamics of human social phenomena (cf. Long 2013, p.xx). The basic building blocks of the socioanalysis of social systems were laid with Bion's studies of group behavior at the Tavistock Institute in London in the 1940s (cf. Bion, 1961). Since then, various socioanalytical instruments – such as social dreaming (Lawrence, 2005), socioanalytical dialogue (Boccara, 2013), organizational role analysis (Newton, 2013) and, more recently, the SPM (Sievers, 2007, 2008, 2013; Serhane, 2012) – have been developed for the study of organizations and as experiential learning methods (for an overview see Long, 2013).

In contrast with objectifying organizational approaches, which focus on measurable and quantifiable aspects, the socioanalysis of organizations assumes that implicit and unnoticed aspects of organizational daily life, work and learning (for example, collectively conditioned frames and labels, habitual forms of argument, unconscious or denied schemas of thought) exert substantial influence on the behavior of an organization's members (Bion, 1984, 1970). Grounded in the socioanalytical tradition, the explicit aim of the SPM is to capture these system-wide unconscious phenomena, and as Sievers (2013, p.134) put it, "to experience [. . .] the hidden meaning of what in an organisation usually remains unseen and unnoticed." Hence, the SPM seeks to address the respective dynamics both on the *individual* and *collective* level of organizational life.

A key psychoanalytic method for capturing hidden and (more or less) unconscious processes is *free association* (see Freud, 1915). In the psychoanalytical tradition, free association is originally embedded in the relationship between the analyst and patient/client and focuses on the *individual* unconscious. In contrast, the SPM, as an explicit socioanalytical method, is concerned with unconscious dynamics at the *collective* or *systemic* level (Sievers, 2013; Serhane, 2012). This involves a less entity notion of free association as a process that unfolds in a plurality of minds, and not in isolation in a single individual's mind. This idea has also been described in more detail by the concept of the *associative unconscious*, which can be understood as a dynamic "mental network of thoughts, signs, and symbols or signifiers, able to give rise to many feelings, impulses, and images" (Long and Harney, 2013, p.8). Another important difference from the original

Freudian concept of the unconscious is that the focus moves far beyond repressed and often negatively framed (clinically analyzed) unconscious dynamics toward the manifold (and potentially more generative) emerging dimensions of what might become real in social systems (Long and Harney, 2013; Lawrence, 2005). Despite these differentiations, what the individual and associative unconscious have in common is that they influence "conscious thinking, feelings, desires, and behaviours in ways of which we are unaware" (Long and Harney, 2013, p.4).

The simultaneous consideration of individual- and collective-level dimensions further holds significant challenges for the SPM setting, which can be met by the *matrix* setting. This specific setting enables a plurality of individuals to become engaged in collective experiential processes without exhibiting the key characteristics (and constraints) of group settings. That is, the matrix setting permits the maintenance of a kind of free space for the individual participant, notwithstanding her or his embeddedness in a collective. As emphasized by Sievers (2013), a matrix setting is distinct from a group setting: "Unlike a group, which often is preoccupied with the maintenance of its identity, rivalry about power and reputation, and, particularly with a work group in an organisation, pursuing its task, the matrix [. . .] is a collection of minds opening and being available for dwelling in possibility" (Sievers 2013, p.130, with reference to Lawrence 2005, p.40). This has implications for the spatial arrangement during the SPM (see the Design section below).

The Nature of the SPM's Core Working Processes

Experiential learning methods in the socioanalytical tradition involve the usage of both *free associations* and *reflection*. With this in mind, the SPM aims to foster both, first by a matrix session with free association sequences, and second, by subsequent reflection sessions (see the Design section, below). These ideas are influenced by Bion's seminal research on experiential learning (Bion, 1984, 1970), which splits the process of "thinking" into two alternating mental activities or stages: first, the stage of the development of thoughts, and second, the stage of the development of thinking to use thoughts.

Accordingly, the SPM comprises two completely different but complementary mental activities. The first mental activity is related to free association and may be characterized as a stance of "receptive opening" toward manifold facets and perspectives of work life. This involves an inclusive attitude and creative mood, which may lead to the intuitive integration of many different perspectives. This first stage is usually characterized by the experience of various and (to our thinking) still surprising or incoherent aspects of social reality. Participants may move toward unsettling existing and often taken-for-granted knowledge. During this stage, patience and frustration-tolerance toward the state of not knowing and ambiguity play an important role in the thinking process (cf. Serhane, 2012; Long and Harney, 2013). Mental activities in this first stage may be forged by using evocative media, ambiguous pictographic signs to express feelings and emotional experiences at work. Beyond that, these dynamics can in principle be supported by any aesthetic material or sense-modality (for example, smell, taste, sound and so on; cf. Springborg, 2012; Sutherland, 2012).

Mental activity in the second stage is of a more reflective nature and relies on the construction of semantic links between pictures, drawings and free associations (Bion, 1970). By connecting various facets of reality, participants may gain increasing coherence of what has been experienced in the first stage. They have the possibility to perceive (new) meaningful insights, which they may contrast with their socially conditioned leadership practice (Serhane, 2012; Mersky, 2012). Experiencing these contrasts may enable participants to critically integrate new thinking concerning their daily leadership practice and related aspects of organizational reality (Sutherland, 2012). Many previously habitual leadership behaviors and related taken-for-granted organizational processes may then appear in a different light.

The Central Role of Photographs in the SPM

Encouraged by the observation that photographs related to the participants' organizations are useful media for both free association and subsequent reflection, Sievers pioneered the SPM as an action-oriented research method in relation to work about social dreaming and organizational role analysis (see Sievers, 2008, 2013). The central role of photographs in the SPM mainly arises from the way they facilitate the forging of associative links, helping to "bridge the gap between the apparently individual, private, subjective and the apparently collective, social, political" (Vince and Broussine, 1996, p.8; Sievers, 2013, p.131). Photographs, therefore, are by no means seen as representing a "true" or objective picture of reality or objects. Photographs are better understood as plastic pictographic signs (Meyer et al., 2013, p.527 f.) that may foster pictographic thinking and help us to gain deeper knowledge about the social systems we live in (cf. Barthes, 1981; Flusser, 2000). Moreover – and particularly because the photographs are taken by participants in their (organizational) context with a certain leadership-related theme in mind – the photographs used in the SPM usually have a strong expressive function (cf. Winnicott, 1971; Sievers, 2013). Photographs in this sense express subjectively experienced and culturally embedded leadership manifestations in organizations, and therefore have many sociocultural functions that may foster reflection about artefacts and symbolic meaning constructions related to our organizational (leadership) roles.

Many work spaces today suffer from the seeming dominance of rational, positivist and mechanistic explanatory models with restricted possibilities for creative expression and comprehensive learning processes embedded in relational contexts (Schyns et al., 2012; Case et al., 2012). In facing these challenges, new leadership approaches that emphasize the relational nature of leadership processes (for an overview compare Endres and Weibler, 2016), as well as the aesthetic dimensions of leadership (see, for example, Barry and Meisiek, 2010; Hansen et al., 2007; Kempster et al., 2015), have more recently been gathering exciting momentum. Against this background, the SPM has gained increasing relevance in the field of leadership in which alternative approaches to leadership development have been called for (Edwards et al., 2013; Mabey, 2013).

The SPM has been applied in numerous contexts relating to organizational development, action research and experiential learning in different organizations or work settings (for example, Autostadt Wolfsburg; University of Wuppertal; JVA Wuppertal; University of Innsbruck; University of Utrecht; Wharton School of Business; University of Pennsylvania; cf. Sievers, 2007, 2008, 2013). Since 2012, the SPM method has been used as an explorative approach in several leadership seminars at the University of Hagen (Faculty of Business Administration and Economics, Chair of Business Administration, Leadership and Organization). Through the application of the SPM in leadership seminars we have explored experiential ways to encourage participants to unveil hidden schemas of thought and behavior patterns, organizational rules and dynamics, and their influence on their views and everyday leadership practice.

DESIGN

In order to unfold the SPM's in-depth reflective power as an experimental leadership development approach, it is used with a specific (leadership-related) thematic focus. We implemented the SPM as an explorative approach in many seminars with various topics such as "Women and leadership," "Reflection and the meaning of work," or "Experiential leadership development from a cross-cultural perspective." Although we apply the SPM in a university context, the majority of participants consists of post-graduate students and employees in managerial roles, who are interested in the exploration and reflection of their daily leadership practice.

Topics of exploration should therefore be mostly practice-oriented. The chosen thematic focus should be communicated in the seminar announcement together with the expected contributions from each participant.

The storyboard and main components of the SPM leadership development program are outlined in Figure 12.1. We successfully implemented a three-stage design involving a pre-phase, a core phase and a follow-up phase.

Stage 1: The Pre-phase of Taking Digital Photographs

Prior to the seminar, participants are asked to take digital photographs related to the seminar topic and to submit these to the seminar facilitator or host via email. Confidentiality must be ensured (for example, via anonymized usage of the photographs during the seminar and beyond). It is helpful to give the participants two or three practical thematic focuses for orientation. It is also advisable to take open questions with an explorative character. For example:

1. How do I experience daily leadership practice (as leadership actor)?
2. What are the underlying assumptions of my/our current leadership practice? How far do they influence my daily leadership behavior?
3. What are the challenges and possibilities for my current (and/or future) leadership practice?

The estimated time required is about three to four months. By taking photographs in their daily organizational environment, the SPM participants have the possibility of translating their subjective (and often implicit) experiences at work into integrative pictographic signs. That is, such subjective and often spontaneously taken photographs will genuinely contain aspects of their work life (both pleasant and unpleasant, easy and difficult) that cannot be divided into "good/bad" or "true/false" leadership experiences or practices. The photographs are saved in a digital archive from which some pictures are selected randomly to be used in the seminar's matrix sessions.

Stage 2: Core Phase

The second stage represents the core of the SPM leadership development program and runs for 1.5 days (with about 15 to 20 participants). Its key components are:

1. a drawing session (30 mins);
2. three matrix sessions with free association sequences (30/60 mins); and
3. two group reflection sessions (45/60 mins).

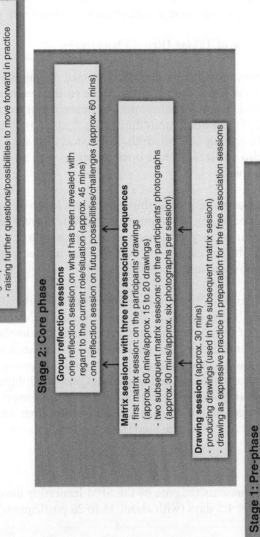

Stage 3: Follow-up phase

Experience exchange and practical/theoretical evaluation
- presenting participants' experience reports /project papers
- group discussion and reflection
- raising further questions/possibilities to move forward in practice

Stage 2: Core phase

Group reflection sessions
- one reflection session on what has been revealed with regard to the current role/situation (approx. 45 mins)
- one reflection session on future possibilities/challenges (approx. 60 mins)

Matrix sessions with three free association sequences
- first matrix session: on the participants' drawings (approx. 60 mins/approx. 15 to 20 drawings)
- two subsequent matrix sessions: on the participants' photographs (approx. 30 mins/approx. six photographs per session)

Drawing session (approx. 30 mins)
- producing drawings (used in the subsequent matrix session)
- drawing as expressive practice in preparation for the free association sessions

Stage 1: Pre-phase

Digital photographs
- taken by the participants
- in their (organizational) environment focusing on a specific leadership-related theme

Figure 12.1   Storyboard and main components of the SPM leadership development program

170

Prior to these core phases, we provide a brief thematic introduction (approx. 60 mins). Its main objective is to provide participants with an overview of questions relevant to the topic and some basics about the SPM method and working instruments, without an explicit normative framing of the topic of exploration (as in no specific leadership theories). Following this more "theoretical" or "factual" introduction, participants' attention should be shifted away from self-centered and rationalizing attitudes toward what is happening at the present moment (for example, via the use of explorative questions, metaphors or stories). Following this, the practical application of the SPM follows by starting with a drawing session (see Figure 12.1).

Drawing session
The integration of a drawing session (that is, producing drawings) and the usage of drawings in a subsequent free association sequence are not essential key component of the original SPM method (as introduced above). In our experience, the drawing session has proved to be valuable for two main reasons. First, the production of drawings may enable the participants to move into an expressive and associative mood, and thus to escape from the rationalization modus. Drawing practice may also help participants to go beyond (positivist) textual and linguistic conceptualizations by increasing the ability to contain different states of experiences with complexity and uncertainty (cf. Ward and Shortt, 2013; Nossal, 2013; Winnicott, 1971). Overall, drawing can be seen as a catalyst in helping leadership actors to express emotional experiences and feelings that may have gone unnoticed and/or been hard to articulate. Hence, it may enable participants to "say the unsaid" (Vince and Broussine, 1996, p.8 f.; Serhane, 2012). Second, the participants' drawings provide a particularly fresh aesthetic medium that may trigger free associations in addition to the photographs in a specific evocative way. The total number of participants' drawings (about 15 to 20) should be used in the subsequent matrix session.

The spatial arrangement of the drawing session should provide enough privacy. With this in mind, several tables (ideally with a visual shield) should be arranged. Of course, good-quality drawing equipment (such as a variety of drawing pencils, colours and paper) also has to be provided. One (assistant) facilitator photographs the finished drawings during a short break and prepares the subsequent presentation of the anonymized drawings in the matrix session.

Matrix sessions with three free association sequences
The term "matrix," first of all, implies a specific spatial arrangement that avoids the perception of being part of a (work) group. Therefore, the chairs

are usually arranged in a semi-circle around the screen (without direct eye contact among the participants). Nevertheless, the collective nature of the matrix method is maintained by the plenary setting of the loosely assembled seminar participants. Ultimately, only through this embeddedness in a collective does the matrix enable amplification and exploration of the associative unconscious with a plurality of minds (as described above). The plurality of the collective, however, is ideally established without any group pressure or normative framing through (common) shared meaning. Of course, this points to some challenging tasks for the hosts (for example, how to forge a democratic peer environment and an appreciative atmosphere without consensus pressure). We will examine this issue later in more depth, together with an overall consideration of the specific roles of the SPM hosts.

As shown in Figure 12.1, we implemented three matrix sessions. In the first matrix session (about 60 minutes) participants' drawings (about 15 to 20 drawings) are used in a random sequence as a source of free associations. In the second and third free association sequences (each 30 minutes), about six photographs are randomly chosen in each case from the overall pool of photographs taken by the participants prior to the seminar. It should be noted that, although it might appear helpful to select a particularly appropriate or "good" photograph to set the tone for the free association sequence, the random selection of photographs is geared to avoid the impression of manipulation (cf. Sievers, 2013). Four to five minutes per picture (drawing or photograph) are needed on average for the free associations.

Participants are invited to freely associate to the pictures. Since it is important that it is not merely (functionalist) descriptions that are expressed, the value of the spontaneous expression of what comes intuitively to mind should be emphasized. During the matrix session, we are interested in the content of photos and drawings as evocative media and not primarily in the skill or technique of the photographer or illustrator. In this context, it has proved helpful to direct the focus to "what this picture tells me," and to let the pictures speak for themselves. In what follows, we provide some illustration of what has been experienced during an SPM application in a leadership development program.

Specimen pictures (drawings and photographs) and corresponding free associations

Participants have expressed the following free associations on the drawing in Figure 12.2:

Everyone says something else – One says where to go /orders – The people are not happy – Over the leader, the sun shines, the other people are standing in

Figure 12.2   Drawing of an SPM participant on the topic "experiential leadership development"

the rain – Leader has completely different view than the others – Leader has an umbrella, he offers it to the other persons – Could also be a sign setting direction (an arrow) – The leader does not listen – It's such a great distance between him and the other people, and one-way communication.

The following free associations were expressed on the drawing in Figure 12.3:

Reaching the top – Being isolated – Trying to graduate/get ahead – The people on the ground are happy – There's shadow under the cloud – No opportunities for advancement /no higher positions – One person is red, unlike the others – The groups are separated from each other – The person at the top sees everybody else, the groups do not see each other – The boss/chief is at the top, at the bottom there are the competing groups – The boss animates/motivates the right group, the left group not – Trying to find the right way – Group is facing a real, not bridgeable gap.

The following free associations were expressed on Figure 12.4:

Swamped colleague – All mine – To get by somehow, the mountains are too high – Public service – Many phones – Stress – Poor health, because of the nasal spray and tea on the table – Trying to integrate privacy, but work outweighs = pressure – Analog work, because of a lot of paper, you have to rifle through until you find something – You do not recognize who is boss and who is employee – Playing with overload = nothing works anymore – One might show nothing – The left mountain is threatening to slip away soon.

Figure 12.3   Drawing of an SPM participant on the topic "experiential leadership development"

The following free associations were expressed on Figure 12.5:

> Boss parking!? – Reserved by numbers/for whom? – To park according to the instruction – To park according to hierarchy – Or the boss has three parking places – But to keep in mind: the boss does not himself drive a car! – Parking with beautiful view onto the green – The parking looks German, standardized, stupid – Are without limit (to park easily?) makes it impossible to crash into another car – provocative parking across all three parking places to annoy the boss – Clean and well maintained, no leaves.

These examples from the matrix sessions, like most of the others, raised associations that loosely cluster around three themes: (1) the experience of hierarchy (privilege, status, distance/differences between leader and followers, resistance); (2) uncertainty, struggle to gain orientation and insight about the (right) way to move forward; and (3) dilemmas, struggle to advance to a leading position, work overload, unhealthy work conditions. As we can further see, during the free association sequence participants related to each other and provided some amplifications. Overall, we perceived an emerging flow of associations to the experienced manifestation of leadership situations. Moreover, some spontaneous initial hypotheses

Figure 12.4   Photograph of an SPM participant on the topic "experiential leadership development"

(for example, concerning what had been experienced given certain cultural and contextual factors, how one could deal with this issue in the given or future situations) were expressed. We would tentatively suggest that the participants moved at least in part beyond a rational and descriptive mode of thinking.

Group reflection sessions
After a break, the reflection sessions start with an explicit movement from the spatial arrangement of the matrix setting into a group setting. The participants are seated at tables in groups of five to seven persons. The group reflection sessions are directed toward two different focuses. The first reflection session (approx. 45 mins) focuses on what has been revealed with regard to the current role and situation. The primary task of the working groups is to describe how as leadership actors they experience everyday leadership practice in contemporary organizations, and to reflect on what different aspects of the current leadership practice the photographs and drawings have shown us. The second reflection session (approx. 60 mins) is directed toward future possibilities. The primary task of the working

Figure 12.5   Photograph of an SPM participant on the topic "experiential leadership development"

groups is then to work out what challenges are faced by today's leadership actors and to develop alternative perspectives, promising and hopeful possibilities for action. Subsequently, the working groups present and discuss their results in the plenary (approx. ten minutes per working group).

The subsequent examples give some impressions of the thoughts that emerged from the reflection sessions in the context of the seminar on "Experiential leadership development." Examples from the first reflection session:

- Control plays an important role in the organizational structure; lack of trust in the employee?
- Structure stands for order and efficiency.
- The lived leadership practice: own office, own parking, creating privileges; distancing; status differentiation.
- Leadership by status symbols.
- People are affected/influenced by structures, norms, rules, artefacts, symbols.
- Everyone works for him or herself.

- No time for social contacts.
- Work pressure.
- Top-down leadership.
- Work–life balance plays an increasingly important role.

Examples from the second reflection session:

- Partial integration of the boss in the team (delayering).
- Team building, task sharing, mutual support.
- Work–life balance (on the job): more time for relaxation, flexible working hours, sabbaticals, parental leave, particularly to increase acceptance for this; wellness facilities.
- Home office (made possible by new technology – but does not replace face-to-face conversations).
- Fostering a positive error culture, constructive feedback, building trust; offering reliability.
- Creating free and unoccupied spaces, breaking out of old patterns; creating spaces for reflection.

Both the free associations and reflections are entered in the minutes (compiled by alternating participants). The individual minutes are then submitted to the seminar facilitator. She or he compiles these notes and returns them to all the participants after a week, together with the respective pictures and drawings. The overall (anonymized) minutes allow all participants to establish further links between the images and thoughts that emerged during the matrix and reflection sequences. Participants may then (critically) relate these results to their (organizational) context, their roles and responsibilities in the organization, and their daily leadership practice. Based on this reflection (and the data from the SPM overall minutes), participants are asked to write a seminar or project paper in the form of an experiential report.

Stage 3: Follow-up Phase

A follow-up workshop (1.5 days) takes place about three to four months following the SPM core phase. It involves the presentation and discussion of participants' experience or research reports – either in the form of seminar papers or project reports. Although both papers focus on reflective practice-oriented presentation, two distinct variations are to be considered: first, the seminar paper, which forms part of a university seminar and examination and involves a more theoretical and methodological treatment of the subject; second, the project report, which is part of an

SPM leadership development program without a university examination. Concerning the university setting, it is important to ensure that only the seminar papers (and subsequent discussion) are subject to examination. The prior SPM phases are explicitly conducted without any assessment or examination in order to ensure an (ideally) pressure-free space as a prerequisite for free association and critical reflection.

Taken together, the main purpose in this follow-up phase is a reflective and critical exchange of experience among participants. The reflection and learning process that was initiated by the SPM method during the prior phases may be continued and ideally gains further momentum through the follow-up process.

REFLECTIONS

Representative proponents of the SPM, primarily Burkard Sievers, have stated that their attempts at working with the SPM convinced them, their colleagues and most participants "that it is possible to gain access to the unthought known and, thus, to the unconscious in organizations through photos taken by their role-holders" (Sievers, 2008, p.249; cf. Sievers, 2013, 2007; Serhane, 2012; Mersky, 2012). Our experience with the application of the SPM to the field of leadership development adds further support to these findings. Most of our participants acknowledged that they identified many new and previously unthought aspects and problems of everyday organizational work and leadership. This was even true after a period of 12 to 18 months after participating in the SPM – although our results are less a comprehensive and more a tentative assessment of the subjective experience of the participants. Overall, the extensive use of the SPM in our leadership seminars has shown that this experiential method may play a significant role in providing more space for dynamic potential for leadership actors to become aware of their habitual (and often unconscious) leadership practices. On this basis they may be able to develop cognitive and sensual abilities to go beyond "the functional stupidity" that entails among other things an "organizationally-supported lack of reflexivity" (Alvesson and Spicer, 2012, p.1196; cf. Adler and Hansen, 2012). At a minimum, this reveals a promising point of departure for critically integrating new thinking into a movement toward expanded possibilities of leadership in practice.

Besides these clearly promising experiences and findings, however, we are well aware that the SPM is still a leadership development methodology in the making that is confronted with various challenges and inherent limitations. As Mersky (2012, p.38) has highlighted, "[t]here are without doubt major challenges in bringing these methodologies to organisations (unfamiliarity with this way of working; complications regarding confidentiality; complexities about who should participate; anxieties regarding drawing and other creative forms, etc.)." She also listed a variety of, in part, quite different tasks of SPM hosts. Depending on the phase of the overall SPM program, hosts need to design, welcome, negotiate terms, communicate, present theory and methodology, give directions, contain, associate and amplify, link and hypothesize, facilitate, set clear tasks and transition work to participants (cf. Mersky, 2012, p.35).

Starting with the pragmatic issues, the overall SPM leadership development program, as described above, involves a lot of organizational work and the smooth provision of technical support. Considering the quantity of tasks alone, we suggest that the SPM is always run with two facilitators, at least one of whom should have experience in conducting an experiential or action-oriented leadership development workshop and in working with groups from a psychodynamic perspective. Conducting an SPM is quite different from moderating a (work) group discussion, or facilitating traditional leadership development training. Essentially, the matrix demands "a different kind of leadership – one inspired by the recognition of the infinite, of not-knowing, of being in doubt and uncertainty, as opposed to knowing and repeating banal facts," as Lawrence emphasized (2005, p.40; Sievers, 2013, p.130). Subsequently, we illustrate and discuss how this idea of "leadership" might be enacted during the hosting of an SPM leadership development course. We relate this discussion and our reflections to key pieces and requirements of our SPM design, and to participants' concerns.

Evocative Work Mediums

Producing evocative working media may not be restricted to photographs or drawings. Other media such as painting, which may offer more expressive space, may also be included. To this end, various tangible or malleable materials (for example, clay, wood, water colors) may be offered to forge a creative and emotionally inviting atmosphere (cf. Taylor and Statler, 2014). The nature and composition of different evocative media may also play an important role by fostering a creative working space.

Concerning the breadth and quantity of evocative working media, the host should be aware of the following challenges. First, an inflationary usage may decrease the "surprise" effect of working with evocative media. It is helpful to have a good sense for narrative saturation and silence by choosing the optimum time to progress to the next picture. Further, superficial usage (for example, through a purely descriptive analysis of the content of photographs) and rational restriction to visible and measurable aspects may have a negative impact on the quality and depth of the free association flow. Free associations (and subsequent reflections) should not be limited to the level of the culturally visible and usually accepted (such as aspects of daily leadership practice that are taken for granted). To that extent, the host may need to intervene clearly, but in a context-sensitive and subtle manner, for example by providing fresh or provocative (alternative) associations, or by taking up a participant's free association and amplifying it in another direction. Thus, the host should occasionally engage in spontaneous leadership without giving the impression of manipulation.

The SPM Participants

Another success factor is the willingness of the participants themselves to engage with evocative work media during the pictographic journey of the SPM. From the beginning it should be made clear that this is not a seminar "for sitting back." Further, the host has to show that the SPM's aim is not to add new skills and concepts in a traditional sense, but to explore and (re) vitalize existing human abilities and qualities. The SPM can only provide a conducive framework for starting an explorative journey; it cannot replace the willingness of participants to move out of their mental comfort zones (Serhane, 2012). Finally, and perhaps even more challengingly, the matrix is based on an assumption that participants are able to temporarily suspend both their individuality and rational (scientific or theoretical) thinking (cf. Sievers, 2013, p.148).

One important task of facilitators is to convey through their presence an appreciative attitude that goes beyond mere knowledge transfer. When an SPM is applied, both the host and the participants are not self-reliant in terms of being autonomous entities, but parts of an ongoing dynamic process. If the facilitator's disposition radiates trust in the ongoing process, this may positively influence the collective working space of the SPM (Springborg, 2012). For example, it may be helpful to use images or narratives of the future that provide enough space to integrate contestable views and ambiguous feelings. Facilitators, on the one hand, should forge an associative mood by being non-judgmental and encourage the participants to spontaneously articulate what comes to mind. On the other hand, they may provide sufficient containment in terms of specific guidance, for example, to contain dominant or narcissistic tendencies among participants (cf. Sievers, 2013). Aside from the danger of dominance by single individuals, the often more subtle influence of the group provides further (and perhaps even more serious) challenges, as we will discuss in relation to the following context-related considerations.

The SPM Context

One of the crucial successful features of the SPM is a working context without peer pressure or pressure for conformity (social or organizational). Emerging dominant and culturally previously known ways of thinking and patterns of interpretation usually undermine any free association flow. Thus, group identifications, or the establishment of subgroups, should be avoided. A matrix in this sense also involves the experience of a democratic environment. An SPM host should realize when participants in the matrix are tending to become possessed by their group perspective and norms (cf. Sievers, 2008, 2013). However, given the collective nature of the matrix concept (as described above), a relevant question to raise is whether it is realistic to hope that participants' associations and amplifications actually are "free from peer pressure, social norms and obligations, power/gender relations or any other form of situational dynamics that may otherwise shape their responses to the images and their willingness to share these with the other members of the matrix" (Warren, 2012, p.92). Should we not instead concede that "regardless of seating arrangements and the depersonalization of the photographs orchestrated by the facilitator of the SPM, the social cannot be escaped, because it is always within us" (Warren, 2012, p.95)? Yet, as Warren highlighted in conclusion (2012, p.97), the "situated social dynamics of the SPM [. . .] do not make the technique invalid by any means." Overall, these tensions inherent in both the collective and psychoanalytical nature of the SPM methodology should always be kept in mind in order to balance it in relation to the context. Further, it might be particularly helpful to consider what has not been said or what has probably been withheld given certain contextual normative constraints. Hosts, therefore, might try to access these "unsaid" and embodied aspects through observation of the participants' reaction during the matrix session. They may then try to subtly introduce their own observations during the subsequent reflection sessions. Provided that ethical concerns are considered, the observation of participants' non-verbal expressions (see for example, Warren, 2012, p.97, on the notion of assessing the "somatic unconscious") might open up further exciting possibilities for advancing the SPM as experiential leadership development method.

KEY TIPS

Although experiences with the SPM as an experiential approach to leadership development are promising, it is still a methodology in the making. Therefore, our design is best understood as an experimental (but relatively well-established) frame within which we raise the following practical suggestions:

- Communicate the required contributions clearly, since this is not a seminar for "sitting back."
- Run the course with two facilitators, at least one of whom should be experienced in psychodynamic work with groups, and able to meet the challenges of enacting the various "leadership" roles as SPM host in a context-sensitive way.
- Contemplate and reflect critically on what emerges both from the free association flow and from subsequent reflection sessions. This involves being attentive toward contextual or normative constraints that may bias or even completely block the articulation of what is actually experienced or thought.
- Embody sensitivity toward the unique culturally embedded and socially constructed nature of each participant's background and leadership experience.

REFERENCES

Adler, N.J. and H. Hansen (2012), "Daring to care: scholarship that supports the courage of our convictions," *Journal of Management Inquiry*, **21**(2), 128–39.

Alvesson, M. and A. Spicer (2012), "A stupidity-based theory of organizations," *Journal of Management Studies*, **49**(7), 1194–220.

Barry, D. and S. Meisiek (2010), "Seeing more and seeing differently: sensemaking, mindfulness, and the workarts," *Organization Studies*, **31**(11), 1505–30.

Barthes, R. (1981), *Camera Lucida: Reflections on Photography*, trans. R. Howard, New York: Farrar Straus & Giroux.

Bion, W.R. (1961), *Experiences in Groups*, London: Tavistock.

Bion, W.R. (1970), *Attention and Interpretation*, London: Tavistock.

Bion, W.R. (1984), *Learning from Experience*, London: Karnac.

Boccara, B. (2013), "Socioanalytic dialogue," in S. Long (ed.), *Socioanalytic Methods: Discovering the Hidden in Organisations and Social Systems*, London: Karnac, pp.279–300.

Case, P., R. French and P. Simpson (2012), "From theoria to theory: leadership without contemplation," *Organization*, **19**(3), 345–61.

Edwards, G., C. Elliott, M. Iszatt-White and D. Schedlitzki (2013), "Critical and alternative approaches to leadership learning and development," *Management Learning*, **44**(1), 3–10.

Endres, S. and J. Weibler (2017), "Towards a three-component model of relational social constructionist leadership (RSCL): a systematic review and critical interpretive synthesis," *International Journal of Management Reviews*, **19**(2), 214–36.

Flusser, V. (2000), *Towards a Philosophy of Photography*, trans. M. Chalmers, London: Reaction Books.

Freud, S. (1915), "The Unconscious," in *Collected Papers, Standard Edition*, 14, London: Hogarth, pp.161–215.

Hansen, H., A. Ropo and E. Sauer (2007), "Aesthetic leadership," *The Leadership Quarterly*, **18**(6), 544–60.

Kempster, S., A. Turner, P. Heneberry, V. Stead and C. Elliott (2015), "The 'finger puppets': examining the use of artifacts to create liminal moments in management education," *Journal of Management Education*, **39**(3), 433–8.

Lawrence, W.G. (2005), *Introduction to Social Dreaming: Transforming Thinking*, London: Karnac.

Long, S. (2013), "Socioanalytic methodology," in S. Long (ed.), *Socioanalytic Methods: Discovering the Hidden in Organisations and Social Systems*, London: Karnac, pp.xix–xxx.

Long, S. and M. Harney (2013), "The associative unconscious," in S. Long (ed.), *Socioanalytic Methods: Discovering the Hidden in Organisations and Social Systems*, London: Karnac, pp.3–22.

Mabey, C. (2013), "Leadership development in organizations: multiple discourses and diverse practice," *International Journal of Management Reviews*, **15**(4), 359–80.

Mersky, R. (2012), "Contemporary methodologies to surface and act on unconscious dynamics in organisations: an exploration of design, facilitation capabilities, consultant paradigm and ultimate value," *Organisational & Social Dynamics*, **12**(1), 19–43.

Meyer, R.E., D.J. Höllerer and T. van Leeuwen (2013), "The visual dimension in organizing, organization, and organization research: core ideas, current developments, and promising avenues," *The Academy of Management Annals*, **7**(1), 489–555.

Newton, J. (2013), "Organisational role analysis," in S. Long (ed.), *Socioanalytic Methods: Discovering the Hidden in Organisations and Social Systems*, London: Karnac, pp.205–26.

Nossal, B. (2013), "The use of drawing as a tool in socioanalytic exploration," in S. Long (ed.), *Socioanalytic Methods: Discovering the Hidden in Organisations and Social Systems*, London: Karnac, pp.67–89.

Schyns, B., A. Tymon, T. Kiefer and R. Kerschreiter (2012), "New ways to leadership development: a picture paints a thousand words," *Management Learning*, **44**(1), 11–24.

Serhane, W. (2012), "Des-integrative Organisationsforschung als psychosozialer Lernprozess. Ein Fallbeispiel zur Sozialen Photo-Matrix" [Dis-integrative organization research as psychosocial learning process – a case study on the social photomatrix], dissertation at Schumpeter School of Business and Economics, University of Wuppertal, Saarbrücken: Südwestdeutscher Verlag für Hochschulschriften.

Sievers, B. (2007), "Pictures from below the surface of the university: the social photomatrix as a method for understanding organizations in depth," in M. Reynolds and R. Vince (eds), *Experiential Learning and Management Education*, Oxford: Oxford University Press, pp.241–57.

Sievers, B. (2008), "Perhaps it is the role of pictures to get in contact with the uncanny: the social photo-matrix as a method to promote understanding of the unconscious in organizations," *Organization and Social Dynamics*, **8**(2), 234–54.

Sievers, B. (2013), "Thinking organisations through photographs: the social photomatrix as a method for understanding organisations in depth," in S. Long (ed.),

Socioanalytic Methods: Discovering the Hidden in Organisations and Social Systems, London: Karnac, pp.129–51.

Springborg, C. (2012), "Perceptual refinement: art-based methods in managerial education," *Organizational Aesthetics*, **1**(1), 116–37.

Sutherland, I. (2012), "Arts-based methods in leadership development: affording aesthetic workspaces, reflexivity and memories with momentum," *Management Learning*, **44**(1), 25–43.

Taylor, S.S. and M. Statler (2014), "Material matters: increasing emotional engagement in learning," *Journal of Management Education*, **38**(4), 586–607.

Vince, R. and M. Broussine (1996), "Paradox, defense and attachment: accessing and working with emotions and relations underlying organizational change," *Organization Studies*, **17**(1), 1–21.

Ward, J. and H. Shortt (2013), "Evaluation in management education: a visual approach to drawing out emotion in student learning," *Management Learning*, **44**(5), 435–52.

Warren, S. (2012), "Psychoanalysis, collective viewing and the 'social photo matrix' in organizational research," *Qualitative Research in Organizations and Management: An International Journal*, **7**(1), 86–104.

Winnicott, D.W. (1971), *Playing and Reality*, London: Tavistock.

PART IV

Place-based approaches

Place-based approaches

13. Developing the practice of framing ... softly, softly catchee monkey

Fiona Kennedy and Ralph Bathurst

INTRODUCTION

Framing is at the heart of contemporary leadership practice and therefore is important for leadership development programmes. However if 'believing is seeing' (Weick, 1995, p.133) then a practice that relies on the prospect that reality could be otherwise can be problematic for those who don't believe it! Nevertheless, with patience and time most managers can 'catch' framing and incorporate it into their repertoire of practices.

We have used the odd phrase 'softly, softly catchee monkey' to suggest the learning conditions that are necessary for developing the practice of framing. This phrase is attributed to the founder of the Boy Scouts, Lord Baden Powell (Baden-Powell, 1898). According to Powell this phrase means 'Don't flurry, patience gains the day.' Others take it to mean 'patience and steadiness will accomplish your goal' ('Softly, softly, catchee monkey', 2013). This can be contrasted with a head-on approach to learning. The latter approach runs the risk of inhibiting learning, driving up anxiety and pushing both facilitators and managers back into their overlearned corners (Weick, 1996). The approach described here is soft in pressure to believe but relentless in asking people to be curious, to explore what they do and do not see, and to practise seeing differently and seeing more.

As the name suggests, a frame creates a boundary, focusing attention within that bounded space, suggesting what meanings and related courses of action are on offer, and what are not. Useful frames can help to cut through ambiguity, surfacing wisdom and new possibilities for action. However, frames are not conjured from thin air (or produced by a marketing department) but evoke and respond to the diverse realities of shifting social situations. As Bennis and Nanus wrote in *Leaders*, 'we human beings are suspended in webs of significance that we ourselves have spun' (1985, p.112). This raises the question of how to notice, reflect on and indeed actively shape webs of significance while acknowledging that we are caught up in them.

Organizational researchers have traced the ways in which leaders negotiate and shape meaning in particular circumstances. In doing so, a crucial relationship between leadership and working with meaning has been drawn. This relationship is conveyed in article titles such as 'Leadership as sense-making', 'Leadership as the management of meaning' and 'Managers as practical authors' (Pye, 2005; Shotter and Cunliffe, 2003; Smircich and Morgan, 1982). However, while organizational researchers have revealed the dynamics of meaning work in action, this does not point the way to developing practice in this area. Furthermore, as Fairhurst (2005) has observed, developing the art of framing amongst managers is far easier said (and seen) than done!

To address these issues we proceed as follows. First, we outline three problems associated with managers developing the practice of framing. Next we outline how meaning work and framing have been conceptualized in relationship to the work of leadership. We then describe an approach to development that enables managers to remain open to meaning work and an activity that helps them to track down their own frames that are influencing their leadership work. Finally we offer some further tips and reflections on creating a leadership development context that enables this work.

THE PROBLEMS WITH FRAMING IN LEADERSHIP DEVELOPMENT

Drawing on the literature and our own experience we notice three problems that crop up repeatedly when framing is translated from theory to practice. First, as we have already observed, some managers are resistant to an 'as if' world (Fairhurst, 2005, p.170). Second is the ubiquity of the transmission metaphor of communication and the implication that framing involves 'delivering' the message to passive recipients (Shannon and Weaver, 1963); and third, but connected to the second, is the risk that framing can imply that managers are an enlightened elite (Uhl-Bien, 2006).

Fairhurst offers a strong case for managers' resistance to an 'as if' world. Approximately a decade after publishing *The Art of Framing* she observed that bringing that art of framing to managers had not turned out to be as fruitful as she had expected, because many managers simply didn't 'get it!' While academics were captivated by a socially constructed world, Fairhurst revealed that bringing this into the training room with managers was quite another matter. In her experience, framing failed to make the translation to practice.

One of Fairhurst's key observations was that underlying assumptions about the nature of communication set up managers to dismiss framing.

Indeed common forms of talk in organizations create a static, technical view of communication, which then makes framing seem quite irregular, or even nonsense. For example, when leaders are exhorted to 'communicate a vision' (Kotter, 1996), what comes to mind is a picture of leaders 'sending a material thing' out into the organization that others 'receive' exactly as it was sent to them, as if the vision was a package in the mail. Ubiquitous phrases in the life of organizations, such as 'delivering the message', create a picture of passive 'receivers' who do not 'shape' the message themselves, but rather extract it whole, with the nuances of meaning and spirit with which it was 'sent' intact. This is quite different to appreciating that organizations are abuzz with people busily handling and reshaping what they hear. As Chandler (2007) claims, 'Meaning is not "transmitted" to us – we actively create it according to a complex interplay of codes or conventions of which we are normally unaware' (p. 11). Thus while framing assumes that communication is dynamic and relational, managers who understand communication as 'delivery' of a message or straightforward baton-passing could be forgiven for steering clear of framing and its implications.

The third and connected problem is the possibility that managers have a greater claim on reality than others and therefore are an elite group. When framing is understood as something that is 'done' to other people (Pye, 2005, p.35) and that derives from managers having a privileged reading of events (Barge, 2004), then managers could imagine that framing is, in keeping with the transmission view of communication, a one-way street. This implication is unavoidable when 'framing' is 'unanchored [from] relationship and context' (Carroll et al., 2008, p.366). Indeed when framing is approached without managers recognizing their own assumptions, and how these shape and filter experience, they can be imagined as an 'enlightened elite' (Alvesson and Sveningsson, 2008, p.176) who stand outside interaction and who consciously craft meaning in order to change or improve others or their situations.

These problems are connected primarily to questions of how framing and meaning work are situated, and the extent to which framing is understood as a technical skill. Over time conceptualizations of meaning work have shifted so that the dynamic, social and contextual nature of 'communication' has become increasingly visible. Therefore we now turn to a brief review of organizational and leadership research related to meaning making beginning in the late 1970s.

RESEARCH: LEADERSHIP AND WORKING WITH MEANING

The late 1970s and the 1980s saw a crack in the dominant rationalist view of organizations. This fracture was wrought by a new interest in the inherent ambiguity of situations and the importance of meaning work for leadership. Arguably, this was set in motion by one of the best-selling management books ever. *In Search of Excellence* (Peters and Waterman, 1982) pushed the human need for meaning to the fore and interrupted the prevailing view that reason was the underlying principle of organizational success. Peters and Waterman created a compelling case for the relationship between organizational excellence and actively working with meaning. In the same year, in the field of leadership, Smirchich and Morgan produced their seminal article 'Leadership: the management of meaning'. They argued that 'leadership is realized in the process whereby one or more individuals succeeds in attempting to *frame* or define the reality of others' (Smircich and Morgan, 1982, p.258, emphasis added). They pointed out that people who emerge as leaders in social situations are those who frame problems in ways that attract and hold diverse groups of people, so that they could come together, see their common purpose and act.

While meaning making seemed a 'new' insight for organizational leadership, history revealed rich examples of meaning work in general and the art of framing in particular. For example, Martin Luther King's 'I have a dream' speech, delivered in August 1963 at the Lincoln Memorial, is frequently used as an example of framing the reality of others (Wright, 2015). In that speech to approximately 250,000 supporters of the Civil Rights Movement, King framed issues of racism with respect to the pursuit of freedom and justice in the United States of America. As Taylor (2012) notes, King's speech 'created a departure, it activated the imagination, and allowed many listeners to go someplace new' (p. 3). Just as Smircich and Morgan (1982) claim, King's framing enabled a new focus for understanding and action.

A decade later the relationship between leadership and the art of framing was firmly established. Fairhurst and Sarr (1996) defined framing as 'the essential tool in the management of meaning' (p. 3) and offered practical activities for managers to become skilled in framing. They drew attention to the choices in framing, the contested nature of reality and the implication of power relations, asserting that:

> To hold the frame of a subject is to choose one particular meaning (or set of meanings) over another. When we share our frames with others we manage meaning because we assert that our interpretations should be taken as real over other possible interpretations. (Fairhurst and Sarr, 1996, p.3)

During this era framing was positioned in ways that drew attention to the agency and skill of particular individuals. It was therefore no surprise that reflecting on the late 1980s and the 1990s Fairhurst (2005) wrote: 'If ever there was an academic warrant for a leadership skill quite new to practicing managers, managing meaning or "framing" was it' (p. 167).

With time the dynamics of meaning making have come to be understood in more active and social terms. This was influenced substantially by Karl Weick's (1995) *Sensemaking in Organizations*, which introduced a way of thinking about meaning making that 'changed the conversation' (Gioia, 2006, p.1710). Weick identified seven constituent dimensions of the process: sense making is a matter of identity, it is retrospective, social, ongoing, built on extracted cues, and is about plausibility and sufficiency far more than accuracy. Weick's seven dimensions of sense making helped to signal the deeply contextual dimensions of meaning making that were not so apparent in the earlier discussions.

Recent accounts reveal a dynamic and relational understanding of meaning making and leadership. For example, Annie Pye (2005) drew on Weick's dynamic, social understanding of meaning work to suggest that sense making was a case of leadership in action. Pye argued that while defining leadership was something of a holy grail it was useful to think of leadership as a sense-making process. Although not using the language of framing, she argued that 'leaders lead by performing an *explanatory function* for others' (Pye, 2005, p.46, emphasis added). She observed that people exemplify these explanations as they respond and, in so doing, 'systems of shared meaning' may be transformed.

In summary, when leadership framing is considered in retrospect, successful framing can appear to be a technical skill, the product of profound situational analysis and communicative expertise. However, the landscape of sense making, of which leadership framing is a part, suggests that framing is less 'managed' and far more situated, emergent and social than earlier accounts suggest. These different 'takes' on framing are consequential for leadership development. The development approach we outline here explicitly draws attention to the ongoing and social nature of meaning making and, with that, the dynamics of an 'as if' world.

SHAPING THE CONTEXT

Bringing visibility to the dynamics of meaning making from the beginning of the first workshop is vital to a softly-softly approach. We aim to establish that frames are everywhere and that an interest in frames will be part of the group's ongoing conversation. This helps managers to stay engaged when the stakes are raised and framing begins to feel more risky.

To help with this, we bring attention to frames when we first get together with a group. We declare frames we are holding with intention, look for opportunities to draw attention to spontaneous frames, and invite managers to consider what frames stir up and attract, as well as what they dampen and rule out. For example, we use the language of framing when we acknowledge that walking into the business school where many of our workshops are held can evoke the 'school' frame. Negotiating throngs of students with their books and bags, searching for a particular room among walls and floors of identical-looking rooms, finally locating the right room – that is set up with whiteboard, lectern, projector screens, a PowerPoint display and blank notebooks and that is populated with a few other people who are looking slightly uncertain – is an experience reminiscent of the first day of class.

As Crevani notes, frames are not real or given but rather 'it is what we say and do when drawing on certain frames that remakes them real over and over' (Crevani, 2015, p.195). Thus, in a recent first workshop, the observation that coming into the business school can evoke a 'school' frame, led one participant – Amy (pseudonym) – to duck down behind another participant, giggling and playing, with an identity of one who plays about in 'class'. In that moment we could take the school frame further, asking managers to notice how this frame ignited identities such as those of students, teachers, and the possibility of class clown or mischief maker. We reflected again on the intransigence of the school frame later, when managers found themselves tangled up with judging themselves as 'right' or 'wrong'.

Having introduced the language of framing and the potential for a 'school' frame to creep up on the learning experience we could then ask managers to consider what notions of right and wrong rule in and rule out, and the identity issues that these notions stir up. Thus the group was invited to be curious and observant about frames and their implications. Moving softly means that frames are brought into the room and people have a chance to name them and play with them, long before we give 'framing' a headline and a dedicated session.

Thus the following activity is designed for a context where the dynamics of meaning making and framing have become part of the conversation. This four-part activity is usually introduced on the second day of a six-day development programme. Each part is illustrated with the experience of a real participant – Joe (pseudonym) – who was a senior manager in a primary healthcare organization. We have drawn on Joe's work in the programme and interviews with him at three-month intervals after the programme had ended.

Figure 13.1   Joe's drawing

Part 1: Drawing

Participants are asked to draw a picture that captures an issue that is calling for their leadership. Instructions for this activity say nothing about framing. Managers are reassured that the quality of their art is not at issue and whether they draw with blobs or stick figures is totally up to them. They are given paper and a range of coloured pens, and instructed not to show their picture to anyone. We ask that they don't talk, and we allocate about ten minutes for them to draw. A contemplative atmosphere usually develops. As participants finish their drawing they are asked to think of what they might say to help others get a feel for the issue they have drawn. They are asked not to simply relay the contents of what they have drawn but to think of a story that will help others 'get' their issue and its land-scape in one minute. Joe's picture is shown in Figure 13.1.

Joe drew a circle with seven stick figures; people with unhappy faces inside the circle and nothing beyond it (see Figure 13.1). In the circle he drew lots of crosses and a few ticks. Joe explained that the circle repre-sented the boundary between his organization and the external world and that the people were all staff. He explained that the crosses indicated that most people 'have bad work practices'.

Part 2: Stories in a Minute

Next, managers are asked to sit in a circle and are reminded not to show others what they have drawn. While they have been drawing, facilitators have created pairs from the group. We pair each person with someone who seems likely to offer their partner a different perspective, as well as being able to relate to the issues that their partner is facing. When people come back into the circle the pairings are made visible, usually via a PowerPoint slide. Joe was paired with Edith (pseudonym) who was also a senior manager in a public-sector organization.

At this point each person is given a maximum of one minute to bring their leadership issue to life for the rest of the group. We use a timer during this activity and give people a 'heads up' when they have only a few seconds left. People are reminded to be particularly attentive when the person that they are paired with speaks. We recommend that they take notes or make a sketch in order to capture key thoughts or impressions. We let them know that they will need to recall their partner's issue, and what they themselves imagined as they listened, for the next part of the activity.

Joe introduced his story as one of an 'unhealthy and unprofessional work culture'. He said:

> There are no processes, nothing exists, people use company cars, come in late, don't turn up for work and this is normal, normal, normal! There is nothing wrong with it . . . We have bad practice, bad behaviour, you name it . . . I am banging my head against a wall and not getting anywhere!

Part 3: the Concept of Framing

At this stage facilitators introduce framing as a concept and as directly linked to the work of leadership. To do so we draw on works cited earlier and use images and examples, including experiences that the group have already shared. For example, when we address the relationship between frames, identities and what people actually do, we might refer to the brief moment when Amy became class clown or when the group became tangled up with ideas of wrong and right. While we address leadership framing we continue to emphasize that frames are always present, with or without conscious intention.

Part 4: Seeing Frames and What They Do

Next, participants move into their pairs and take 15–20 minutes to consider the frames that are suggested by each person's image. While frames can be obvious once they are brought into view, before that they can be elusive. As the British psychiatrist R.D. Laing quipped with respect to rules: 'Unless we see through the rules we only see through them rules' (Laing, 1969, p.105). The same could be said for frames. We use language such as exploring and turning things this way and that to describe the *feel* of this work. The following questions guide this work:

- What is not in this picture or at the very edge, that could well have been in the picture?
- What would happen if features that are absent or at the edges were in the centre?
- What is the main idea, theme or metaphor conveyed by this picture?
- What relationships and identities are called up by this idea, belief or metaphor?

Before participants move into their pairs the whole group works together to consider these questions in relationship to a picture that one of them has drawn. When a pair gets stuck we often get the whole group to work together to find their way with the above questions.

Joe's example:

- What is not in this picture or at the very edge, that could well have been in the picture?
- What would happen if features that are absent or at the edges were in the centre?

As we have already noted, frames relegate some aspects of the situation to the background, rule out others and bring still other aspects to the fore. The above questions invite participants to play with issues of figure and ground and, in doing so, to consider that other, equally valid frames might be possible. For example, Edith was struck by the circle that divided the internal organization and the external world, and she noticed that the space beyond the circle was empty. She and Joe identified many stakeholders that were not in the picture and who could have been included. These included funders, clients, client's families, other organizations, board of directors, executive director, past staff and people in the local community.

At the time of this activity what was *not* in the picture seemed abstract to Joe, although the absence of clients bothered him. He tried putting the organization's clients at the centre of the picture but this felt contrived to him. He resisted imagining what would happen if clients were at the centre, arguing that they would never be at the centre *until* the bad practices of staff had been addressed. However, he was struck by the limits of a frame that focused exclusively on staff and their behaviour:

- What is a central idea, theme or metaphor conveyed by this picture?
- What relationships and identities are called up by this idea, theme or metaphor?

These questions help participants to see that frames are inherently social and dynamic, and shaped by who we understand ourselves to be. In Joe's case the question of the theme was quite apparent. However, this is not always the case. When themes are elusive we often prompt pairs to consider a theme, or a story that would sit in tension with, or be complementary to the one that they are considering. For example, if Joe and Edith had become stuck it might have helped them to think about an historic view or a three-dimensional perspective, because Joe's view shows one part of the organization in the present.

Joe and Edith focused on the ticks and crosses and the implication that what the staff were doing could be understood with respect to right and wrong. They described this as a strong performance theme and Edith suggested that this cast Joe firmly into identities of one who knows the answers and what is right and wrong, such as those of judge, priest, technical expert or teacher. They recognized that these identities would encourage Joe to give answers, correct, guide, reward, absolve and sanction.

Approximately three months later Joe elaborated on the meaning of these dynamics in his workplace. He observed that as the youngest in a Pacific Island family he was expected not to have a voice in decision making but to do as he was told. His focus on poor practices and performance problems sharpened the tension with older staff who shared Joe's cultural background and who saw him as engaged in unacceptable practices because he was talking out of turn. He observed: 'They see me as the youngest one so every time I talk it's like, "Oh, where does he get all these ideas from?"'

As Smircich and Morgan observed in their 1982 article, 'while individuals may look to a leader to frame and concretize their reality, they may also react against, reject or change the reality thus defined' (p. 259). Frames, as Smircich and Morgan note, are embedded in context. In Joe's prior place of work he had learned that systems for monitoring performance defined the successful manager. Yet this same frame was contributing to stress and conflict within his current organization.

Edith also noticed that Joe was not in the picture at all, although it was understood that he was the person allocating ticks and crosses. He was there but not there, as someone with a bird's-eye view of things. Edith suggested that identities of this sort would make it difficult for Joe to enjoy regular relationships with staff, making it unlikely that he would be alongside people, involved with their situations or sharing a joke with them. Indeed, the performance frame and notions of right and wrong rattled Joe. Several months after this activity and after the programme had ended, he described questioning himself and asking: 'Is it me? Am I doing it the right way? Am I the one with the problem and everyone else is right?' Looking back a year later Joe said: 'I was the most hated person back then . . . I was the loneliest man in the world.'

REFLECTIONS

The framing process described here builds on several years of working with framing in leadership development. We are not concerned with learning new skills or with the technical elegance of particular frames but with an orientation that is alert to the here-and-now dynamics of a socially constructed world. Our interest is persistent and steady, and represented by Baden Powell's phrase 'softly, softly catchee monkey'. For some managers the implications of framing will flicker in their peripheral vision like a monkey's tail in the forest, and they will catch hold of it only after the programme has finished.

This was the case for Joe. He was despondent at the time of the framing activity outlined here, was on the verge of leaving his job and was sceptical that anything (let alone alternative frames) could offer something to the situation. Questioning his taken-for-granted realities disturbed him. Looking back he described the first day of the leadership programme as utterly bewildering: 'The first day, honestly my head, I was like, what the . . .? What's this? It played with my mind. I thought, what's this? What is this? Honestly, when I was driving home I thought, what the hell was that?'

However, with time, Joe 'caught' the concept of framing and began to experiment with frames other than that of poor performance. He also worked with frames as material, tangible objects, realizing how they could highlight and contain spaces, hopes and memories by providing a border for them. For example, he created a collage out of photos of the organization's clients, including some that showed clients in situations of extreme poverty. He put his collage in a wooden frame and carried that with him to a meeting with staff where the literal picture became an intermediary object for their conversation. Almost a year after the first workshop Joe set up a retreat day for staff and board. He literally framed the meeting room with printed email responses to a question he had asked of everyone in preparation for the day: 'What are your hopes for our retreat day?' Looking back he attributed a successful day to framing:

Staff didn't know I was going to print out their expectations of the day and put them all around the wall. I believe that was key . . . To me, this was framing: staff and board walking around and looking at these so they would be in the space to contribute to the day.

However, there was no straight line, cause-and-effect relationship between the workshops, the framing activity and people in Joe's organization reconnecting with a sense of purpose that had fallen out of view. The framing activity began Joe's exploration of his own frames, helped him to 'see' his focus on 'bad practices' and to ask questions as to whether staff performance was a frame that would enable the work of leadership in his organization. Moreover, as Shotter (2008) notes, 'meaning is created by, with and for people in their collaborative meetings with each other' (p. 2). Joe's collage picture played a part in jogging people out of their malaise, but the identity that emerged as Joe built the collage and framed it was different than the frustrated man who was judge, priest, technical expert or teacher. Indeed, he came to see that fixing systems and processes, judging and correcting things, would never create engagement and change. Looking back he reflected:

It wasn't about the processes, it wasn't about the systems. Before, I sort of focused on their performance. I said 'Don't do this. That's not government policy. That's not right.' But when I started pointing back to the reality of the families that we're working with . . . (we have 20 individuals living in a garage) . . . once you start telling that story it then goes back to what they believe.

TIPS

1. We do not recommend using classic examples of framing such as King's 'I have a dream' speech to introduce framing to managers. Examples such as this entice people to craft great frames and, with that, to escape the more fundamental work of noticing frames, including their own. While noticing one's own frames tends to create a sense of strangeness, not knowing and not being in control of the latter invites the prospect that managers can be masters or possessors of their world (Shotter, 2008, p.217). We separate the work of identifying frames outlined here from the craft work of framing. (In the course of a six-day programme we often introduce framing on the first day and do not address crafting frames until the final day.)
2. We recommend that facilitators 'frame' this work for themselves as an ongoing strand rather than a learning module. Whereas a module stops and starts, a strand runs through an entire programme and

beyond. Holding framing as a strand helps us to be patient. This approach helps us to realize not that some people 'can't catch frames' but that they haven't caught framing *yet*.

3. Finally, it is important to remain mindful of the pull to conflate leadership development with personal development. When managers notice their own frames they can be shunted into questions they did not see coming, related to who they are and what they take their world to be. The activity outlined here takes the work of leadership, *not* personal development, as its purpose. We see personal development as a by-product of leadership development and as a different proposition. We find it helpful to be conscious of our choices in responding to those moments when managers have lost their footing. We aim to remain connected to the work of leadership when the conversation tugs in a personal direction.

REFERENCES

Alvesson, M. and S. Sveningsson (2008), *Changing Organizational Culture: Cultural Change Work in Progress*, New York, NY: Routledge.

Baden-Powell, R.S.S. (1898), *The Downfall of Prempeh: A Diary of Life with the Native Levy in Ashanti 1895–96*. London: Methuen & Co.

Barge, J.K. (2004), 'Reflexivity and managerial practice', *Communication Monographs*, **71**(1), 70–96.

Bennis, W. and B. Nanus (1985), *Leaders: The Strategies for Taking Charge*, New York, NY: Harper & Row.

Carroll, B., L. Levy and D. Richmond (2008), 'Leadership as practice: challenging the competency paradigm', *Leadership*, **4**(4), 363–79.

Chandler, D. (2007), *Semiotics: The Basics*, 2nd edn, London: Routledge.

Crevani, L. (2015), 'Relational leadership', in B. Carroll, J. Ford and S. Taylor (eds), *Leadership: Contemporary Critical Perspectives*, London: Sage, pp.188–212.

Fairhurst, G.T. (2005), 'Reframing *The Art of Framing*: problems and prospects for leadership', *Leadership*, **1**(2), 165–85.

Fairhurst, G.T. and Sarr, R.A. (1996), *The Art of Framing: Managing the Language of Leadership*, San Francisco, CA: Jossey-Bass.

Gioia, D.A. (2006), 'On Weick: an appreciation', *Organization Studies*, **27**(11), 1709–21.

Kotter, J.P. (1996), *Leading Change*, Boston, MA: Harvard Business School Press.

Laing, R.D. (1969), *The Politics of the Family, and Other Essays*, New York, NY: Random House.

Peters, T.J. and R.H. Waterman (1982), *In Search of Excellence: Lessons from America's Best-run Companies*, New York, NY: Harper & Row.

Pye, A. (2005), 'Leadership and organizing: sensemaking in action', *Leadership*, **1**(1), 31–50.

Shannon, C.E. and W. Weaver (1963), *The Mathematical Theory of Communication*, Chicago, IL: University of Illinois Press.

Shotter, J. (2008), *Conversational Realities Revisited: Life, Language, Body and World*, 2nd edn, Chagrin Falls, OH: Taos Institute.

Shotter, J. and A.L. Cunliffe (2003), 'Managers as practical authors: everyday conversations for action', in D. Holman and R. Thorpe (eds), *Management and Language*, London: Sage, pp.1–37.

Smircich, L. and G. Morgan (1982), 'Leadership: the management of meaning', *Journal of Applied Behavioral Science*, **18**(3), 257–73.

'Softly, softly, catchee monkey' (2013), accessed 20 June 2017 at www.worldwide words.org/nl/fjyn.htm.

Taylor, S.S. (2012), *Leadership Craft, Leadership Art*, New York, NY: Palgrave Macmillan.

Uhl-Bien, M. (2006), 'Relational leadership theory: exploring the social processes of leadership and organizing', *Leadership Quarterly*, **17**(6), 654–76.

Weick, K.E. (1995), *Sensemaking in Organizations*, Thousand Oaks, CA: Sage.

Weick, K.E. (1996), 'Speaking to practice: the scholarship of integration', *Journal of Management Inquiry*, **5**(3), 251–8.

Wright, M. (2015), '"I have a dream": a call for intergenerational dreaming', *AI Practitioner*, **17**(2), 27–8.

PART V

Reflections on practice

14. Facing the monsters: embracing liminality in leadership development

Beverley Hawkins and Gareth Edwards

PURPOSE

Understanding the liminal aspect of the learning experience can maximize the potential for transformation within the leadership development space. We show how this can be useful for learners and facilitators of leadership development by emphasizing three phases of liminality in learning: separation, the liminal space itself and reincorporation. We offer a series of exercises drawing on the liminality within learning, and show how they enable recognition to surface about the specific challenges that learners face, and promote a more reflexive approach to the student/educator relationship.

UNDERPINNING RESEARCH

Conceptualizing Liminality in Leadership Development

The concept of liminality was originally used by Victor Turner (1979), and within the discipline of anthropology more widely, to explore how people undergoing cultural transitions experience a state of 'being on a threshold' (Turner, 1979). This originally applied to participants of tribal cultural rituals that symbolize the transition between one stage of life and another, such as weddings or coming-of-age ceremonies, or carnivals celebrating the transition to a new year. These moments are thought to be important because they involve the suspension of the traditional relationships and ways of thinking that hold individuals in place. Instead, participants occupy a liminal space where 'anything is possible'.

Transitioning through this space and emerging on the 'other side' is proof of some kind of self-transformation: often, on leaving the liminal space, participants are awarded a new identity or status. Wedding ceremonies are prime examples of liminal moments, where participants leave behind their status as 'single person', and undertake a ritual where they are transformed into a married person with altered responsibilities.

More recently, scholars have suggested that liminality resonates beyond the formal cultural rituals identified by anthropologists. Scholars of organization studies have used liminality to address the experiences of temporary contract employees (Garsten, 1999) and management consultants (Czarniawska and Mazza, 2003), who are not fully in or out of organizational boundaries. The spaces between public or front-stage and private, back-stage workspaces are considered liminal spaces, and can become especially meaningful to employees as places of possibility, where important identity work is carried out (Shortt, 2015). Often this research refers to the precarious, in-between status of many organizational members. This is particularly salient in the light of trends towards a so-called post-industrialist society where firm boundaries are more permeable, and there is increasing reliance on temporary project teams. Tempest and Starkey (2004) point out the implications of such transient organizational forms for learning, suggesting that 'liminality breeds ambiguity' (2004, p.507) in ways that create risks and opportunities for learning. Being embedded in an environment with characteristics of liminality might enable workers to challenge the taken-for-granted aspects of organizational structure, and develop more fluid and innovative ways of working. However, these same characteristics make it more difficult for liminal employees to access formal training, engage in post-project reflection and develop learning systematically, rather than in an ad hoc fashion. Understanding the liminal implications of these trends may draw more attention to their disorientating aspects, than does the more neutral term of 'flexibilization' (Garsten, 1999).

Following Turner (1969), some aspects of organizational life might be better characterized as *liminoid*, rather than *liminal*. Liminoid contexts can invoke the suspension of norms and social relationships, and the potential for surprise or challenge that are also features of the liminal. However, the term 'liminoid' might speak particularly to ongoing processes of uncertainty that have no clear end, or those instances that represent a playful 'break' from society, rather than a contribution to social structure. Full liminality, according to Turner, 'is a state of great intensity which cannot exist very long without some sort of structure to stabilise it' (Homas, 1979, p.207). It is perhaps this definition that is most helpful for leadership developers working with participants over a defined period, and which we seek to address here. We focus attention on the identity work and transformations embedded in the transition to new learning (Hawkins and Edwards, 2015; Cook-Sather and Alter, 2011; Tempest and Starkey, 2004). This is particularly important for leadership development, which often connects working on leadership practice to working on the self, leading to transformations at the level of practice and at the level of identity (Ford and Harding, 2007). As Warren Bennis has said, 'becoming a leader is much the same as becoming an integrated human being' (2009, p.5). Therefore, understanding learning as a liminal space, which develops selves as well as skills, enables learners and facilitators alike to maximize the transformative potential of leadership development.

In a previous article, we (Hawkins and Edwards, 2015) have shown how students of leadership experience aspects of liminality. We draw attention to three key phases of liminality, originally identified by Van Gennep (1960) – separation, the limen and reincorporation – and illustrate why they are relevant to leadership development. Each of these phases are discussed in further depth below.

Phase 1: separation
This phase involves the dissolution of previous understandings and connections to the world. It is not always a physical or geographical separation, although some leadership development 'away days' may involve a change of physical location (Ford and Harding, 2007). It can also involve the leaving behind of old ways of understanding or practising leadership, or the unravelling of previous identities (Nicholson and Carroll, 2013). For many of our leadership students, this has involved abandoning prior convictions about the 'heroic' nature of leadership, or assumptions about where (and by whom) leadership is practised. It may involve letting go of old practices that are comfortable and familiar, but ultimately unhelpful.

Phase 2: the limen or liminal space
This phase represents the moment of transition, where possibilities are open and there is rich potential for transformation. Liminal spaces are opportunities to try out, question and reject possibilities and alternatives that might not be 'thinkable' in a non-liminal space. This means that liminal experiences contain great potential for self-development, but this potential is not without challenge. It is not easy to reject previously held ways of looking at, and being in, the social world (Van Gennep, 1960; Hawkins and Edwards, 2015). Letting go of old convictions and self-understandings can be disorientating. In the liminal space 'anything might happen' (Turner, 1979, p.465) – and this means that these spaces are not always positively experienced. Modern interpretations of liminality incorporate a sense of fear, upheaval and dissolution; they can be places where people get 'stuck' and feel unable to move on. For leadership developers, the challenge here is to create a space that feels comfortable but 'apart' from the rest of the world, for the purpose of encouraging reflection and a sense of fellowship

or togetherness, which Turner (1969) calls 'communitas'. For an example, see Kempster's (2009 and elaborated in this volume) use of tents as spaces for reflection, in an activity designed to help participants acknowledge and share their earliest recollections and experiences of leadership, and link these to their current practice (see also Mackay, 2012).

Phase 3: reincorporation

The final stage of liminality is characterized by the return of the participant to the social world, albeit with – hopefully – an altered understanding and sometimes, also, a more developed sense of self (Van Gennep, 1960). Usually, reincorporation implies a higher social status – as when a student is reintroduced to the world as a 'graduate'. Often, the subject is expected once more to conform to standardized social conventions: graduates are often expected to 'settle down' and begin a life of employment. After undertaking a leadership development programme, participants also often return to the world of work – in the same workplace or elsewhere. The challenge for them, and for facilitators, is to ensure that the learning accomplished during the liminal learning experience is not stifled or hampered once more by familiarity or convention. Research suggests that this might be enabled through the provision of spaces for continued reflection on practice at work (Tempest and Starkey, 2004). In this way, facilitators and managers can retain some of the 'liminoid' characteristics of the development programme, within a more structured, ongoing work environment.

Experiencing Liminality: Tackling 'Liminal Monsters'

The anthropologist Mary Douglas wrote that tribal rituals often centre on the subject battling a 'symbolic monster'. Overcoming the monster is a sign that the transition has occurred: the subject has left liminality and re-entered society, potentially with a new social status. This theme is repeated often in folkloric tales or fantasy fiction, where the hero navigates a quest-like journey across liminality, during which he or she battles various 'dragons', and after which s/he emerges with a new status or having 'grown' in some other way. Tolkien's *Lord of the Rings* is a good example (Grint, 2010), but so too is much young adult fiction, including the *Hunger Games* and *Mazerunner* series (and perhaps this is unsurprising, given the emphasis during this transitional phase of life on physical, social and existential 'growth'). Often, these stories invoke traditional 'heroic leadership' models, but simultaneously emphasize the importance of collaboration and community – the hero makes mistakes, and is never alone in tackling the fire-breathing dragon or draconian totalitarian regime. Therefore in popular culture, liminal spaces are emotional, intellectual and/or spatial landscapes where leaders emerge, and where communities and fellowships are brought together to experience challenge, catharsis, triumph and hope.

Hawkins and Edwards (2015) note that in the leadership learning experience, liminal monsters often take the form of doubt and uncertainty about how to study and practise leadership. Much of this uncertainty comes because of the subjective and contextual nature of leadership, which indicates that there is never a 'best' way to do or understand it. Common 'monsters' that our students grapple with include certain 'threshold concepts' that, whilst difficult to learn, often open doors to new understandings once they have been grasped (Meyer and Land, 2005; Yip and Raelin, 2012). They also struggle with the interdisciplinary nature of leadership, which means that there are 'many ways to think like a leadership scholar', rooted in psychology, philosophy, sociology, history and so on (Hawkins and Edwards, 2015). But these 'monsters' have implications for practice, as well as theory. Doubt-monsters are essential to leadership learning, because *doing leadership* itself is said to require familiarity with doubt (Weick, 2001a). Leadership involves navigating uncertain waters, and trying out solutions to never-before-seen problems (Grint, 2007). If doubt can never be conquered, perhaps the best that leaders can hope for is to learn to accept uncertainty – indeed, Weick has suggested that recognizing uncertainty as a central part of our experience is crucial to developing leadership wisdom (Weick, 1998, 2001b). Therefore, experiencing and perhaps embracing 'doubt-monsters' in the leadership learning process might help learners to become familiar with doubt's inevitable presence (Hawkins and Edwards, 2015; Locke et al., 2008). Facilitators of leadership development walk a difficult tightrope here: they must allow for doubt to emerge within the learning experience, but must provide enough support that participants feel they can manage this experience (Hawkins and Edwards, 2015). Therefore, there is a role for leadership educators in helping learners to recognize and unravel their monsters of doubt, and we discuss this in more detail in the next section.

Leadership Developer: 'Host' and 'Trickster' of Liminal Spaces

Our original article on liminality (Hawkins and Edwards, 2015) explains that, from the learner's perspective, the leadership developer is the permanent occupant of liminality – and this itself is an ambiguous role, not without danger. Leadership developers are the hosts of the liminal learning space, walking alongside liminal subjects in their journey back to reincorporation. Returning to the anthropological literature, we see this role likened to a 'master of ceremonies' by Mary Douglas (1966) or to a spirit guide or paraclete by Joseph Campbell (1993). In fact, the role of 'host' has been addressed in the leadership literature as an alternative to the hero metaphor at the root of much Western leadership thought (Wheatley, 2004), because it allows us to think of leaders as people who enable and empower others to collaborate in, and with, a particular context, rather than as people who enforce, direct or decide for others. Much of the suggested exercises in this chapter draw on the idea of 'hosting' a collaborative space for learning. However, the image of host is countered by an alternative archetype: that of the trickster. Tricksters are known to enact and perpetuate misunderstandings. They work to confuse and to lead astray, often first by lulling the subject into a false sense of security. For learners, leadership educators who promote one approach to understanding leadership – before asking students to consider an alternative perspective as equally valid – might be seen as 'tricksters'.

Applying this treacherous archetype to leadership development brings to light the power dynamics embedded in the student–educator or even the mentor–mentee relationship. Many writers have acknowledged that the leadership development space is not absent of power and that the learning that is achieved in these environments is not 'neutral', but always shaped through power (Nicholson and Carroll, 2013), and the emotional and political journey of learning (Gilmore and Anderson, 2012; Vince, 2011). The views of educators or coaches are often taken for granted by students, because power relations construct them as 'legitimate' forms of knowledge. This can make it hard for students to question the assumptions embedded in arguments presented by leadership educators. Clearly, learners are not unquestioning dupes who passively absorb everything that takes place in a leadership development context. But tricksters can make false promises (Hawkins and Edwards, 2015). These can take the form of a 'one size fits all', prescriptive approach to doing leadership, which ignores the importance of situated experiences and context. They might also perpetuate the idea that achieving leadership positions is not simply a meritocratic race, in which privilege is irrelevant and at which anybody, regardless of race, class, gender or (dis)ability has equal chances. Being aware of these nuances enables educators to use the development space as a chance to explore the way that leadership learning and practice are territorialized by power and privilege. Nonetheless, leadership development spaces themselves have potential to act as a mechanism for symbolic violence when they silence or marginalize alternative discourses about leadership practice (Smolovic-Jones et al., 2016). These are not easy things to discuss, but one of the exercises below offers a way to surface their implications.

DESIGN: ACTIVITIES TO MAXIMIZE THE LIMINAL LEARNING SPACE

In this section of the chapter, we offer some ideas from our own experiences of helping students to achieve liminal transitions. We offer three exercises, each of which are designed to draw on the liminal context of leadership development to build capacity for leadership practice. The suggestions here are not leadership 'how to' guides, but are designed to give participants opportunities for reflection on situated practice, to develop abilities for community building, and to encourage familiarity with navigating the unknown.

Exercise 1: Photographing Power

Aim

To encourage discussion about the connections between leadership and power. For many of our students, power is a 'threshold concept' that is hard to understand and apply to practice, but once understood, has the potential to change understanding of how leadership operates in organizations. Nonetheless, students often find it too 'abstract' and hard to relate to their own experience. This exercise aims to disrupt participants' understandings of power as a tool used by leaders, and encourages them to think of the 'hidden' ways that power acts on followers and leaders themselves.

Duration

Up to 1 hour.

Method

Split the cohort up into groups of between two and four people. Ask them to leave the classroom/development space, and spend about 15–20 minutes exploring their local environment (workplace building or nearby streets). Ask them to take at least one photograph, which symbolizes 'hidden forms of power' – smartphone cameras are ideal for this. After 20 minutes or so, the cohort gathers together again to identify and discuss the power dynamics expressed in the photographs. Encourage discussion about how far social norms and expectations act as forms of power, shaping organizational practice in the actions of leaders *and* followers. If possible, ask the cohort to email you the photographs so that they can be projected on screen, or shared with the rest of the class.

Questions for the cohort

- Where is the power in this photograph?
- Who or what is power 'acting' on?
- Is power always in the hands of leaders? Or are leaders also influenced by power?
- What kind of social norms or conventions are shaping action in this photograph?
- Does power restrict, or enable, action?
- How is action being justified or legitimized here?
- What forms of inclusion/exclusion are represented in this photograph?
- Is this kind of power necessary? What can we do to mitigate against its effects?

Important points

- Remind the cohort to secure proper consent before taking photographs of any people. Remind them to avoid taking photographs of power that emphasize faces or identifying features.
- Offer a few example photographs. Examples we have used in our own practice include:

  (a) A lecture theatre, to illustrate how power embedded in architecture shapes the possible actions of both teacher as active, speaking 'expert' and student as passive, constrained 'learner'.

  (b) A supermarket car park, to show how shoppers are encouraged to regulate their actions by parking 'between the lines'.

  (c) Security keypads on office doors, reception areas and other spaces, which symbolize or legitimize organizational hierarchies.

In our experience, this exercise offers students a new way to access alternative understandings of power, so that they can think beyond power as a 'possession', and understand the more subtle forces shaping social interactions at work. The two examples and explanations below come from undergraduates who participated in this activity as part of a second-year leadership module. Of course, they relate to the students' own experiences as members of a business school, but they exemplify the quality of insight that can come from this exercise.

A photograph of the sign for a 'Dean's Office' on a university campus. The group who took this photograph explained that this sign was placed in an area where students rarely venture – perhaps because students are not expected to have regular contact with the dean (or to know how to find his/her office). They located the office at the top of several flights of stairs, guarded by a secretary's desk. On returning to the classroom, a discussion emerged about whether a sign like this, combined with the 'high-up' office location, serves to reinforce the 'them and us' dynamic between senior university staff and students. Students pointed out that the sign emphasizes the dean's official status rather than his or her name (as other lecturers' offices do). They interpreted this to mean that part of the dean's power comes from this detached, impersonal public office or rank. The students' interpretation of the photograph emphasized the uneven, hierarchical power dynamics in the university community.

A photograph of an assignment feedback sheet, with sections for reviews of 'analytical thinking', 'originality' and 'structure'. Here, our students identified that feedback sheets represented power in the forms of norms governing what scholarly writing looks like, and discussed how far this seeks to standardize writing and its evaluation. This led to a discussion about the power dynamics between lecturers and students, including a debate about who decides what a 'good essay' is, whether another person's knowledge can ever be objectively evaluated, and whether these feedback sheets marginalize or discredit other forms of knowing, which might be more accessible to some students. In turn, this opens up difficult discussions about how 'learning' privileges some people over others, and how this might be addressed in teaching and learning. For participants in less student-based, more corporate settings, other forms such as performance review evaluation sheets might be used as equivalents.

Exercise 2: Your 'Leadership Toolkit' – a Peer Coaching Exercise

Aim
To help pairs of participants develop the next steps towards achieving goals. Research suggests that by learning to help others manage uncertainty, people improve their resilience when facing uncertainties in their own life. One technique that is useful here is peer coaching, which has been articulated as a 'helping relationship that has the intent of promoting growth, development, maturity, improved functioning [and] improved coping with the life of the other' (Rogers, 1973 in Parker et al., 2008, p.488). Quick peer mentoring/coaching exercises like this one can address the liminality in leadership in two ways. First, they bring participants into contact with uncertainty and doubt, and second, they develop community and connectedness, which as Edwards (2015) points out, connects liminality to leadership. Meyer and Land (2005) point out that paired dialogue and even role play exercises make the most of the suspension of traditional

relationships that is a feature of liminal space. They help participants to overturn their preconceived ways of looking at things, and to surface alternative possibilities (Parker et al., 2008). Additionally, when using a reflective (rather than directive or rhetorical) approach, questioning places value on the respondents' own experiences and rejects the idea of a 'quick solution' to problems (Romme and van Seggelen-Damen, 2015).

Reflective questioning draws on the importance of 'doubt' as a catalyst for identifying new pathways for practice (Locke et al., 2008). Each question has a specific aim related to managing uncertainty in liminal spaces. The first question encourages participants to look again at their context: to identify previously taken-for-granted information that may have been overlooked, and build situated knowledge. The second question focuses on building connectedness by helping participants maximize their relationships. This maintains a recognition that leadership is embedded in relationships rather than an individual's practice. The final two questions maintain the reflective approach, but focus on developing structure and helping the respondent to navigate their way out of uncertainty.

The questions given below under 'Method' comprise a *very* simple exercise aimed at developing situational awareness and building this into 'next steps' for practice. Incorporating a series of reflective questions, this exercise aims to open out rather than close down discussion. It acknowledges the value of situated experience, but asks participants to reconsider their assumptions about what they know about their own context.

Duration
Twenty to thirty minutes.

Method
Divide the cohort into pairs. Ask each partner to think of a specific challenge they are currently facing at work, which would make a difference to their working life. Ask them to describe it to the other half of the pair within two minutes. Then, one partner asks the following questions of the other, in fairly quick succession:

1. Can you think of any additional information that would help you to improve your response to this challenge?
2. Can you identify other people who can access or help you find this information?
3. Do you know of any other places you can look for this information?
4. Can you reflect on the next steps you might take to pursue this information?

Important points

- Peer-mentoring conversations can be challenging for participants, particularly given the always political and emotionally charged nature of learning (Vince, 2011). Facilitators need to be aware of the emotional (and practical) risks as well as the benefits for participants of these techniques, use careful judgement about when they are likely to create tension or discomfort, and prepare the ground with warm-up activities. Effective dialogue is said to be grounded in mutuality, reciprocity and trust (Rogers, 1973). This reflects Turner's (1969) point that liminal contexts develop *communitas*, a spirit of comradeship, trust and togetherness – but, it must be noted, there is potential for liminal tricksters to emerge here too. The role of the questioner is important here: ideally they should support reflection with additional prompts, but avoid rhetorical or 'closed down' questions ('why don't you . . .') which might result in the respondent becoming defensive.
- While the respondent reflects, the questioner should make notes on their answers. This enables the respondent to take away a list of new information sources, a set of new relationships or contacts to develop, and a possible timescale for practice: a 'toolkit' that is not universal, but which addresses their specific challenge.
- After 10–15 minutes the pairs should swap roles so that each member experiences the dialogue from both 'sides'.

Exercise 3: Trickster Reflection Exercise

Aim
This exercise offers participants a chance to explore the implications of the trickster archetype for their leadership practice, and can be used as a reflection exercise for both leaders/facilitators, and leadership developers. It was designed originally as part of a local authority continuous professional development (CPD) workshop for professionals working in family support services. Participants included teachers, healthcare professionals, social workers, police officers and non-governmental-organization employees. The workshop offered participants a chance to discuss the complex nature of their work supporting families deemed 'at risk' due to *inter alia* addiction problems, experience of domestic violence, histories of abuse and/or social and economic deprivation. Discussions focused on how client families saw support workers as occupying a 'trickster' role: they offered access to resources that could improve the family's quality of life, but also embodied the risk that their circumstances might be 'judged' in some way,

with possible unwanted consequences for the family – such as the removal of children into care. The workshop encourages critical reflection and discussion as to how participants might engage with and navigate these tensions, how they impact on the possibility for dialogue and trust to emerge, and whether these tensions might be resolved.

In particular, this activity draws on the liminality of learning by incorporating elements of creativity into the reflection process, which 'suspends reality and exaggerates possibility' (Kempster et al., 2015, p.3). The process of modelling or drawing 'trickster figures' encourages talk and collaboration amongst participants, but also opens up the liminal space as an aesthetic moment, which enables new opportunities for inventive and critical reflection on the challenges of managing people (Sutherland, 2013; Ward and Shortt, 2013). Our experience with family support works suggests that creative activities can be very helpful in developing discussions about topics that are important, but uncomfortable or very difficult to articulate.

Duration
Sixty to seventy minutes.

Materials
Flip charts and marker pens, modelling clay.

Method

1. (10 minutes) Divide the cohort into groups of around four. Explain how the trickster archetype presents as a way of articulating the agenda-filled, persuasive nature of leadership and facilitative work. Offer examples of tricksters from popular culture and folklore: whose leadership role can be extremely powerful and supportive, but can be perceived as bound up with subterfuge, manipulation, trickery and cloaked agendas. Examples might include the Norse god Loki, Roald Dahl's Willy Wonka and Captain Jack Sparrow from the *Pirates of the Caribbean* franchise. Offer a chance for the group as a whole to discuss the tensions embedded in leadership practice.

2. (20–30 minutes) Ask participant groups to explore how the trickster archetype relates to their own experience of leading/facilitating others, using the following technique:

   (a) Draw (or model, using clay) a trickster figure that represents your own experience of this work.

   (b) Consider the features of this trickster. In what ways might they be perceived as 'harmful' or 'dangerous'?

    (c)   What is in the trickster's immediate environment? What tools does s/he carry?

    (d)   What does the trickster say? What kind of language does s/he use?

    (e)   Are there any common preconceptions or misconceptions about the trickster's agenda?

3.   (20–30 minutes) In our own experience, the models and pictures acted as useful prompts for discussion across and between groups. Encourage the groups to share their models or pictures with the rest of the cohort, and to explain the significance of this particular trickster's appearance. Then encourage groups to explore the following discussion questions:

    (a)   What are the challenges of 'trickster' work?

    (b)   What has enabled you to create a trusting and supportive environment in this context?

    (c)   Is it possible to resolve the competing tensions in your work? If not, how do you navigate them?

    (d)   Is there a role for collaboration and reflection in helping you to work with trickster elements of your practice?

CONCLUSION

This chapter has reflected on the value of liminality as a lens for understanding the leadership development learning space. It has emphasized the potential and the dangers of liminal spaces for both facilitator and participants. We have pointed out that liminality enables participants to suspend their conventional social relationships and assumptions, and offers opportunities for playfulness, self-examination and critique of practice. We set out three exercises aimed at capturing this spirit of liminality, but many other activities are documented in the literature that recognize the creative potential and separation of liminal passage. These include the use of 'finger puppets' (Kempster et al., 2015, and Turner in this volume) and 'doll-making' for reflecting on leadership practice (Wicks and Rippin, 2010), role play as a mechanism for trying out new identities and worldviews (Meyer and Land, 2005), and 'walking around' as an invitation to practical, embodied learning (Zundel, 2013).

We conclude by pointing out the significance of the final phase to liminality identified by Van Gennep (1960) – reincorporation back into society. For leadership developers, this phase might be the ultimate challenge of the liminality in learning. Participants in liminal leadership development spaces can be exposed to new ways of understanding the world, or, emboldened by communitas, may have engaged in trusting dialogue with colleagues or peers, which might make them vulnerable on return to the workplace. What happens when these individuals return to an existing workplace context, fraught with political agendas? More research needs to be conducted on how leadership developers might guard against the risks of leaving liminality. Nonetheless, creating further spaces for follow-up discussions and feedback might be one way of enabling participants to navigate their return to non-liminal contexts, and bring their learning to bear, constructively, on their continuing leadership experience.

REFERENCES

Bennis, W. (2009), *On Becoming a Leader*, New York: Basic Books.

Campbell, J. (1993), *The Hero with a Thousand Faces*, London: Fontana.

Cook-Sather, A. and Alter, Z. (2011), 'What is and what can be: how a liminal position can change learning and teaching in higher education', *Anthropology & Education Quarterly*, **42**(1), 37–53.

Czarniawska, B. and C. Mazza (2003), 'Consulting as liminal space', *Human Relations*, **56**(3), 267–90.

Douglas, M. (1966), *Purity and Danger: An Analysis of Concepts of Pollution and Taboo*, London: Routledge.

Edwards, G. (2015), *Community as Leadership*, Cheltenham: Edward Elgar.

Ford, J. and N. Harding (2007), 'Move over management: we are all leaders now', *Management Learning*, **38**(5), 475–93.

Garsten, C. (1999), 'Betwixt and between: temporary employees as liminal subjects in flexible organizations', *Organization Studies*, **20**(4), 601–17.

Gilmore, S. and V. Anderson (2012), 'Anxiety and experience-based learning in a professional standards context', *Management Learning*, **43**(1), 75–95.

Grint, K. (2007), 'Learning to lead: can Aristotle help us find the road to wisdom?' *Leadership*, **3**(2), 231.

Grint, K. (2010), *Leadership: A Very Short Introduction*, Oxford: Oxford University Press.

Hawkins, B. and G. Edwards (2015), 'Managing the monsters of doubt: liminality, threshold concepts and leadership learning', *Management Learning*, **46**(1), 24–43.

Homas, P. (1979), *Jung in Context – Modernity and the Making of a Psychology*, Chicago: University of Chicago Press.

Kempster, S. (2009), *How Managers have Learnt to Lead: Exploring the Development of Leadership Practice*, Basingstoke: Palgrave Macmillan.

Kempster, S., A. Turner, P. Heneberry, V. Stead and C. Elliott (2015), 'The "finger puppets": examining the use of artifacts to create liminal moments in management education', *Journal of Management Education*, **39**(3), 433–8.

Locke, K., K. Golden-Biddle and M.S. Feldman (2008), 'Making doubt generative: rethinking the role of doubt in the research process', *Organization Science*, **19**(6), 907–18.

Mackay, F. (2012), '"I don't have to be like my principal": learning to lead in the post-compulsory sector', *Educational Management Administration & Leadership*, **40**(3), 392–409.

Meyer, J.H.F. and R. Land (2005), 'Threshold concepts and troublesome knowledge: epistemological considerations and a conceptual framework for teaching and learning', *Higher Education*, **49**, 373–88.

Nicholson, H. and B. Carroll (2013), 'Identity undoing and power relations in leadership development', *Human Relations*, **66**(9), 1225–48.

Parker, P., D.T. Hall and K.E. Kram (2008), 'Peer coaching: a relational process for accelerating career learning', *Academy of Management Learning & Education*, **7**(4), 487–503.

Rogers, C.R. (1973), 'The interpersonal relationship: the core of guidance', *Interpersonal Growth and Self Actualization in Groups*, **32**, 176.

Romme, A.G.L. and I.C. van Seggelen-Damen (2015), 'Taking nothing for granted in management education: a systemic perspective on the role of reflective questioning', *Organization Management Journal*, **12**(2), 76–86.

Shortt, H. (2015), 'Liminality, space and the importance of "transitory dwelling places" at work', *Human Relations*, **68**(4), 633–58.

Smolovic-Jones, S., O.S. Jones, N. Winchester and K. Grint (2016), 'Putting the discourse to work: on outlining a praxis of democratic leadership development', *Management Learning*, **47**(4), doi: 1350507616631926.

Sutherland, I. (2013), 'Arts-based methods in leadership development: affording aesthetic workspaces, reflexivity and memories with momentum', *Management Learning*, **44**(1), 25–43.

Tempest, S. and K. Starkey (2004), 'The effects of liminality on individual and organizational learning', *Organization Studies*, **25**(4), 507–27.

Turner, V. (1969), 'Liminality and communitas', in *The Ritual Process: Structure and Anti-structure*, Chicago: Aidine Publishing, pp.94–130.

Turner, V. (1979), 'Frame, flow and reflection: ritual and drama as public liminality', *Japanese Journal of Religious Studies*, **6**(4), 465–99.

Van Gennep, A. (1960), *The Rites of Passage*, London: Routledge.

Vince, R. (2011), 'The spatial psychodynamics of management learning', *Management Learning*, **42**(3), 333–47.

Ward, J. and H. Shortt (2013), 'Evaluation in management education: a visual approach to drawing out emotion in student learning', *Management Learning*, **44**(5), 435–52.

Weick, K.E. (2001a), 'Leadership as the legitimation of doubt', in W. Bennis, G.M. Spreitzer and T.G. Cummings (eds), *The Future of Leadership*, San Francisco, CA: Jossey-Bass, pp.91–102.

Weick, K.E. (2001b), *Making Sense of the Organization*, Malden, MA: Blackwell.

Wheatley, M. (2004), 'Servant Leaders', *Executive Excellence*, **21**(7), 15–16.

Wicks, P.G. and A. Rippin (2010), 'Art as experience: an inquiry into art and leadership using dolls and doll-making', *Leadership*, **6**(3), 259–78.

Yip, J. and J.A. Raelin (2012), 'Threshold concepts and modalities for teaching leadership practice', *Management Learning*, **43**, 333–54.

Zundel, M. (2013), 'Walking to learn: rethinking reflection for management learning', *Management Learning*, **44**(2), 109–26.

15. Leadership exchange: contextualized learning about how leadership is accomplished and personalized leadership development

Jonathan Gosling and Simon Western

I have spoken to many people about the leadership exchange which was both fascinating and useful, and suggested that we scrap every other form of management development!

NHS chief executive writing to his exchange partner following their exchanges

INTRODUCTION

The main question addressed in this chapter is 'how is leadership accomplished – in practice, in a specific setting, in real time?'

The problem is the same if we are looking at management, responsibility or organization: the accomplishment of all these is complex, context specific and infinitely variable, involving social and personal forces, intentional and unconscious actions, mixed and often juxtaposed motives; the question is affected by specific technologies, organizational politics, group dynamics, individual styles and preferences, relational emotions and constantly negotiated meanings. No wonder experienced students baulk at the simplified generalizations of management theory. 'Real life', they say, 'is far more complicated than that'. So the leadership exchange described in this chapter is a way to explore, in a disciplined and rigorous manner, real-time practices and outcomes by combining objective observation with subjective reflection on leadership as it happens. Our fundamental assumption – justified in experience and shared with many others – is that this level of self-awareness is a highly effective basis for improved performance.

This approach is at once simple and profound. It involves practising leaders taking time out to observe each other in the everyday acts of leadership, within a carefully structured framework of training, peer feedback and coaching. The results, as we will show, are often immediately useful and also offer long-lasting insight. In order to understand how these outcomes arise from an apparently simple process we employ Kleinian psychoanalytic ideas. These help us to appreciate the complexity of the underlying dynamics and to make some important generalizations about leadership and management development.

The early design for our management exchange programme was based on a simple hypothesis: if one manager could observe another, with the focus being on leadership – picking up the details, the minutiae, whilst also seeing the context and big picture with fresh eyes – they would bring rare insight to the process. At the same time the person being observed could contribute insider information on what he or she intended, and the emotional experience of being in that position. This method was tried and tested on an international executive master's programme – The International Masters Programme for Managers (IMPM) (www.impm org) and was a great success in the eyes of the participants. Research by the authors (Western and Gosling, 2000) then led to deeper understandings of what worked well and why, in the light of which we designed a new stand-alone leadership exchange process that we called *Lead2lead* and we came to use the exchange as a core activity of coaching and organizational development (OD) interventions. In both settings, within a conventional education programme and as a stand-alone intervention, the mixture of excitement and anxiety generated by the exchange needed careful containment, and outcomes were much enhanced if participants understood the role interdependence of reciprocal research, and were trained in reflective, reflexive and observational skills.

We noted that the most successful exchanges on the IMPM had proved successful because both parties had gone beyond knowledge seeking, for example benchmarking best practice, gaining new knowledge and skills, and having learnt something new about themselves that they could relate to their work role.

The first part of the chapter will discuss the IMPM management exchange and highlight our learning from this. The second part will describe the *Lead2lead* stand-alone individual exchange programme in some detail, before showing a case study of a corporate change programme built around internal leadership exchanges. Finally, the chapter will highlight the theoretical thinking behind the process and arrive at conclusions and identify areas for further enquiry.

THE BASIC OUTLINES OF THE LEADERSHIP EXCHANGE PROCESS

Participants choose or are allocated a partner and arrange a three-day visit in each direction, with a task to find out 'how management and leadership are accomplished' in the course of a normal week's work. During the week they talk to each other to test out impressions and interpretations, and at the end of the visit they sum this up in the form of 'working hypotheses'. The visitor may give feedback to their observed host on how the host took up his or her management role, with comments on management style and behaviour and any challenges or cultural differences observed; and seeking to compare the perspectives of the observer with those of the actor – objective and subjective views. This process is repeated in reverse and at the end of the exchanges a debriefing and coaching session helps them to draw out both (1) lessons about how leadership is accomplished in their own workplace, their own role in that, and further pointers to improved practices; and (2) general understanding of leadership, management, organization and responsibility. On certificated programmes where grades must be awarded each participant writes a reflective paper as a course requirement on what they had learnt from being both host and visitor on the management exchange.

We have noticed two distinct approaches to the learning opportunities, described in Figures 15.1 and 15.2, below.

PROCESS OF LEARNING THROUGH THE MANAGEMENT EXCHANGE

The exchange process naturally prompts people to be reflective because they are aware of someone else watching them; and even the observers often find themselves comparing their own responses with what they see someone else doing. But the depth and extent of this can be varied, and we wanted to improve the willingness to think creatively once jolted by something new or unexpected; to see new patterns emerging, reflect on one's own behaviours and styles and appreciate how these interact with organizational culture and process. We noted that in choosing partners many would select a comfortable partner, a friend and an easy visit rather than one to stretch themselves. We surmized that this is why many shadowing or buddying programmes run out of steam, because whilst they are interesting they are often reduced to little more than tourist visits lacking the rigour to challenge those undertaking the programme. Those participants who did stretch themselves on the management exchange, through

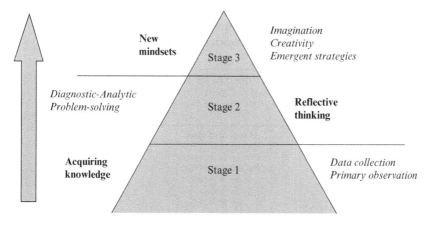

Note: This diagram depicts the qualities of learning that the visitors may attain through the exchange. Some participants stayed in the first stage we have labelled Knowledge Acquisition. Others moved to the Reflective Thinking stage and a few worked their way into New Mindsets. The latter showed evidence of sensing a wider and deeper range of feelings and group behaviours, questioning their own worldview. Here the learning is less linear, more dynamic in nature. The knowledge gained from stage 1 can be very valuable in its own right and may include benchmarking, business tips and personal feedback. However, to make the most of the management exchanges, and to develop managers' sensitivity, which seems so important in contemporary leadership, the aim should be to increase their capacity to reach stages 2 and 3 of the triangle.

Source: Western and Gosling (2000).

Figure 15.1 Linear learning process

choosing a challenging partner and/or place to visit, seemed to get much more from the exchange process. This is described in Figure 15.2.

OBSERVATION SKILLS, 'THE MARKETPLACE' AND ROLE CLARITY

To make it more likely that people would extend their learning approach we added structure and depth to the process. One step was to enhance the training in observation skills, with has three benefits – they notice more; they become aware of how each person notices different things and can thus learn more from each other; and practising the skills enables them to more confidently inhabit an observer role in meetings and office visits, boosting their objectivity.

We have also brought more attention to the process of selecting an exchange partner through an event called 'the marketplace'. Participants

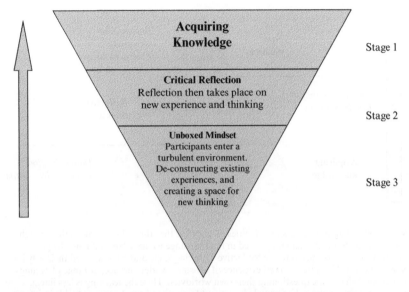

Stage 1

Stage 2

Stage 3

Note: Figure 15.2 describes how some participants use the exchange to learn from practice in a non-linear way. They chose (or found themselves) in a new, different or turbulent environment. From facing turbulence and a starting point of 'not knowing', of being bewildered, the visitor is immediately confronted with the opportunity of learning something new. Some participants when confronted with this experience are able to engage and use it, rather than retreat to a place of safety and control. It is a bit like a group of tourists visiting a very different culture on a foreign holiday. Some would stay in the tour group and observe the culture from a safe place, never venturing out alone. Others would go out alone after building up some confidence and then would experience something more challenging. A minority of others would leave the tour group immediately, taking a back-packing approach and throwing themselves into unpredictable and new experiences, revelling in the excitement, joy and even danger of discovery. It is from being immersed in the difference that they learn and reflect.

Source: Western and Gosling (2000).

Figure 15.2　Non-linear learning

are taken through the models depicted in Figures 15.1 and 15.2 above, and are then asked to focus on what would be a useful exchange for them, taking into account the personal profile of someone they would learn from, the geographical place, the sector and working environment. For example, if their US company had business interests in Asia would a visit to Japan or India be useful, or would a visit to a completely new culture help open their mindset and increase their innovative thinking? Finally we focused on what sort of organization would be most useful to visit: one similar to your own, or to something different in sector, size or strategy? Participants draw up a 'wish list' and a 'what I can offer' list. They then coach each other in threesomes, taking turn as client, coach and observer. The coach aims to help and challenge the client in their choice of exchange partner to ensure they seek someone who offers the best learning potential. After this process they take their 'wish list' and 'offer list' to the marketplace. Here the participants mingle and mix, checking each others' lists and informally discussing the possibilities of exchanging with each other.

The instructions for this process are simple and important:

> *Don't choose your first love! Make sure you play the field first. No one has finally chosen their partner until everyone has chosen a partner.*

The process of choosing and being chosen (or perhaps left stranded) raises anxiety levels, so the first instruction aims to prevent a manic flight towards selecting the 'nearest or easiest person'; not because the partners are well matched but because the anxiety is so powerful (Miller, 1990).

The second instruction pushes the group to take responsibility for ensuring that everyone has a satisfactory partner (even if not a perfect match). Participants discuss and negotiate with each other and we facilitate this process, clarifying and asserting the main purpose of learning. This has proved a useful though challenging exercise in distinguishing sentient from task priorities, with applications to other aspects of team formation. But it takes time and patience; and often participants see the value of it only after they have completed the exchange and look back on it as formative. It is not a good bet for facilitators dependent on instantly positive happy-sheet evaluations!

We have also found it important to clarify what participants were to do on the exchange, that is, what is involved in taking up a role as either an observer or a host, and as co-learner in feedback and reflection sessions after the visits. Some of the tools for doing this are described below. We also clarify expectations on any written work and make it clear that the learning and reflection process began when choosing a partner and continued beyond the final visit on the exchange.

CASE STUDY 1:   IMPM MANAGEMENT EXCHANGE

A manager from a British telecom company visited the CEO of a large family-owned bakery in India, and was prompted to reflect on his own priorities. Commenting on his Indian colleague's determination to focus on strategy, he noted: *'He only attends the business for four to five hours a day. The rest of the time he is reflecting on the direction of the business and formulating his change initiatives and growth plans.'* Contrasting this with his own work patterns and that of other colleagues he continues: *'I spend approximately twelve hours a day at work and usually return home exhausted. On return home I think about food, family, football and other non-work topics but certainly not strategy. I'm far too knackered. During my working week I attend to strategy for a small proportion of the time. Most of the week is consumed in operational issues and this week's latest greatest panic.'*
   He continues to comment on observations of his host:

> *He has a clear agenda to encourage growth in individuals, to encourage them to take responsibility, to fulfil their potential. He is not focused on 'control'. He has also limited his work time at the business premises, leaving him with the necessary energy at the end of the working day to reflect on current issues and plan for the future. Undoubtedly the group is a success and it has reached this level of achievement as a direct result of new and changed strategies in the bakery industry.*

Finally he reflects about his own culture and decides that he should modify his behaviour as a result of this experience:

> *There is something very Anglo-Saxon about my own insistence on knowing everything that is happening in my ambit of responsibility and controlling any half-important activity. I see it about me at work in many of my colleagues also. And we compound the problem by working long hours and saving little or no energy for the equally important issues of strategy. If Narayan* [his exchange partner] *practises 'management by thinking', my personal bias is towards 'management by doing' ... I hope to modify my own behaviour as a manager.*

LEAD2LEAD: DEVELOPING THE METHODOLOGY

The learning from the IMPM management exchange enabled the authors to design and deliver a successful leadership exchange programme to individual leaders exchanging between companies.

The Leadership exchange process

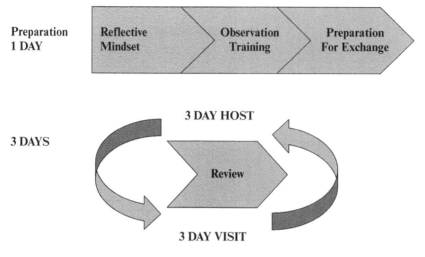

⇒ Write a <u>report</u> and give verbal feedback to host on how they took up their
   leadership role on final day of visit

Figure 15.3   The leadership exchange process

Stage 1: Reflective Mindset

As Figure 15.3 shows, the participant goes through a preparation process
that entails a three-hour training session called 'the reflective mindset'.
This explores the participant's perception of him/herself as a leader. We
ask them to reflect on any previous feedback they have received and use
artwork as a tool to cut through the well-defended layers of language with
exercises, as shown in Figure 15.4.

Reflective mindset exercise
Draw yourself in each box without using any words:
   Participants are invited to 'Draw yourself in each box without using any
words (being an artist is not important – symbols, rich pictures, do it in any
way that feels comfortable)'.

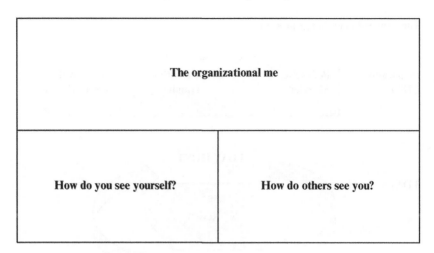

Figure 15.4   Reflective mindset exercise

Example: The coach interprets the pictures in a safe but robust way with the client, based on a standard open-systems distinction between person, role and task (Miller and Rice, 1967). For example, a male participant drew himself balancing with a pole on a tightrope to show how others at work saw him. His interpretation was that he was seen as a well-balanced team player, a man who could be trusted and was sure-footed. The coach suggested he might also feel himself to be in a precarious position, drawn to dangerous risk. During the coaching session we used this to discuss his possible move to an emerging economy as a national director of the company. This job, he said, would make or break him; if successful he would have turned round a hugely difficult situation and would gain great respect within the company, but if he failed he would definitely minimize his chances of reaching board level, which was his stated goal. The drawing and interpretation led him to the realization that he was indeed a risk taker, and that was recognized in the company – one reason he had been offered the move. It was from this newly realized view of himself that he was able to make a clearer decision, and think about what changes he needed to make to be seen as both a risk taker and yet one who could also represent a safe pair of hands with the gravitas to join the board.

At the end of this coaching session we get the leader to identify the exchange that would be most beneficial; taking into consideration the role of the other, the company or other organization and the geographical place. Often a client comes to the session with a fixed view of the exchange they want and, through this process of exploration and challenge, leave with a different idea completely.

Stage 2: Observation Training

Managers become adept at sizing up a situation quickly and decisively. But we encourage participants to go beyond their usual learning patterns of developing knowledge and to create a new space that enables creativity to flourish. To do this our experience shows that managers need training in observing others and, more importantly, observing themselves *in the process of observing* (which includes editing out what they pre-judge to be uninteresting, irrelevant or too painful to notice). Reflection is an oft-used term but in reality it is a very challenging task for busy managers brought up on a diet of goal-oriented attainment and technical knowledge and skill.

Observation training exercise: the window and the mirror
In this exercise we outline some observation skills and then send participants out into a 'busy place' (a café, a railway station, an airport lounge) to undertake two exercises. Ideally, these are done in pairs, sitting side by side to observe the same scene. The first exercise is called 'the window': participants are asked to observe for ten minutes, as if they were a video recorder, without taking any notes until the end and then to write down everything they saw during the ten minutes. If with a partner, they should only then speak to each other after they have done this, comparing observations.

The second exercise is called 'the mirror': to stay in the same place and do exactly the same except they are to observe their emotions and thinking process whilst observing the external world; for example, if you see a homeless person, how does it make you feel? If you lost focus and your mind wandered, where did it wander to and how might that be linked to what was going on at the time?

Our aim is to heighten the observers' sensitivity to the context, to make them aware of what their emotional and cognitive responses are, and to disentangle the relationship they have with them. As well as the skills and personal insight, they also internalize what it is to be an observer. Debriefing this is crucial as it is the basis for entering the exchange in a disciplined and rigorous way – to make it more than a shadowing exercise. When on the exchange (as both visitor and host) participants should continuously reflect on their relationship with the context, and how it impacts on the ways in which leadership, authority and responsibility are enacted.

Stage 3: The Exchange

Once partnerships are agreed (as described above) they plan the logistics of the visit. Sometimes we provide tools such as mapping techniques to chart relationships between individuals and departments; and journaling techniques based on the psychoanalytic concept of 'free association'. (Participants record their host's behaviours, the organizational context and their own reactions, and then speculate freely about the images these excite.) These and other techniques aim to enhance and deepen the creative potential of the exchange – avoiding an evaluative judgement of leadership style or competence.

The host is advised to inform colleagues that s/he will have an observer with him/her for a three-day period and they are to take up an active role of encouraging feedback and observation. The visitor is to take up the role of observer for three days – a tough assignment!

On the final day the visitor is asked to write a report based on his or her observations and journal records as this forms the basis for a later feedback session to the host, and subsequent joint analysis of their findings about how leadership is enacted.

Stage 4: Coaching Debrief

When both participants have been host and visitor they face the significant task of making sense and making use of the experience. It is normal for each to have a one-to-one coaching session to digest it all, relating the feedback they received, the thoughts they had as an observer, and issues arising from comparing their own organization to another.

But it is also important that they work together to focus on generalizable lessons from the two specific examples of leadership in practice. The focus depends on each case, but refers to issues of hierarchy, gender and other structures of inequality; accountability, responsibility and corporate culture; and the intermingling of all these along with personality and team agendas. Often the exchanges are set up specifically to address one of these – responsible leadership, for example – and the debrief sessions can be designed accordingly.

Corporate Applications

Beyond individual exchange programmes we have found a market for this idea within large companies. HR directors and senior executives are often

CASE STUDY 2: CORPORATE EXCHANGE CASE STUDY

Company Profile (all details disguised to ensure anonymity)

International company working in engineering, one year into a three-way merger; making synergies in the face of continuing losses and overcapacity in the market; and creating flatter management structures.

Let 100 Flowers Bloom

Following the success of a small series of individual exchanges for the four executive directors (with peers in external companies), we were invited to design a programme involving the 100 most senior managers. In preparation we issued online questionnaires aimed at engaging the participants in a self-reflective process before the observation training. The questionnaires were also used to help decide on the exchange partnerships, along with knowledge of individuals, the businesses they came from and where networks needed building and communication channels opened up. We briefed participants on the observation and exchange process in groups of six to ten at a time. Within three months we had 100 managers visiting and being visited across the company – all in one partnership – and just two people didn't manage it. We decided from the outset that the debriefing had to be personal and we arranged as many face-to-face coaching sessions as we could, and picked up the rest via telecoaching.

There were three key outcomes to this work: individual learning through observing and being observed and sharing feedback; improved corporate communication and integration; and strategic innovation through thinking outside the functional silos.

Some examples of the value derived form the exercise can be seen in these illustrative quotes:

1. Communication:

   This exercise has caused both of us to reflect on the critical importance of communication skills among managers, and to consider whether we are making optimum use of communication tools and styles for the most effective and efficient communications within our organization.

2. Leadership styles:

   I need to learn how to say no, my visitor told me I can't be everybody's darling.

   I used negative examples to highlight the seriousness of the situation. It was pointed out to me that this sometimes freezes people. I needed to find ways to motivate people, to get them to focus on how they could achieve success and the opportunities for doing this.

   The positive feedback confirmed me as a positive leader.

Common reflections after the exchange were around the difference between a technical/expert leader and an empowering/facilitating leader. Questions were discussed between exchange partners of how much detail one should have and how too much can inhibit delegation whilst not enough detail leaves too many gaps:

Their preparation for meetings was excellent and it showed in the outcomes from the meetings – I must spend more time on preparation as it is more efficient in the long term.

3. Connectedness:

What does he need to do a good job? This should be the question we ask of our internal customers. We need to be concerned for their success as well as our own.

We realized how much our work impacted on them; the problem wasn't theirs but both of ours. They couldn't solve it alone. We went to lunch and worked out a plan to present the issues to the boss so we could resolve it.

How do we harmonize and create a management style that motivates – this is the key to our success.

Realizing the commonalities as well as difference was insightful:

Through the visit I was introduced to an IT specialist and we shared the same problems: I have now liaised with him and we have started to work together on this issue.

The exchange process seems to have improved the sense of connectivity and integration of effort across the company. Conclusion:

Multiply [my] learning by 100 leaders and the micro changes that take place with individuals represent a significant change programme within the company.

troubled by the difficulties in dealing with the key issues of communication, alignment and improving collaborative working within their complex organizations. We have designed and delivered an organization-wide series of exchanges that pair up managers to observe each other's leadership practice across different functions as well as national boundaries and old 'bloodlines' when working with acquisitions and mergers.

The results of this series of 50 internal corporate exchanges were indeed powerful and widely diffused. Though impacts are notoriously difficult to measure, narrative methods are able to assess outcomes, individual learning and corporate patterns, using the verbal and written data gathered through the stories, reports and one-to-one coaching debriefs. The independent coaching team analysed this data, checking prejudices and biases before offering findings and hypotheses to the HR team, who then added their own hypotheses. We were thus able to accomplish a cultural audit of the company carried out by their own managers, who in effect had been action researchers using ethnographic skills to make sense of the whole, and contribute to new networks and communication channels being formed whilst also working on their own personal development and supporting a peer in their leadership development.

THEORETICAL DISCUSSION

The theoretical stance informing our work draws on psychoanalytic theories of group behaviour, some aspects of which we discuss below. Specifically, we focus on unconscious aspects of:

- pairing;
- containment; and
- observation and voyeurism.

Pairing: A 'Basic Assumption'

One of our early premises was that 'pairing', two people becoming exchange partners, formed an essential bedrock of the leadership exchange process. Bion (1961) describes pairing (BaP) as one of three basic assumption states that groups take up unconsciously, the others being dependency (BaD) and fight/flight (BaF). Each basic assumption state allows the group to unconsciously protect itself against anxiety that arises naturally in all the uncertainties of work and group membership. In BaD the group members act 'as if' a leader (or doctrine, ideology or strategy) will protect and sustain the members, that is, will make them feel safe. The group members avoid the responsibility of developmental activity and individual responsibility due to a pathological dependency. The BaF group assumes a danger or enemy, which should either be attacked or fled from. Through this mechanism they constantly focus on the enemy and avoid the work in hand. The pairing group (BaP) works on the belief that a future event will save them, so they look to a pairing within or a pairing between the leader of the group and an external person or pairing with an idea or fantasy figure; a pairing that will miraculously conceive a resolution to their problems. The group unconsciously places this hope onto a union that will bring them salvation. However, as Bion says, the hope is futile because 'The Messianic hope must never be fulfilled. Only by remaining a hope does hope persist' (Bion, 1961, p.151).

Such basic assumption states are unconscious processes that undermine the developmental growth of individuals and move the group away from fulfilling their given work or primary task. Bion noted, however, that these basic assumptions can be changed to a 'sophisticated state' whereby they act as a basis for the workgroup, which engages with reality and fulfils its tasks (Obholzer, 1994). For example, the BaD is useful as a premise in the medical profession where a degree of dependency on behalf of the patient is a necessity. We would add here that it is also useful within education, as the induction of students to a school or university creates a dependency ritual enabling the new intake to take up the role of learners or students. BaF is of course useful in the military or emergency services, who have to psychologically be prepared for fight or flight in order to carry out their job. Likewise in normal commercial competition BaF will also be a useful mode to function in; but when exaggerated in a takeover defence, for example, it can make the job of subsequent integration much harder. Thus it becomes important to mobilize hope in the new pairing, BaP. The sophisticated use of BaP also underpins the pairing in a therapeutic or coaching relationship as it supplies the hope that is required to sustain the treatment and to work through painful realities.

Groups and individuals move between the three basic assumption states and between the basic assumption state that is in denial and the work group that focuses on performance. In essence these basic assumptions can be unconscious collusions to avoid reality and work tasks and/or they can underpin the unconscious culture in a group or team to take on the task in hand. An important leadership task is to harness the correct basic assumption state to the team and organization. Likewise when planning a leadership development activity, engaging with the most appropriate unconscious culture to enhance the learning potential is an often overlooked aspect of development design work (Western, 2013). The leadership exchange process encourages and utilizes the basic assumption of pairing and the hope it inspires as a leverage point to create a stimulating desire for development.

Reciprocity and pairing
Notably in this form of paring there is inherent symmetry, as both parties are reciprocally dependent on the other. By contrast, coaching relationships lack this reciprocity; the coach is a paid 'expert' and assumes authority from the role, which reproduces a distinct power relationship similar to teacher–pupil, despite attempts to ameliorate that through non-directive coaching approaches.

Sexuality
One interesting observation to note from the pairing assumption is the unconscious sexual nature of 'the pair'. To produce a messiah the unconscious fantasy is a sexual liaison, the fertile couple will give birth to the new. This is not dependent on gender, nor on real events; it is a persistent but mostly unconscious fantasy.

A work group likely to stimulate the basic assumption of pairing . . . is likely to reveal sexuality in its central position. According to my view of the pairing group, the group must assume that if two people come together, they can only do so for sexual purposes (Bion, 1961, p.176).

When planning and running the IMPM management exchanges the notion of sexuality was indeed prominent. The management exchange group would joke about getting into bed with the right partner, or when we tried to set up a threesome to exchange – due to odd numbers in the group – jokes about a *ménage a trois* were abundant, despite it being three males exchanging. It is important therefore to confront this early in the process, and to assert the primacy of work-oriented collaboration, while allowing the 'hope' – the unconscious by-product of 'pairing' – to thrive as a form of leverage for leadership development.

Containment

First, as Anna Freud says, build the house; first, as Klein says, introject the good breast; first, as Bion says, you have to have an adequate container; first, as Bowlby says, have a secure base. (Alvarez, 1992, p.117)

Our second theoretical stance was that for any learning to take place the appropriate containment is necessary. In Kleinian psychoanalytic terms 'maternal containment' underpins the quality of relationship an infant receives from its primary carer to manage (contain) anxiety and therefore leave a space for thinking to take place (Klein, 1959; Bion, 1961; Hirschhorn, 1990). In adult life, containment comes in many forms but is a vital enabler for thinking and learning to occur. For example, when we were developing the leadership exchange the container was the IMPM. The IMPM is an institution made up of high-quality universities; as an institution it provides a well-thought-out framework, professional faculty, supervision and marking systems and the recognition of a master's degree. All of these factors constitute a 'containing environment' in which learning can take place.

As a stand-alone activity the leadership exchange requires a containing environment or what Winnicott (1971) refers to as a 'holding environment', which we have carefully fostered by basing our work on research, sections such as this paragraph affirming that this has been thought through and has been tried and tested over a number of years. Care must be taken to support learning and contain the anxiety created through taking people beyond their comfort zones. We were very aware that the idea of being observed and observing others brings with it conscious and unconscious fantasies. Becoming an observer means giving up a familiar (and often distracting) active role, and taking up a new role, which will initially leave the participant feeling inactive and passive and impotent. To be given the task of focusing wholly on observing another, without rushing too quickly to describe, explain or assess what is going on, is a counter-intuitive learning process. It can bring unconscious associations of voyeurism (Peeping Tom behaviour – see below) and of being critical and judgemental. To be observed can also be a daunting prospect. In contemporary society it often stimulates anxiety associated with surveillance, with being in trouble or with being audited and judged. As any child, parent or teacher will know, a school going through an Ofsted inspection can turn from being a place of learning into a place of frenetic anxiety. Yet being observed is also part of being noticed and valued. So again, it is important to recognize the anxiety of being observed while emphasizing the positive experience of being recognized, respectfully seen and heard. The reciprocity referred to above is crucial to this, because in the leadership exchange there is actually no external assessor – there is only the role of observer that is put at the service of both participants in turn. So here the rigour and clarity of the task and the roles contributes to the containment – everyone knows what they should be doing throughout, and recognizes that each is part of a process with a foreseeable progression.

Observation and Voyeurism

Having drawn upon the sophisticated stance of pairing to stimulate the hope needed for learning, and having worked on the design to create the container for the learning to take place, we now turn to the actual learning itself that draws on observation and, unwittingly, voyeurism!

Observation and auto-reflection

When in the role of observing someone else, one has to refer to one's own experience in order to make sense of what one observes. In this way reflection is triggered automatically. The design also ensures that the participant in the role of host – being observed – reflects on what he or she is doing. The very fact that they become an object of another's gaze creates a self-reflective stance. One becomes aware of one's own behaviour. The creation of an audience means that one becomes an actor performing on an overfamiliar stage, the office. The theatre is the workplace, the host becomes the star actor, his or her team in support roles, and the visitor becomes the audience. The stage, the support actors and the self all become (re)viewed in a new light through the introduction of an audience specifically trained to place you into their gaze.

Using the metaphor of theatre brings us to a central tenet of the work.

The leadership development we offer through coaching, training and the exchange process is far more than the sum of the parts. The ancient form of theatre provides a creative and dynamic form in which ideas are shared. As in the theatre, there are many roles and without each of them the play doesn't work. An actor cannot be an actor without an audience, and the quality of both is vital to the success of the play. The programme points a spotlight for actors and audience alike on how one person takes up and interprets his or her leadership role in relation to others.

Voyeurism
We have described the double-edged significance of pairing and hope; of anxiety and containment that support the observation and learning process. In a similar way the exchange triggers the unconscious excitement of looking at that which is forbidden: that is to say, to spend three days observing another at work is an unusual – and may be considered a voyeuristic – task. Laura Mulvey, in her classic (1975) paper 'Visual pleasure and narrative cinema', draws on Freud's thinking on scopophilia (in *Three Essays on the Theory of Sexuality*, 1905) and relates this to attractions of going to the cinema:

> He [Freud] associated scopophilia with taking other people as objects, subjecting them to a controlling and curious gaze. His particular examples centre around the voyeuristic activities of children, their desire to see and make sure of the private and the forbidden (curiosity about other people's genital and bodily functions, about the presence or absence of the penis and, retrospectively, about the primal scene). (Mulvey, 1975, p.9)

Consuming tips and skills and benchmarking is a useful and engaging activity. Seeing what is forbidden is for the visitor an exciting, stimulating and naughty prospect, particularly for those drawn to the more open and adventurous levels of learning described in Figures 15.1 and 15.2 above. This may produce discomfort, along with pleasure, because having seen 'the forbidden', an unconscious fear is that one may become the target for a vengeful attack or exile, as having eaten too much of the fruit of knowledge. This is one reason that observers so often hide behind a clip board, a check list or competency framework – a kind of lattice through which they can peep at others, while disguising their scopophilia. By properly establishing the role and skills of the observer, and the reciprocity of the exchange process, we acknowledge the curiosity, avoid the need for subterfuge and legitimize the excitement of discovery.

The opposite experience to being a voyeur is that of being an exhibitionist, the pleasure derived from being seen. Many high performers are obviously drawn to perform to others; this is often linked with transformational leadership (Bass, 1995) and charisma, though of course many leaders are more reticent and introverted. The media have cashed in with relish on this dynamic; reality TV shows are profuse and play on the audiences' voyeurism and scopophilia. It seems there is no shortage of people vying for the opportunity to be exhibitionists and to put themselves through all kinds of demeaning processes in order to be seen by others. Presumably for some people this may be part of the appeal of the leadership exchange, but the experience of exposure is already intrinsic to corporate life.

The competitive environments of most organizations can cause constant self-doubt and comparison, and also a regressive infantile unconscious reaction . . . 'will they be better than me' (will his/hers be bigger than mine?) or 'will I be exposed as a fraud' (does he/she have one?). As visitor or host (voyeur or exhibitionist) there will be an element of pleasure and pain based on the individual's confidence and personal preferences. Providing a balance between stimulating the unconscious desires to engage in these learning processes and just enough containment of anxiety is a delicate balance that relies on a well-thought-through pedagogical process. Our task was to utilize the pleasure gained from the observation of another 'scopophilia' and make this a safe-enough experience to turn the observer's gaze back on themselves using the reciprocity, the role clarity and the coaching, to maximize the reflective process.

It is helpful in this regard to recognize the second element of Freud's work on scopophilia, again set out by Mulvey (1975) in terms of cinema viewing: 'the cinema has structures of fascination strong enough to allow the temporary loss of ego while simultaneously reinforcing the ego' (Mulvey, 1975, p.11).

In short, the observer is encouraged to temporarily lose their ego and enter the world of the other . . . as one does at the cinema. Thus one may identify with the other, as in the cinema one comes to empathize with the movie stars and their cognitive and emotional predicaments; in the leadership exchange this takes place through the identification with a peer facing workplace predicaments. This explains why certain types of experiential learning are both powerful and sustainable, because they become internalized into the self rather than knowledge bolted onto the self.

Our goal has been to design a way to help leaders to 'look awry' firstly at the other, then at themselves and their own workplace. We believe this promotes a more 'ecological leadership' stance (Western, 2013) that enables them to relate to the ecosystem they are working within in a more embedded and contextually aware way. Being able to locate oneself with greater clarity and to be able to see patterns in the whole and engage with the wider system with a greater sensitivity to others are some of the building blocks of great leadership practice . . . well that's our assumption and our hope!

KEY TIPS

1. This is about enquiring into how leadership, influence, membership, loyalty and motivation are accomplished in the specific circumstances of the participants; and generating insights about their own part in this. It is not helped by advocating an ideal model of leadership style or process. There may be some aspect of self-assessment and feedback.
2. It is key to stress 'reciprocity': the exchange partners should be encouraged to act as a team to enquire into leadership as practised in real life, providing for each other the benefits of two perspectives – the actor and the observer – in each location. Beyond the exchange phases, they should be facilitated to review their learning and to articulate what they now understand to be the ways in which leadership is accomplished.
3. The exchange should be for a minimum of two full days in each direction. We know that a one-day visit can be very interesting, but the benefits of the second day are more than twice as much data – it brings depth and nuance.
4. A practical tip – equip exchange partners with good-quality notebooks, and give them some training in taking field notes – for example, drawing a vertical line down each page and noting what you see externally on one side, and your internal thoughts and feelings on the other.

CONCLUSION

The apparently simple process of 'shadowing' another practitioner both reveals and disguises a number of dynamics that are often overlooked in the enthusiasm for learning. The most naive account of learning emphasizes the 'consumption' of facts and techniques. The learner is pictured as a gatherer filling his or her basket with useful tips in the expectation of being able to unpack and apply them later. There is no need to change: the learner and the learned are in an unproblematic subject–object duality. In its purest form this would seem to be exemplified by the act of dispassionate, uninvolved observation in a traditional work-shadowing process. And yet we have found that this simple duality is confounded by emotional and psychological responses. These responses – including anxiety, surprise, creativity and a dynamism linked to primitive and unconscious sexuality – explain why this exchange process is both so powerful and, also, how without the appropriate containment could easily go amiss.

REFERENCES

Alvarez, A. (1992), *Live Company*, London: Tavistock/Routledge.
Bass, B. (1995), 'Theory of transformational leadership', *The Leadership Quarterly*, **6**(4), 463–78.
Bion, W. (1961), *Experiences in Groups*, New York, NY: Basic Books.
Freud, S. ([1905] 1953), 'Three essays on the theory of sexuality', in *The Standard Edition of the Complete Psychological Works of Sigmund Freud*, VII, London: Hogarth Press and Institute of Psychoanalysis.
Hirschhorn, L. (1990), *The Workplace Within*, Cambridge, MA: MIT Press.
Klein, M. (1959), 'Our adult world and its roots in infancy', in A.D. Colman and M.H. Geller, (eds), *Group Relation Reader 2*, Washington DC: Rice Institute Series.
Miller, E. (1990), 'Experiential learning in groups: the Leicester model', in E. Trist and H. Murray, *The Social Engagement of Social Science Vol.1: The Socio-psychological Perspective*, London: Free Association Books, 165–98.
Miller, E. and K. Rice (1967), *Systems of Organization*, London: Tavistock.
Mulvey, L. (1975), 'Visual pleasure and narrative cinema', *Screen*, **16**(3), 6–18.
Obholzer, A. and V.Z. Roberts (eds) (1994), *The Unconscious at Work*, London: Routledge.
Western, S. (2013), *Leadership: A Critical Text*, 2nd edn, London: Sage.
Western, S. and J. Gosling (2000), 'Learning from practice', presented at the British Academy of Management Conference, Edinburgh.
Winnicott, D.W. (1971), *Playing and Reality*, Harmondsworth: Penguin Books.

16. Walking with Wordsworth: exploring leadership as purpose through *The Prelude*

Steve Kempster and Simon Bainbridge

'WAS IT FOR THIS . . .?'

This question, taken from *The Prelude*, captures the essence of the walk (1979, p.1). It was with this question that Wordsworth began the writing of what became his masterpiece, an epic poetic autobiography in which he examined his own growth and development. Wordsworth began writing the poem in 1798 at a time of vocational crisis, when he was struggling to fulfil another ambitious creative project. In jotting down 'Was it for this . . .?', Wordsworth was starting to ask himself about all the influences that had shaped him, made him who he was, and brought him to his current position. He was also beginning to think about his future role and all that he hoped to achieve. In other words, Wordsworth was embarking on what would become possibly the greatest single exploration of the purpose of being a poet, a role that for him involved a strong sense of leadership.

Purpose in leadership is deeply paradoxical. It is at the heart of the phenomenon. Broadly leadership can be conceived as a process of influence to achieve a societally desired purpose. Wordsworth himself was deeply committed to such a sense of leadership. It took him seven years to write the first full version of *The Prelude* and he concluded it after over 8,000 lines of poetry, with a powerful articulation of his own role as poet as one who sought through influence to achieve a societally desired purpose. In the poem's closing lines, Wordsworth describes how he and his fellow poet Samuel Taylor Coleridge will be 'joint labourers in the work [. . . of men's] redemption' (1979, p.482; XIII. 439–41). As 'Prophets of Nature', he and Coleridge 'will speak / A lasting inspiration, sanctified / By reason and by truth' (1979, p.482; XIII. 442–4). By asking himself the question 'Was it for this . . .', Wordsworth had confirmed his own vocation as poet and discovered his sense of purpose.

However, unlike Wordsworth, few managers readily distil what their societally desired purposes are (Kempster et al., 2011). Yet purpose infuses in the language of leadership – objectives, vision, key performance indicators (KPIs). In a sense the word has been corrupted by what Alasdair MacIntyre (1985) would describe as a loss of virtue practices and the decline of internal goods in organizational activity in what appears to be a mutually exclusive pursuit of external goods. External goods are tangible outputs such as profit, salaries, bonuses, titles, KPIs, products and services – they are extrinsic assets possessed by people (Kempster et al., 2011). All these are necessary transactions that are part of modern life, but alone not sufficient. Wordsworth himself provides a critique of the modern world's tendency to focus on such external goods in a sonnet that opens 'The world is too much with us', arguing that 'Getting and spending, we lay waste our powers' (2000, p.270: 1–2). By contrast, internal goods are the product of transactions and exchanges but whose value or asset is for society rather than personal acquisition. Examples might be a cabinet maker crafting a piece of furniture, a nurse offering delicate care, an architect designing an exquisite building, a poet creating a poem, a scientist explaining gravitational waves, or a leadership developer stimulating a desire in a manager to search beyond external goods, or a banker who seeks to enrich society through responsible finance. MacIntyre suggests that internal goods are derived from practice virtue dispositions – our everyday activities that we invest in to achieve these outcomes. Why do we invest ourselves in such a way? Again MacIntyre is helpful here. He connects virtue practices and internal goods with Aristotle's notion of 'telos' – a quest to understand and seek to achieve a contribution that is good for humankind; and someone will only feel fulfilled with a sense of purposefulness if they journey towards their telos (Kempster et al., 2011, p.321). It is with the possibility of such fulfilment that Wordsworth concludes *The Prelude*; he tells Coleridge that the two of them will be 'Blessed with true happiness if we may be / United helpers' in the task of mankind's redemption (1979, p.482; XIII. 437–8). Drawing on Aristotle, Howie interprets telos as 'a purpose outside that "being", for the utility and welfare of other beings' (1968, p.41). It is not sufficient to just have an idea about purpose but to pursue its fulfilment: 'the highest good for man consists not merely in the possession [of a purpose] but in the exercise of it [. . .] Knowledge [of a purpose] merely possessed and not put to use is ineffective and useless' (1968, p.47). Telos becomes the purpose that gives alignment and commitment to invest oneself in virtue practices and the associated output of internal goods. Again, Wordsworth emphasizes this sense of the exercise of a purpose in his conclusion, his commitment to speaking 'A lasting inspiration' so that 'what we have loved / Others will love, and we may teach them how' (1979, p.482: 444–5). Wordsworth and Coleridge's task is nothing less than transforming the way in which people understand the world around them and their place in it. It is leadership in the highest sense.

The purpose paradox is a consequence of the decline in virtue practices and internal goods as a consequence of a lack of attention to leadership enabling people to discover and pursue their purposes. Kempster et al. (2011) gave illustration to this argument through empirical insights from hybrid middle managers within the National Health Service (NHS) – clinicians who have moved into management roles. Even in the health context the external goods of money, titles and targets had, like a cuckoo, 'kicked out' the internal goods of patient care. The evidence in the Francis Report on the failings of the UK Mid-Staffordshire Hospital sought to readdress the balance. The report made recommendations (in response to the NHS crisis of care and responsibility) placing significant emphasis on putting human welfare to the forefront in decision making – a duty of candour alongside a duty of care (Francis, 2013).

So the work we have undertaken through creating the Wordsworth Walk has been an overt intent to bring purpose to the fore in leadership work through making salient life course, vocation and sense of place. Wordsworth's poem *The Prelude*, unknown at the outset to almost all participants on the walk, provides one of the greatest literary explorations of the connections between purpose, internal goods and virtue practices.

The Prelude, as an exploration of Wordsworth's life course, is complementary to Steve Kempster's chapter in this volume ('Tents', Chapter 8). The aspects covered there will not be repeated here, except to emphasize that the underpinning theoretical insights of life course leadership learning (captured in Steve's chapter 'Tents') are applicable to our theme here of leadership purpose. For example, aspects of hardships, crucibles, trigger moments and notable others were significant to Wordsworth and are similarly significant to the managers who have engaged in the walk.

WALKING WITH WORDSWORTH

We were introduced to each other as a result of a mutual colleague, Oliver, standing in the graduation procession queue with Simon. We met for a coffee and each of us outlined our work. The fit surprised us both, with particular resonance around life course, and purpose. Steve was module leader on the International Masters in Practising Management (IMPM) and we explored the possibility of using Wordsworth on the module. The cohort would comprise approximately 25 senior managers drawn from around the world. Timing would be the last week in April, so a pleasant spring day was assured. A real sense of excitement and potential synergy occurred when Steve explained that the first module of the 'International Masters in Practising Management' was on 'The Reflective Mindset' to explore management practice. The notion of reflection was the first common ground between us. Simon described how Wordsworth could be seen as perhaps the greatest poet of 'Reflection' in the English language. While Wordsworth is best known as a nature poet, to many literary critics his true significance as a poet lies in his pioneering exploration of the idea of the self and its development over time. As such, he can be seen as a major figure in the literary movement known as Romanticism, which places the individual at the centre of the creative process. Wordsworth was committed to reflection on his early childhood experiences and believed that these experiences were formative in making him the person he became, writing that 'The Child is Father of the Man' (2000, p.246: 7). Such a belief has clear overlaps with the pedagogic philosophy of the IMPM and its core principle that managers grow through reflecting on experience. For both Wordsworth and the IMPM, reflection is a crucial process and vital for an understanding of our sense of purpose.

Our excitement grew as Simon explained to Steve that Wordsworth's sense of purpose and vocation were very closely linked to the specific area around the villages of Rydal and Grasmere in the Lake District in the north-west of England. Wordsworth's sense of purpose and vocation were highly place specific and his decision to rent Dove Cottage in Grasmere in 1799 was a key moment in his poetic development. Dove Cottage was a place where Wordsworth could 'dwell', to use his own term for the coming together of vocation, location and purpose that he found so stimulating and that enabled him to produce his greatest work. Wordsworth continued to live in the Grasmere area until 1813 when he moved two miles further south to Rydal Mount, where he resided until his death in 1850. We decided that a walk between these two villages of Grasmere and Rydal would provide the ideal environment to explore the three key Wordsworthian themes that would provide a valuable framework for the students on the course. The first of these themes would invite participants to reflect on their past experience through Wordsworth's concept of 'spots of time'. In *The Prelude* Wordsworth states that 'There are in our existence spots of time', key moments in our lives that shape our development and make us who we become. These 'spots of time' have a continuing role in our lives, Wordsworth argues, providing '[a] renovating virtue' and 'nourish[ing]' and 'repair[ing]' 'our minds' (1979, p.428: XI. 257–64). For the second theme, we went to another key idea in Wordsworth, the concept of 'vision'. Whereas the first theme would focus on the past, this one would look to the future and to what participants hoped to achieve (which could be defined in whatever way the participants chose, be it personal, familial, domestic, organizational or societal). For our third theme we drew on Wordsworth's collaborative working practices to emphasize the importance of other people in the fulfilment of our visions. Throughout *The Prelude*, Wordsworth stresses that he would not have been able to create his masterpiece had it not been for the support, encouragement and constructive criticism of his sister, Dorothy, and his friend and fellow poet, Samuel Taylor Coleridge. As we have already seen, Coleridge was central to Wordsworth's own sense of purpose as a poet.

Mapped against these three themes were aspects of leadership learning through life course. For example, the 'spots of time' might reflect hardships (McCall, 1998) or trigger moments (Luthans and Avolio, 2003); or vision and aspiration linked to the desire people have to achieve and develop their careers and sense of aspirational identity (Kempster, 2009); collaborative and relational leadership (Uhl-Bien, 2006) linked to narrative authenticity (Shamir and Eilam, 2005).

We had the framework. Steve wanted an experiential process in the module as most of the inputs were classroom sessions, an idea that again paralleled Wordsworth's own thinking. In a poem entitled 'The Tables Turned', Wordsworth instructs his reader to quit his or her books and step outside: 'Come forth into the light of things. / Let Nature be your teacher' (2000, p.131: 15–16). The good news for us and the emerging design was that the classroom was the Langdale Country Club in the heart of the Lake District – very nice!

Mike Palk (who ran his own outdoor leadership development business, and had worked a few times with Steve) was called to the next coffee session. We mapped the phases of the framework to the physical location of Rydal Water – the essence of Wordsworth's inspiration. Mike's knowledge of the area and outdoor expertise made it possible to incorporate Wordsworth's own images and ideas into the physical experience of the walk itself. The key metaphor of *The Prelude* is that of the journey of the river of life that flows from a 'blind [dark] cavern' out to sea (1979, p.468; XIII: 174). On hearing this, Mike immediately suggested that as the symbolic start of the walk we could use the 'blind cavern' of Rydal cave, a disused slate quarry on the side of Loughrigg Fell. Entrance to this cave would involve a short rope scramble that Mike and his team would oversee. Starting at this cave, our walk could then follow the course of the local river, the Rothay. While we couldn't reach the sea, the ultimate destination suggested in *The Prelude*, we could trace the Rothay's course as far as Grasmere Lake. For Steve, Wordsworth's metaphor of the journey of the river of life was a particularly valuable one that he could link to many of the other module sessions, such as the participants' mapping of their own 'life lines'. It provided a powerful image for the day, for the module, the IMPM and, of course, for the participants' own life journeys, linking to the ideas of 'telos' that Steve was keen to explore.

The 'blind cavern' of Rydal cave also provided the ideal location for the first of our three themed reflective exercises. In his elaboration of his 'Spots of time' concept, Wordsworth draws heavily on the idea of 'darkness' as he seeks to describe the state of mind created by these key formative experiences. After one such experience, Wordsworth describes how 'In my thoughts / There was a darkness' and how he feels cut off from the normal world from which we take our bearings – he sees 'no familiar shapes / Of hourly objects, images of trees, Of sea or sky, no colours of green fields' (1979, p.50: I. 420–24). We realized that we could use Rydal cave to create a similar experience of darkness for the participants. After their roped scramble up to the mouth of the cave, they could enter it holding lighted candles that they would then blow out to re-create the atmosphere of the 'blind cavern'. By cutting off the participants from the world of 'familiar shapes', we could enable them to focus on their own 'spots of time' – the key formative moments in their lives. For many participants, this period of reflection on their 'spots of time' in the 'blind cavern' would prove to be one of the most powerful elements of the entire IMPM.

Wordsworth himself identified the location for our second themed exercise, the viewpoint of Loughrigg Terrace above Grasmere. In 'Home at Grasmere', a poem written in the same period as *The Prelude*, Wordsworth describes how he himself had his most important moment of vision from this very place. As a young boy, he looked down on the beautiful scene and recognized it as a location where he could fulfil his own purpose. He describes how the beautiful landscape went from being a physical image to a mental one:

> From that time forward was the place to me
> As beautiful in thought, as it had been
> When present to my bodily eyes . . . (2000, p.175: 44–6)

Wordsworth also describes the continued and sustaining power of this vision for him over the next 20 years, offering 'a gleam of light' even in times of 'sorrow' and 'gloom'. It is one of the great literary descriptions of the power of vision and its link with purpose, in this case Wordsworth's own embracing of the role of poet. What better place could there be for participants to consider their own sense of vision than standing in Wordsworth's own footsteps, looking at the beautiful landscape that had inspired his sense of purpose and where he would write much of his greatest poetry.

For our third and final themed exercise, inspired by the creative collaboration of Wordsworth and Coleridge, we turned to the history of the poets themselves. The two friends liked to row from Wordsworth's home at Dove Cottage out to Grasmere Island, a small piece of land in the middle of the lake, where they would make tea and discuss their ideas. Mike designed a similar adventure for us that initially involved paddling rafted canoes across the lake to the island – an exercise in itself for the development of relational leadership that exemplified 'the value of others'. After reaching the island, we would then cast our canoes adrift, enabling participants to float, contemplate and consider the importance of their own collaborators to their sense of purpose.

REFLECTIONS

This section is written as two letters: the first from Steve to Simon, and then in response from Simon to Steve. We use this approach for a number of reasons. First, a letter is of purposeful intent of 'writing to someone else with the expectation of a response' (Clandinin and Connelly, 2000, p.106). Steve was the first to write. Simon's then is a response, in part stimulated by the first letter in terms of the content – some perspectives previously shared, but also some new insights. Second, each letter is an intention to make sense of the experiences and express this to each other through a 'conversational tone'. Third, this form of writing offers the notion of an obligation to consider, make sense and respond to the content. Fourth, as Richardson (2000) helpfully highlights, writing is in itself a process of inquiry and a letter enables deep reflective dialogue (Cunliffe, 2001) through being written at a moment conducive in which feelings and thoughts can flow relatively freely (Davies, 1996, in Clandinin and Connelly, 2000). Fifth, an exchange of letters acts as provocation to become reflexive (Ramsey, 2011). Sixth, letters were very important for Wordsworth, a major form of communication in the period that involved an almost daily walk to collect them from Ambleside (usually by Dorothy). Finally, we might say this epistolary exchange seeks to parallel that between Wordsworth and Coleridge. Wordsworth addressed *The Prelude* to Coleridge; he knew the poem as 'The Poem to Coleridge' and frequently includes phrases such as 'To thee' and 'my friend'. When Coleridge read *The Prelude*, he responded with a similar (though shorter) work in the same style called 'To Wordsworth'. These exchanges were part of an ongoing dialogue through which the two writers developed their sense of their roles.

Dear Simon,

Leadership studies have been much the weaker for the absence of an interdisciplinary approach. Using The Prelude *has been most illuminating. Not simply because I come from Stevenage (the wastelands of culture), but for the opening up of so many possibilities and contributions. Recalling the first time we did the walk, the rain pouring down, us all eventually scrambling into the deep cave. Candles blown out and dripping water all around we stand quiet. Then stumbling out of the darkness and seeing the sun glistening through the rain and the Korean chap in tears, grabbing my arm and saying 'Was it for this? No it wasn't! I've got to get things sorted and be clear on what a difference I'm here to make.' (Of course that's the Stevenage lad's translation rather than the Seoul transcript). The manner of this senior manager, and the many others, to translate Wordsworth's autobiography to their current lives seemed most natural, very unforced, and captured the embodied essence of reflexive insight.*

So to the first of my questions. Why do you think this is so, and have you experienced similar translations elsewhere with humanities subjects informing management?

I have been blessed to have an expert in Wordsworth and the Lake District on my doorstep. However the purpose of this chapter is not to replicate the walk. Rather it is to show the opportunities of connecting the humanities with leadership development, with a bit of exercise thrown in! So my second question. What do you think is the scope for linking leadership studies with humanities? What is the basis for making this succeed?

As I wrote this question I wondered whether it was the resonance of the romanticism that spoke to people. A sense of people dreaming of possibilities of time long since gone where work and home were more closely connected – that powerful reframed sense of 'dwelling'. Whether the sense of purpose and vocation connected with bigger pictures has become too disconnected? Or perhaps the world of business feels in some way ugly and people want to connect with notions of beauty. Adler makes the point strikingly in her paper 'leading beautifully' that so chimes with the work we have done: 'twenty-first century society yearns for a leadership of possibility, a leadership based more on hope, aspiration, innovation, and beauty than on the replication of historical patterns of constrained pragmatism' (2011, p.2008).

So humanities have a big place in leadership development. I'm wondering how much further can we go? You have undertaken this exercise so many times and with many different people. What are the possibilities? What are the variations? Could this be undertaken in the classroom? Or perhaps a walk around campus, or even around Stevenage?

The very serious global challenges that impact on every daily life require of us a greater perspective. Perhaps humanities have many more offerings to make that need to be embraced. Why have we not heard more from you and your colleagues? Is it that the management and science disciplines are the cuckoos in the nest?

> *My friend, I await you your insights.*
> *Best*
> *Steve*

Dear Friend (to use Wordsworth's means of addressing Coleridge in The Prelude*),*

Our work with Mike Palk creating the 'Wordsworth Walk' has been one of the most surprising, stimulating and enjoyable projects of my career. Thank you for taking the initiative (and risk) in inviting a literary scholar to contribute to a leadership programme, an unusual and daring act that shows an admirable desire to look beyond disciplinary and faculty boundaries in seeking answers to the global challenges that confront us.

We were fortunate in the outset, I think, that there was such a strong sense of shared philosophy between The Prelude *and the IMPM, both with their emphasis on the value of reflection. Had the Lancaster module not been 'The Reflective Mindset', it might have been more difficult for us to make Wordsworth's autobiographical poem as central as we did. We were also 'blessed', as Wordsworth would say, in our location and our ability to design the walk within 'Wordsworth Country', one of the most beautiful parts of England that is so closely bound up with the writer's poetry. The power of this landscape, which Wordsworth felt made him the poet he became, contributes significantly to the experience. The exercises designed by Mike, scrambling into Rydal cave and rowing across Grasmere Lake, offer different ways of interacting with this landscape and generate a sense of team spirit even, or perhaps more so, on the wettest of days! And we should not underestimate the value of the walking and talking that are central to the experience. Wordsworth and Coleridge spent much of their most productive time in walking together, planning, creating and feeding back on each others' ideas. Walking was central to Wordsworth's own creative practices; he often liked to compose outside while moving and would then write up or dictate his poems once he had returned home. There is a strong sense of authenticity to the experience we designed, enabling participants to walk in Wordsworth's footsteps and to visit the exact location where he underwent what he tells us was the most important moment of vision in his life.*

In one way, then, the 'Wordsworth Walk' we have created is unique; there is nowhere else in the world where it would be possible to bring together such a landscape and a literature that speak so directly to the idea of purpose. In another way, though, I think the walk illustrates the potential and perhaps wider value of the humanities to leadership development. What Wordsworth provides for participants on the course is a framework that they can use to explore the key elements of their lives – their past, their future and the value of others. The Wordsworthian reflections we do on the walk have much in common with more familiar leadership development exercises. The 'spots of time' exercise, for example, has parallels in the writing of 'lifelines' or 'timelines' (though these rarely occur in a 'blind cavern'). Similarly, the 'vision' exercise could be compared to target-setting or strategy-defining processes. (I have taught a number of classroom-based versions of the vision exercise for senior managers on a 'Transition and resilience' course). While Wordsworth's The Prelude *provides a less familiar and perhaps more elevated version of certain leadership development processes, it perhaps has most power on the walk as an expression of 'purpose'. For Wordsworth, these processes of reflection on the past and envisioning of the future were central to who he was and what he wanted to achieve.* The Prelude *is a major landmark in the literature of self-reflection, which took Wordsworth seven years to write in its first full version and which he continued to revise for most of the rest of his life; the poem was only published for the first time after his death in 1850. It remains one of the fullest and most complex answers to the question that stimulated it in the first place, 'Was it for this . . .?'*

There are other areas in which literature has been used as part of leadership development, including a range of courses that use Shakespeare's plays and courses taught at Harvard Business School. Strikingly, it seems to me that the initiative in bringing humanities into the field of leadership studies is coming mainly from those in management. I was struck, for example, when attending at your invitation

> the 'New Romantics of Responsible Management' conference at Lancaster in 2014, by how many papers made use of literature (including poetry) as part of their approach. Similarly, I have been repeatedly delighted by the open-mindedness, engagement and curiosity of those who have participated in the Wordsworth Walk whenever it has run. My experience suggests that it is perhaps those in the humanities who need to think about the value of their work for those beyond their own disciplines and also beyond the academy itself. Working with you on the Wordsworth Walk has enabled me to bring my own research to a much wider and diverse audience than would normally be the case; well over 1,000 people have now taken a Wordsworth Walk in a range of different forms. The experience has also caused me to reconsider Wordsworth himself, re-evaluating him as much more of a poet of social responsibility than I had previously recognized.
>
> It is perhaps with this sense of the importance of social responsibility to Wordsworth's sense of purpose that I should conclude. In many ways, Romanticism – of which Wordsworth was a key spokesperson – was a utopian movement. Many critics have linked its origins to the French Revolution and the political attempts to create a new world, despite what Wordsworth ultimately came to see as the revolution's failure. Wordsworth's establishment of a 'home' in Grasmere can also be seen as a utopian project, seeking to find a new way of living and working that would fulfil his sense of purpose and enable him to find 'true happiness'. In such an endeavour, he remains an inspiration today.

We hope this chapter has illuminated possible novel ways in which the humanities can be a deeply complementary companion to leadership development. The rich value of interdisciplinary collaboration offers avenues of imagination, possibility and insight that are rewarding for collaborators and participants alike.

REFERENCES

Adler, N. (2011), 'Leading beautifully: the creative economy and beyond', *Journal of Management Inquiry*, **20**(3), 208–21.

Clandinin, D.J. and F.M. Connelly (2000), *Narrative Inquiry: Experience and Story in Qualitative Research*, San Francisco: Jossey-Bass.

Cunliffe, A. (2001), 'Reflexive dialogical practice in management learning', *Management Learning*, **33**(1), 35–61.

Francis, R. (2013) *Independent Inquiry into Care Provided by Mid Staffordshire NHS Foundation Trust January 2005–March 2009*, London: The Stationery Office, HC375-1.

Howie, G. (1968), *Aristotle*, London: Collier-Macmillan Ltd.

Kempster, S. (2009), *How Managers Have Learnt to Lead: Exploring the Development of Leadership Practice*, Basingstoke: Palgrave MacMillan.

Kempster, S., B. Jackson and M. Conroy (2011), 'Leadership as purpose: exploring the role of purpose in leadership practice', *Leadership*, **7**(3), 17–31.

Luthans, F. and B. Avolio (2003), 'Authentic leadership: a positive development approach', in K.S. Cameron, J.E. Dutton and R.E. Quinn (eds), *Positive Organizational Scholarship*, San Francisco, CA: Berrett-Koehler, pp.241–58.

MacIntyre, A. (1985), *After Virtue: A Study in Moral Theory*, 2nd edn, London: Duckworth.

McCall, M.W. (1998), *High Flyers: Developing the Next Generation of Leaders*, Boston, MA: Harvard Business School.

Ramsey, C. (2011), 'Provocative theory and a scholarship of practice', *Management Learning*, **42**(5), 469–83.

Richardson, L. (2000), 'Writing: a method of inquiry', in N. Denzin and Y. Lincoln (eds), *Handbook of Qualitative Research*, 2nd edn, London: Sage, pp.923–48.

Shamir, B. and G. Eilam (2005), 'What's your story? A life-stories approach to authentic leadership development', *Leadership Quarterly*, **16**, 395–417.

Uhl-Bien, M. (2006), 'Relational leadership theory: exploring the social processes of leadership and organizing', *The Leadership Quarterly*, **17**(6), 654–76.

Wordsworth, W. (1979), *The Prelude: 1799, 1805, 1850*, ed. J. Wordsworth, M.H. Abrams and S. Gill, New York and London: W.W. Norton.

Wordsworth, W. (2000), *The Major Works*, ed. S. Gill, Oxford: Oxford University Press.

17. 'Collaboratory' as leadership development

Steve Kempster, Eric Guthey and Mary Uhl-Bien

GLOBAL CHALLENGES AND LEADERSHIP DEVELOPMENT

The leadership development industry is enormous. Scholars have estimated that organizations spend in excess of US $12.5 billion per annum on leadership development training in the United States alone (Sowcik and Allen, 2013, p.56), and over 15 years ago was in excess of $50 billion globally (Fulmer and Wagner, 1999; see also discussions on spending in DeRue et al., 2011). The staggering size of this industry raises a series of simple yet important questions: leadership development for what? That is, what does all of this activity and effort seek to achieve on behalf of clients and other sponsoring organizations? Better leaders? The question remains: better leaders *at doing what, and towards what ends*?

Meanwhile, the vast majority of leadership research to present has focused on how leadership gets done – on how to lead. Very little research has paid attention to the ultimate purpose of all this leading, and the ways that a stronger sense of leadership purpose can connect team, organization and society in new ways (Kempster et al., 2011). This is relatively unsurprising given the private-sector context in which most leadership development takes place. Private-sector organizations have a strong tendency to frame the purpose of leadership as the delivery of shareholder value, and to direct leadership development efforts towards cascading this very narrow definition of purpose down to middle managers through key performance indicators (KPIs). Leadership scholars have not done a good job in questioning this orthodoxy. Granted, Burns (1978), originally conceived of transformational leadership as a matter of raising followers to higher levels of purpose. But as this notion became widespread, it became translated and refined into forms of transactional and transformational leadership in which authenticity and purpose were no longer core, but more often marginalized with a passing reference to idealized inspiration or some such. In many ways such translation sought to resonate and reflect dominant organizational discourses and directives about performance.

Leadership development practitioners have been somewhat braver than leadership scholars in this regard. In our experience many leadership developers perceive and promote broader connections between the practice of leadership and societal purpose. Often considerable talent is demonstrated in disguising these kinds of higher ideals within their programme designs. Meanwhile, in the public sector prevailing conceptions of the purpose of leadership present a paradox. On the one hand the primacy of purpose is ever present and axiomatic within everyday public-sector activity – for example, the purpose of a hospital is to care for people, and this is what everyone is there to do. On the other hand, as MacIntyre (1985) wisely anticipated, public-sector organizations and their leaders have slowly but steadily yielded to the pressure to mute or even to abandon notions of higher social purpose in favour of the private-sector discourse of efficiency, financial management, KPIs and performance management. The Francis report (2009), into the Mid-Staffordshire hospital crisis in the United Kingdom is testament to a shift away from a focus on the virtue of care towards the fetishism of financial performance and the sad consequences that can follow from this. Kempster et al. (2011) have discussed the inability and/or lack of desire to place a discourse of societal purpose at the heart of leadership talk and leadership practice among both leaders and followers in both the private and the public sectors.

Things are changing, however, and these changes will only gather pace. Many organizational actors increasingly recognize that they are systemically embedded in a multitude of stakeholder relationships, and that shareholder value can only be maximized by cultivating stakeholder value in a very broad sense: employees, customers, suppliers, communities, and broader notions of society and environment. As Unilever CEO Paul Polman has emphasized, 'one thing is clear: the scale and magnitude of the changes we face are too big for any one organization, or even one nation, to deal with alone' (2014, p.xiv). Under Polman's watch, Unilever has launched a 'sustainable living plan' that attempts to engage 1 billion people (customers), in an appreciation of the systemic challenges facing individuals, organizations and humanity as a whole. Of course this is 'savvy', it generates brand value enhancement, and Polman is on record for confirming this relationship.

And here's the thing. Leadership development can provide a powerful lever for engaging managers in understanding and *tackling* the systemic stakeholder value that generates shareholder value. We emphasize the word 'tackle' as this is the purpose of collaboratory leadership development – tackling important social challenges in a way that can provide the common ground that connects stakeholders. Such challenges offer a clear and tangible, communal yet also personal, sense of societal purpose by means of which leaders and managers can readily connect themselves, their teams and the organization – in terms of both extrinsic value generation and intrinsically worthy activity that can provide a greater sense of fulfilment.

In this brief introduction we have argued that the nature of the grand challenges that face humanity require our attention in the context of leadership development practice. As we will argue, we can move this process forward by reconceiving of leadership development as a form of collaboratory, because the foundational elements of the collaboratory model effectively connect identified best practices of leadership development (James and Burgoyne, 2001), with the process of design science (Van Aken, 2004). We will therefore draw upon and further refine the concept of the collaboratory as a model of resource mobilization and innovation that can engage a network of diverse stakeholders to address pressing social and organizational challenges on a global scale. In order to exemplify our point, we will then describe three interconnected collaboratory events we have helped to organize, and discuss the strengths and the potential challenges of pursuing such an approach. We will conclude by reflecting on the opportunities currently available for the leadership development industry to help tackle pressing social challenges and to contribute towards meaningful change by crowdsourcing collaborative practices that will mobilize leaders and managers to foreground this very important question: *leadership for what?*

COLLABORATORY AS LEADERSHIP DEVELOPMENT

The original conception and organization of collaboratories took place in the realm of pure science (Wulf, 1993), where perhaps the most prominent example is that of the CERN particle physics project in Switzerland. In this context, the term 'collaboratory' combined equal parts *collaboration* and *laboratory* in order to emphasize the importance of collective experimentation and problem solving on a grand scale (Wulf, 1993). Taking the latter half of this portmanteau word first, the notion of a research laboratory highlights the process of examining an issue, challenge or problem. The laboratory metaphor – not even really a metaphor in the context of CERN – invokes an ongoing trajectory, rather than a one-off event, because a laboratory exists to pursue, to test and to experiment with ideas over time. This process can even take place in parallel and multiple locations or settings, multiple laboratories, facilitated by technologies of virtual communication, with the intent to return to an event such as a collaboratory workshop to compare insights, results and progress. For these reasons Wulf defined a collaboratory as a 'center without walls, in which the nation's researchers can perform their research without regard to physical location, interacting with colleagues, accessing instrumentation, sharing data and computational resources, [and] accessing information in digital libraries' (Wulf, 1989, p.19). The mobilization across multiple locations gives emphasis to many people in different contexts engaging and working on the challenge. In this sense a collaboratory is not just a fancy name for a one-off workshop, but rather an ongoing process. This process seeks to examine scientific problems that are characterized by a depth of complexity that requires an interdisciplinary perspective cultivated and enriched via multiple experiments in multiple settings. In this way a collaboratory is more of a collective action research project, but it is different to action research. We shall explain the difference below through the ideas of design science.

The Collaboratory: A Co-creative Stakeholder Engagement Process for Solving Complex Problems

Muff (2014) proposed an outline for the deployment of this method within the context of management and organization research, where interdisciplinary research and exploration have become ever more important given the increasing complexity of organizational activities and challenges. Towards this end Muff and colleagues translate the collaboratory concept from the virtual realm of scientific data production and distance collaboration to define an actual physical space in which collaboration and experimentation can occur to address social and organizational challenges. They define a collaboratory as 'a place where people can think, work, learn together, and invent their respective futures', and as 'an inclusive learning environment where action learning and action research meet' (Muff, 2014, p.23). On this basis Muff and colleagues describe a set of facilitation techniques for achieving collaboratory goals. They even go so far as to specify the arrangement of chairs and the protocols for interaction and dialogue within the collaboratory, and they stress the important role of facilitators, whom they describe as 'highly experienced coaches who act as lead learners and guardians of the collaboratory space' (Muff, 2014, p.24). As these authors themselves recognize, this tight emphasis on the design and facilitation of a time-limited collaboratory event, in a particular physical locale, crowds out sufficient attention to the experimenting, testing and exploring process that needs to occur between collaboratory workshops. As they conclude, '[w]e propose that the next evolutionary step of the collaboratory will include both the broader community of researchers engaged in collaboratories around the world, as well as stakeholders in management education who seek to transform themselves by providing responsible leadership.' This is precisely the next step that we suggest must occur within the context of leadership development. To explain further what we mean, we would do well to return to the roots of the collaboratory concept within design science.

Design science draws from such fields as medicine, architecture, engineering and psychotherapy (Van Aken, 2004, p.224). Drawing on generic principles and evidence of what has been applicable and useful in prior projects, it seeks to use these in order to understand how to design solutions in specific contexts. This evidence base gives prominence to theories that are useful and pragmatic in terms of 'what works' rather than 'whether something is true' (the latter reflecting much management theory, see Hodgkinson and Starkey, 2011, p.609). In a most complementary manner to the notion of a collaboratory, design science points towards a problem-led, transdisciplinary approach. In this sense it requires collaboration between diverse sets of people – those seeking to generate knowledge and those seeking to apply knowledge in practice (Keleman and Bansal, 2002). For this reason, design science holds out considerable promise with respect to the central purpose of this chapter – that is, to stimulate interest among scholars and practitioners in addressing complex global challenges:

> The idea of design involves inquiry into systems that do not yet exist. Will it work rather than is it valid or true? Rooted in pragmatism as underpinning epistemology, design science seeks to produce knowledge that is both actionable and open to on-going validation. Importantly it has a latent aspirational orientation to action where approaches to 'design involves human beings using knowledge to create what should be' (Romme, 2003, p.562).

So this is all very interesting and potentially exciting, but how exactly does it link to leadership development? Here is the thing: the key principles commonly identified as the foundation of best practice in leadership development (James and Burgoyne, 2001), also undergird the design science behind the collaboratory approach. First, leadership development needs to be anchored to organizational priorities. We have already argued that the global challenges exert an impact on individuals and organizations alike – they are systemically connected. So we make an assumption that organizations engaging in collaboratory activity can and should connect participation with a perceived organizational need. Organizations cannot avoid the far-reaching effects of the global challenges.

Second, and a corollary of the first point, leadership development organizational participation in efforts to address pressing social challenges will lead to the delivery of change in the organization itself. The process of testing and experimenting in a collaborative manner engages many others in the organization, especially when senior management have a vested interest in the possible outcomes and when they receive regular reports on progress achieved. Top-level sponsorship also provides opportunities for those undertaking leadership development to engage with senior role models in the form of mentoring, coaching and networking. It may be that at the first collaboratory senior managers accompany their colleagues to frame the issues and anchor the purpose to organizational priorities.

Third, there are strong connections between the kinds of experimentation and problem solving at the heart of the collaboratory approach, on the one hand, and the central tenets of action research for leadership development on the other. The major difference between action learning and collaboratory is the manner in which the latter combines a forward-looking vision of what might be/should be (for example, engaging with the possibilities of addressing the global challenges), with a set of principles/prescriptions to guide the research journey. In understanding and applying the principles of collaboratory an implicit executive education dynamic occurs. The first collaboratory functions as an interdisciplinary deep dive into the theme associated with the challenge being addressed; a potentially challenging and hopefully enlightening process that can act as a form of 'purpose awakening' among participating individuals.

Fourth, the design science behind collaboratory leadership development differs from action research in that it does not represent an isolated process within a single organizational context. Rather, parallel research is being undertaken in multiple settings. The orientation seeks to develop an evidence base to help refine the principles for guidance in the current organizational situations, but also in subsequent settings. In this way the design science behind collaboratory leadership development seeks to reach beyond 'mode 2' knowledge production and application and reach towards 'mode 3' where knowledge is being developed to enhance the human condition (see Huff and Huff, 2001). We shall return to the possibilities of a growing evidence base connected to leadership development crowdsourcing in our final section to this chapter, the reflections.

Fifth, the ongoing nature of the process of participating with a range of collaboratory colleagues from a variety of contexts offers the opportunity for action learning. The challenges of undertaking the experiments in organizational settings can be assisted through questioning and comparing circumstances – supportive conversations that not only give insight to progressing with the action in hand but also have a most powerful social-comparison learning dynamic. Steve has explored how observational learning (Bandura, 1986), and social comparison (Greenberg et al., 2007), are most influential in stimulating leadership development (Kempster, 2009; Kempster and Parry, 2014); the greater the variety of people to observe and compare to undertaking similar roles the greater the assimilation and transferability of learning. The interdisciplinary nature of the collaboratory offers up such variety, and with people from contexts that are likely to be most novel and stimulating. For example, a private-sector manager in an action-learning set with a manager from a non-governmental organization (NGO). There is not just the difference in context, circumstances and challenges, but also different sense-making of purpose and leadership practices.

Finally, the mere fact of working together to address a pressing global or social need puts participants in a position to confront significant developmental challenges – intellectual, emotional and moral. The process also brings to the fore key issues and debates about purpose and meaning. We highlighted earlier that everyday leadership practice is typically devoid of discourse that addresses the higher-order purposes of work. Such discourse is more prevalent within the leadership development industry – for example, the practice of service learning, gives priority to issues of purpose and meaning. Many interventions seek to make this prominent. Each of us have undertaken similar types of activities, taking managers to challenging contexts to participate in service learning projects. Service learning often exerts striking impact, but it can also unsettle and destabilize, sometimes to the point of causing participants to reassess their purposes and to seek careers in alternative places (Larsson and Holmberg, 2015). Whilst not seeking to comment on the virtue or otherwise we would seek to suggest that there is a moral duty to the participant manager and the host organization in the leadership development process. Our view is that collaboratory process building on design science can offer a more grounded and emergent engagement, and is in some ways less romanticized by working alongside collaboratory colleagues and understanding the realism of the work at hand to address the global challenges.

THREE COLLABORATORY WORKSHOPS

In the first part of this chapter we have outlined the rationale for pursuing a model of leadership development as a collaboratory process of resource mobilization and innovation that draws on a diverse network of stakeholders to address specific and pressing societal and global challenges and to help bring about constructive change. The next part of the chapter provides insight into the workings of such a process via a description and evaluation of three interconnected collaboratory events that we helped to organize during a six-month period: a workshop on the dynamics of cross-sector partnerships between the Danish Red Cross and a number of private-sector organizations working to support refugees in the process of integration, hosted in Copenhagen, Denmark in May 2016; a NATO-funded workshop on the dynamics of leadership in fragile and post-conflict environments, hosted in Geneva, Switzerland in September 2016; and a workshop on inclusive and grass-roots leadership in the context of refugee resettlement, hosted in Atlanta, Georgia in the United States in November 2016. The common threads connecting these three collaboratory workshops included, first of all, the various members of several loosely coupled, overlapping networks working in tandem, and second, the concerns shared by members of these networks to define and to begin to address the pressing leadership challenges posed by fragile and post-conflict environments, and by the global displacement, migration and refugee crisis. Each of these events brought together a different and very diverse combination of participants, among them leaders from the United Nations as well as other NGOs and civil society organizations, refugee leaders, government officials, military officers, managers and other private-sector company representatives, socially engaged artists, entrepreneurs, activists, leadership development professionals, leadership scholars and graduate students. In each instance the intention was to leverage the diversity of expertise in the room by minimizing formal presentations and maximizing emergent dialogue and creative problem solving.

Before describing these three events in more detail, we should clarify their role and significance in the broader framework for collaboratory leadership development we propose. These collaboratory workshops themselves are not the collaboratory per se – they are rather one of three crucial elements of the broader process of resource mobilization and change we propose to define as a collaboratory. The other two elements are the *collaboratory network* and the process of *collaboratory experimentation*. The three workshops functioned effectively to bring together a collaboratory network and to facilitate an emergent process of dialogue and exchange among the diverse stakeholders at the table. The crucial next step will be to undertake a process of collaboratory experimentation that takes concrete steps to effect change in the face of real-world problems, and then to cycle the lessons learned from those experiments back into the collaboratory in order to mobilize more dialogue, more action and more change in an iterative process akin to action learning on a grand scale.

Because we emphasize mobilization as the key characteristic of the collaboratory process, it is helpful to understand this process through the lens of social movements theory, as articulated by Gerald Davis and Christopher White in their book *Changing Your Company from the Inside Out: A Guide for Social Intrapreneurs.* Davis and White canvas their own and others' research on social movements (such as the civil rights struggle in the United States or the Arab Spring in the Middle East), and social innovations in organizations (such as the development of a service learning corps inside IBM or the establishment of a Code of Basic Working Rights inside the Ford Motor Company), in order to isolate the four key elements of change in these contexts. According to the authors these are:

1. *Opportunity structures* are the answer to the question *'When* is the right time for change?' (Davis and White, 2015, pp.6, 31). They consist of a combination of temporal, structural, institutional, political and cultural elements that determine when the timing is right for the mobilization of an effective movement for change.
2. *Framing mechanisms* answer the question *'Why* is this a compelling change?' (Davis and White, 2015, pp.6, 31). They consist of the language and the story that can connect to key values and concerns shared by stakeholders in a manner that articulates a convincing argument for the necessity for change.
3. *Social networks* answer the question *'Who* should be involved?' (Davis and White, 2015, pp.6, 31). An understanding of the power of social networks makes it possible to map out potential allies, decision makers, leaders and opponents of the movement for change.
4. *Mobilizing platforms* answer the question *'How* should they press for change?' (Davis and White, 2015, pp.6, 31). They are the vehicles by means of which change occurs, and they can include everything from an institution like the Black church, as in the case of the Civil Rights Movement, to online tools such as Facebook and Twitter, as in the case of the Arab Spring.

This framework helps us better understand the collaboratory process we have been seeking to mobilize. In our instance, the opportunity structures are primarily twofold. On the one hand, they consist of the ever more urgent need for mobilization and change with respect to pressing social and global challenges such as the refugee crisis or the impending devastation of climate change. On the other hand, they consist of the apparent lack of response to such pressing challenges on the part of leadership research and development, and on the perceived need for new approaches to leadership theory and leadership development practice that can make up for this lack of response. The central and compelling framing mechanism that can galvanize such efforts is the simple question 'leadership for what?' and the effective articulation of the need to connect leadership more directly to purposes that matter. We have already described the breadth of the network that populated our three collaboratory workshops – members include artists, activists, aid workers, politicians and government officials, military leaders, diplomats, corporate executives, scholars, students and leadership development practitioners. Finally, our proposed redefinition of the concept of the collaboratory revolves around the issue of mobilizing platforms. As we described earlier, the group connected to CERN understood the mobilizing platform that energized the collaboratory primarily as the virtual mechanisms and communication tools that connected the collaboratory network. Muff and her colleagues understood the collaboratory workshop itself as the key mobilizing platform. We argue that all three key elements of resource mobilization we have described function in tandem as mobilizing platforms: the collaboratory network, the collaboratory workshop and, crucially, the collaboratory process of iterative experimentation and action. With this latter, third crucial element of resource mobilization in mind, we can add a fifth question to Davis and White's framework in order to further specify the similarities and differences between their social movements framework and the collaboratory process:

5. *Collaboratory experimentation* poses the key question '*What* is the nature of the change that has to take place?'

In the process of collaboratory resource mobilization, the four questions 'When?' 'Why?' 'Who?' and 'How?' necessitate the asking of the further important question 'What?' There is no easy answer to this question, which is why it requires the kind of iterative process of trial-and-error experimentation coupled with collaboratory reflection and dialogue, as we described above. We turn to a description of our three collaboratory workshops in order to drive home this point.

Cross-sector Collaboration and Leadership on Refugee Issues in Denmark: An Action Research Workshop Hosted by the Danish Red Cross and the Leadership Collaboratory at Copenhagen Business School, Denmark, 25 May 2016

All three of the collaboratory events described in this chapter emerged as opportunities as the authors followed the thread of a long-term dialogue with their extended network about how to connect leadership research and development to pressing global challenges. As part of this evolving conversation, Eric Guthey began to direct the efforts of a fledgling effort called The Leadership Collaboratory at the Copenhagen Business School towards addressing the global displacement, migration and refugee crisis. Without question, forced displacement and migration represent the sorts of challenges about which leadership research and leadership development should have something important to say. The United Nations High Commission on Refugees (UNHCR), has estimated that by the end of 2014 there were 59.5 million people in the world who had been forced from their homes as a result of violent conflict or persecution, and this number continues to grow. Roughly 1 in every 120 people on the planet today is either a refugee or an internally displaced person. From 2014 to 2015, the number of persons seeking asylum in Europe skyrocketed from under 700,00 to 1.3 million. Just under 20,000 of these sought asylum in Denmark, which was also a record number. These numbers have led to a heightened sense of tension, to a more rancorous public and political discourse connected to displacement and migration, and to considerable strain on the organizations responsible for accepting and welcoming refugees into European countries like Denmark.

Eric reached out to a number of such organizations in Copenhagen, including the Danish Refugee Council and the Danish Red Cross. Members of the latter organization expressed the ambition to figure out how to work more effectively with their private-sector partners, which led to the organization of a day-long collaboratory workshop hosted at Copenhagen Business School. The purpose of this workshop was to share knowledge and best practices generated by successful partnerships between the Danish Red Cross and private-sector organizations, and to develop new opportunities for more such collaboration into the future, with a specific focus on partnerships that support the Danish Red Cross's mission with respect to refugees and integration in Denmark. Towards this end the workshop brought together relevant Danish Red Cross staff and leadership, representatives from current private-sector partner organizations, representatives from potential new partners, faculty and graduate students from the Copenhagen Business School, and Steve Kempster from the Lancaster Leadership Collaboratory.

In the months prior to the event, the Danish Red Cross had published two important documents – 'Not Business As Usual – Partnerships Between CSOs and Businesss' and 'Cross Sector Partnership Guideline'. These two documents resulted from a three-year multi-stakeholder project funded by the Danish International Development Agency entitled 'Future Partnership Models for Strategic CSR'. For very good reasons, the bulk of case studies and many of the recommendations contained in these documents focused on Red Cross partnerships in key international contexts such as Bangladesh, Ethiopia and Kenya. One key goal of the workshop was to explore how to render the recommendations and guidelines contained in these two documents to be specifically relevant and actionable in the context of Danish Red Cross efforts to meet challenges related to displacement and integration in Denmark. Towards this end the workshop consisted of three parts: (1), an extended working-group session in which small groups reviewed and discussed instances of existing collaboration and partnership through the lens of the 'Cross Sector Partnership Guideline'; (2), a plenary session in which the small groups came together to generate recommendations for translating the 'Cross Sector Partnership Guideline' into action steps for developing and managing future partnerships that address displacement and integration in Denmark; (3), a meeting between the working groups and the Danish Red Cross leadership, in which the working groups presented their recommendations and participated in a discussion of the leadership issues and challenges related to the implementation of these guidelines and recommendations.

The unfolding of a collaboratory dialogue should move in two directions at once: towards an examination of the underlying influences and forces that shape the problems and challenges under discussion, and towards the generation of potential solutions that can be tested in practice. Making progress in the conversation about underlying causes is challenging enough when dealing with wicked problems and intractable challenges. But in precisely these contexts, generating solutions proves even more difficult. The workshop did generate a number of directions and proposals to present to the Red Cross leadership regarding future cross-sector partnerships. Topics included, for example: the necessity for the Red Cross to deeply engage with partners at the earliest stage to understand what generates value in the partnership for both sides; the exploration of tensions in projects that seek to address refugee employability without connecting activities to enhancing social inclusion; considering non-traditional approaches to social inclusion through social entrepreneurship and venture funding. In this last example, discussions opened up to consider a future collaboratory that might draw on examples from elsewhere in the world that have addressed social inclusion for other excluded groups not necessarily refugees.

But the Red Cross collaboratory did not fully succeed in anchoring down concrete steps for future action. We were not able in the event to shape or to refine action in terms of the following questions: what discrete activities? How might these be explored/tested? Are these occurring in parallel and by whom? What outcomes are to be achieved and by when? Who is coordinating the various activities in terms of interim meetings, timescale moving towards the next collaboratory? Granted, these were grand ambitions, but from a leadership development perspective it is almost irresistible to push for clarity on these aspects, as such clarity can lead to the formation of action-learning sets, exchanges between managers to observe project activity, and to engage senior managers to sponsor projects to be reported to the board. We know from previous research that these sorts of mechanisms can exert considerable impact on leadership development processes inside organizations (James and Burgoyne, 2001). At the end of this collaboratory, the question remained: how can we leverage the participants' palpable sense of purpose and appreciation of how to engage more effectively in cross-sector projects? And how can we capitalize on the very clear and positive notions of shared value generation to exert impact in the area of refugee resettlement and integration moving forward? In short, 'what is the crucial what?' As we will describe, a similar challenge over how to proceed further presented itself in the context of the other two collaboratory events we helped organize in 2016.

Leading Sustained Cooperation in Fragile Environments: Steps toward Long-term Security and Defence, Geneva, Switzerland, 14–16 September 2016

Another emerging node in the burgeoning 'Leadership for What?' network was anchored by Patrick Sweet of the Center for Creative Leadership (CCL), in Europe. Patrick had helped arrange financial backing to the 2014 International Studying Leadership Conference at the Copenhagen Business School as a means to open up an exploratory dialogue between CCL and Eric Guthey and Steve Kempster's network of leadership scholars about the future of leadership research and development. At the same time, Patrick himself was in conversation with Peter Cunningham of the Geneva Center for Security Policy (GCSP), – an international foundation, think-tank, and provider of executive education in peace, security and diplomacy circles – about what would evolve by 2015 into the CCL-GCSP Alliance for Advancing Leadership in Peace and Security. In early 2016, the Leadership Alliance successfully requested funding from (North Atlantic Treaty Organization), NATO's Emerging Security Challenges Division to convene a three-day, advanced research workshop on leading cooperation in fragile and post-conflict environments – with Eric's leadership collaboratory serving as academic adviser to the funding initiative. The collaboratory network was expanding further, and the stage was set for an in-depth, multi-stakeholder conversation on leadership challenges of crucial importance.

Fragile, war-torn and post-conflict regions pose a set of particularly complex leadership challenges connected to the establishment and maintenance of sustainable, productive cooperation among diverse stakeholders, many of whom may have previously taken opposite sides to the conflict or who may otherwise see the world and their own interests in radically different ways. For this very reason a key ambition for the Geneva workshop was to assemble a wide range of perspectives by bringing together a diverse range of experienced professionals familiar with leading in fragile contexts (peace-builders, diplomats, leaders in humanitarian organizations, security experts), with international leadership and peace-building scholars. Altogether 35 participants joined the event, roughly 10 scholars and 25 practitioners, hailing from Afghanistan, Austria, Belgium, Denmark, Egypt, Germany, Kosovo, Libya, Switzerland, the United Kingdom and the United States. This mix of participants resulted in a fairly level playing field – the peace-building professionals were mostly too busy in their daily working lives to keep close tabs on recent advances in leadership research, while the scholars came from a research environment overly focused on conventional commercial organizations, with an underdeveloped sense of the complex, charged and fragile nature of transitional and conflict-affected environments. In other words, the participants all had a lot to learn from each other.

The CCL-GCSP Leadership Alliance, working with the participating scholars, designed the event to bring these diverse stakeholders into dialogue around five key themes chosen for their consistent reoccurrence as 'recognized barriers to, or failures in, maintaining long-term peace' across numerous peace-building efforts:

1. engendering long-term international political and donor support for international missions;
2. fostering common vision among nationals and internationals that engenders national ownership that is not simply tilted towards international agenda;
3. creating civil and military governance transformation beyond coordination, such as leading efforts to civilianize and democratize leadership that is, typically, initially formed out of rivalling, battling and military/paramilitary factions that are not democratic;
4. empowering women in governance and peace-building efforts in ways that are stronger than gender presentation;
5. ways and approaches for mission leadership to introduce and create local ownership of (sometimes less-welcomed), issues on the longer-term agenda of the international political donors: for example, preventing violent extremism in peace missions.

Small groups pursued each of these themes and contributed to non-directed, emergent conversations in the plenary, in a manner that involved all participants. The resulting dialogue was open-ended, far-reaching and often intense. Slowly, consensus and recurring themes began to emerge, in particular around the insufficiency of hierarchical and leader-centred approaches to leadership; around the intransigence and inertia of overly bureaucratic organizational structures; and around the need to emphasize the importance and impact of practical and collaborative leadership practices and trust building, to fill institution-building efforts with true, trusted, cooperative human agency in order to effectively lead towards sustained peace. The enthusiastic participation of Mary Uhl-Bien, one of the founders of complexity leadership theory, provided the practitioner participants with a new vocabulary to articulate and to analyse the complexity and turbulence they encounter in their daily working lives. Two results emerged. The first was the realization that the United Nations (UN) activities give little focus to engaging businesses within peace-building processes. A follow-on collaboratory is being explored with participating businesses to examine where value is generated for businesses in participating in such peace-building activities. The second result emerged only after the event was over – given Eric's connections with the International Leadership Association (ILA), he proposed that Patrick Sweet and the Leadership Alliance offer to serve as programme coordinators for the ILA's next global conference in Brussels in 2017. After a few transatlantic phone conversations, the next stage was set for the further expansion of the network, and the continued engagement with the collaboratory's concerns in another, much larger forum.

Inclusive Leadership in Refugee Resettlement: Local and Global Perspectives, Atlanta, Georgia, USA, 1–2 November 2016

The third collaboratory workshop we helped to organize in 2016 followed the pattern of the previous two. The opportunity to launch the workshop emerged out of a combination of intense dialogue about what to do next, energetic networking and happy coincidences. The event took shape as a pre-conference offering of the ILA's annual conference in Atlanta, Georgia, around the theme of 'The Dynamics of Inclusive Leadership'. Eric Guthey and Steve Kempster had served as board members to the ILA, but needed a local contact to explore whether a workshop on refugee issues would ignite interest in Atlanta. Through personal connections, they got in touch with Letitia Campbell, who works for the Candler School of Theology at Emory University as Director of Contextual Education and Clinical Pastoral Education, and as the Senior Programme Coordinator for the Laney Legacy Chair in Moral Leadership. Letitia coordinates programmes in the context of which Emory Masters of Divinity receive extensive pastoral training through working with refugee families and organizations, especially in the Atlanta suburb of Clarkston, Georgia. This suburb is one of the most successful refugee resettlement communities in the United States, and consequently one of the most culturally diverse 1.4 square miles of real estate in the entire country.

On 16 November 2015, Georgia Governor Nathan Deal had issued an executive order to try to halt any state involvement in the resettlement of Syrian refugees, a move that reflected the kind of divisive blindly anti-Muslim leadership that went on to characterize now President-elect Donald Trump's campaign for higher office. On that same day, Clarkston Mayor, Ted Terry, spoke out on the side of compassion, reason, inclusion and an altogether different type of leadership. 'The reality is that extending a welcoming hand and relief for people who, through no fault of their own are caught up in this civil war, is an incredibly smart and powerful way to engender confidence and friendship across the Middle East and across the entire world', said Terry. As he pointed out, Clarkston had already opened its doors to 125 Syrian refugees and fully intended to do more. By January 2016, the town had made good on Mayor Terry's promise, welcoming 50 more Syrian refugees and further cementing the town's reputation as the 'Ellis Island of the South' and the largest and most successful refugee resettlement in the country. A PBS documentary on the changing demographics of US communities has highlighted Clarkston as a community that has shifted from 90 per cent white to less than 14 per cent white over the last few decades, largely as a result of welcoming nearly 60,000 refugees during that period. As the *Christian Science Monitor* has pointed out, four out of five refugee families become economically self-sufficient within six months of arriving in Clarkston. A series of articles in the *New York Times* told the inspiring story of the Fugees, a soccer team that has united and nurtured refugee children from Afghanistan, Bosnia, Burundi, Congo, Gambia, Iraq, Kosovo, Liberia, Somalia and Sudan.

Clarkston is a place where the global meets the local, and where informal, community and grass-roots leadership is at least as important as formal and political leadership. Many resettled refugees play important leadership roles in Clarkston, working alongside a number of social entrepreneurs and service organizations to empower other members of the community. For these reasons, and with Letitia Campbell's hard work and leadership, the collaboratory assembled local area community leaders, leadership development practitioners, international scholars and students to explore what inclusive leadership looks like on the front lines of the global refugee crisis, in a local community helping displaced persons and families to establish new homes and new lives in the face of cultural, political and economic barriers of exclusion. The network was expanding yet again, bringing in more expertise and more diverse perspectives. Our goal was to uncover new insights and perspectives that we can incorporate into research, teaching and development practice, but more importantly in order to cultivate the kinds of leadership that can address one of the most complex challenges facing the world today.

On the eve of the event, Candler screened a new film entitled *The Crossing*, about a group of Syrian friends who make the journey from Egypt across the Mediterranean on a smuggler's ship, and about what happens to them in refugee camps in Europe afterwards. After the film, members of the Emory community and several collaboratory participants engaged in a dialogue with a panel that included local volunteers and members of some of the refugee families with whom they work. On the morning of 2 November, the 50 or so participants converged on the Clarkston Community Center and met with Mayor Terry and a number of refugee leaders. In the afternoon, the group moved to the Candler School at Emory to pursue small group and plenary discussions on four key areas related to refugee resettlement: youth and families, religious organizations, political and government contexts, and refugee aid and assistance organizations and programmes. Energy was high, and insights and ideas flowed around the room. Perhaps the most significant moment came towards the end of the workshop, when local refugee leader Hussein Mohammed put his finger on the tension in the room, which was no doubt connected to the fact that the US presidential elections were just six days away. Depending on the outcome of the elections, Hussein said, many of the very refugee families we were talking about would be in an even more difficult, stressful and even perhaps terrifying situation, one requiring even higher levels of leadership from the bottom up.

REFLECTIONS

In our reflective space we wish to think big. We are sure that the people who put together the CERN project thought big and with great ambition. The CERN project is a most wonderful example of scientists being able to come together to address research that could only be undertaken through collaboratory process. The stats on the CERN project are most illuminating: people – in excess of 12,000 scientists – half of the world's particle physicists – come to CERN for their research; locations – 111 nations involved that includes 600 institutes around the world (for example, in the UK 20 research sites involved); cost – approximately £5 billion; purposes – to test the existence of the Higgs Field that is postulated to give particles mass through identifying the Higgs Boson and to identify the existence of dark matter and dark energy; outcomes suggest strong evidence for the Higgs Boson, and detected photons, that give a hint towards dark energy.

This achievement (which of course is ongoing), has occurred through much coordination, skill, passion, lobbying and commitment.

Imagine if the leadership development industry had similar ambitions. It is not that we do not have connection to resources. As we have earlier stated, our industry spends in excess of US $50 billion per annum, so if we could coordinate sponsoring organizations to aligned activity in some way then we have the potential for considerable leverage. And here's the thing (again). The leaders we are working with have the potential power through networks and roles to make considerable change happen. A major criticism of leadership and management studies, and related development, has been the severe limitations of relevance and impact (Hodgkinson et al., 2001). We suggest that there are two major causes for this. The first is levelled at the lack of coordinated theme or purpose leading to considerable frag- mentation and utter differentiation of research – mostly in pursuance of universal truths and law-like regularities. Our quest is not the pure scientist quest (as with particle physicists). Rather research and development needs to align with pragmatic orientations: what helps managers and organi- zations in their everyday endeavours? What helps to advance humanity through everyday leadership endeavours? To address these questions the approach of design science has so much to offer.

So what might be? Well alignment requires a common ground. We have that palpably facing all of us – the grand challenges. Collaboratory leader- ship development offers a process to engage with such challenges, and it utilizes best practices of leadership development. However, that still does not address being able to make a considerable difference. How can we create our 'CERN' leadership challenge(s)? How can we – leadership devel- opment practitioners, leadership researchers, leaders and their sponsoring organizations (private, public, NGOs) – come together for the changes we collectively desire for our organizations and for society?

Our reflections on these questions have led us to explore the notion of crowdsourcing as an answer – an answer that has potentially great possi- bilities. Wikipedia is a most prominent example. It has enabled the estab- lishment in quick time of the most extensive encyclopedia the world has known. We may question many aspects defined therein but it is the illustra- tion of the process that is of importance here. The CERN project is a form of crowdsourcing – many minds being drawn together focused on aligned pieces of research. Leadership development could do the same thing. The grand challenges require many minds working on possible solutions being tested out in multiple locations. If collaboratory leadership development interventions became coordinated along themes, then, as with Wikipedia, we could pool insights from all stakeholders: public, private and third sector; academics and leadership development practitioners; politicians and foundations. The design science approach would continually distil and refine design principles that are most effective in guiding the interdisciplinary community of stakeholders in their concerted action to addressing the common agenda of the global challenges.

We suggest a virtuous circle of activity. First, the principles and approaches to developing and refining the collaboratory approach to leadership development would be continually advanced. Leadership development practice would gain a data source, insights and designs to structure and implement leadership development interventions. There would be frameworks for evaluation and clear indicators of effectiveness. The crowdsourcing would enable networks to be strengthened through symposia, conferences and webinars, and the creation of publications suited to the various audiences. Second, academics would similarly have greater and greater data to draw on and the publications would be both rigorous and relevant. Impact would be assured. Third, institutions – public, private and third sector – would be advancing change in their organizations, alongside and through the advancing of skills, capabilities and sense of purpose burgeoning in the leadership cadre engaged in the collaboratory process. Fourth, for leadership scholars and practitioners to be able to reach out to foundations and philanthropists to fund various collaboratory initiatives. Fifth, there would be greater potential to influence government policy to support further action and intervention, as well as connect between governments to align engagement.

In essence, collaboratory leadership development can become the 'research and development' dynamic of leadership academics and leadership development practitioners – connecting theory and practice for great impact. A group of leadership centres have come together to commence this journey and pilot collaboratory leadership development in the manner we have described; that is, focusing on the grand challenges. It is but one small group of 15 centres (at the time of writing), from eight different countries. However, the possibilities of illustrating the potential have at least commenced.

By dreaming big all things seem possible, of course. It is most doable if there is a common will. There should be – because we have a common cause. The global challenges will only become more pressing on humanity. The leadership development industry has a major role and influence to bring to bear. We already have over US \$50 billion to play with, if we can just get our act together. They did at CERN . . .

KEY TIPS

- Briefing papers on the global challenge and the concept of collaboratory.
- First collaboratory workshop to build in evening gathering as pre-event process.
- Expectations of collaboration emerging from the first collaboratory need to build trust; a sense of agreeing the next date rather than naming the children!
- Experiments to be tested in organizational contexts need to be capable of subsequent comparison when returning to second and subsequent collaboratories.
- Action-learning sets to be set up and aligned to the experiments.

REFERENCES

Bandura, A. (1986), *Social Foundations of Thought and Action: A Social Cognitive Theory*, Englewood Cliffs, NJ: Prentice-Hall Inc.

Burns, J.M. (1978), *Leadership*, New York: Harper and Row.

Davis, G.F. and C.J. White (2015), *Changing Your Company from the Inside Out: A Guide for Social Intrapreneurs*, Boston: Harvard Business Press.

DeRue, D.S., S.B. Sitkin and J.M. Podolny (2011), 'From the guest editors: teaching leadership issues and insights', *Academy of Management Learning and Education*, **10**(3), 369–72.

Francis, R. (2009), *Independent Inquiry into Care Provided by Mid Staffordshire NHS Foundation Trust January 2005–March 2009*, London: The Stationery Office.

Fulmer, R.M. and S. Wagner (1999), 'Leadership: lessons from the best', *Training and Development*, **53**(3), 28–32.

Greenberg, J., C.E. Ashton-James and N.M. Ashkanasy (2007), 'Social comparison processes in organizations', *Organizational Behavior and Human Decision Processes*, **102**(1), 22–41.

Hodgkinson, G.P., P. Herriot and N. Anderson (2001), 'Realigning the stakeholders in management research: lessons from industrial work and organisational psychology', *British Journal of Management*, **12**(SI), S41–S48.

Hodgkinson, G.P. and K. Starkey (2011), 'Not simply returning to the same answer over and over again: reframing relevance', *British Journal of Management*, **22**, 355–69.

Huff, A.S. and J.O. Huff (2001), 'Refocusing the business school agenda', *British Journal of Management*, **12**(SI), S49–S54.

James, K. and J. Burgoyne (2001), *Leadership Development: Best Practice Guide for Organisations*, London: Centre for Excellence in Management and Leadership.

Kelemen, M. and P. Bansal (2002), 'The conventions of management research and their relevance to management practice', *British Journal of Management*, **13**, 97–108.

Kempster, S. (2009), 'Observing the invisible: examining the role of observational learning in the development of leadership practice', *Journal of Management Development*, **28**, 439–56.

Kempster, S., B. Jackson and M. Conroy (2011) 'Leadership as purpose: exploring the role of purpose in leadership', *Leadership*, **7**(3), 317–34.

Kempster, S. and K. Parry (2014), 'Exploring observational learning in leadership development for managers', *Journal of Management Development*, **33**(3), 164–81.

Larsson, M. and R. Holmberg (2015), '"It's the organization that is wrong": learning of conceptual models as a resource for identity work in leadership development programs', ILA Conference, Barcelona.

MacIntyre, A. (1985), *After Virtue: A Study in Moral Theory*, London: Duckworth.

Muff, K. (2014), 'Defining the collaboratory', in K. Muff (ed.), *The Collaboratory: A Co-creative Stakeholder Engagement Process for Solving Complex Problems*, Sheffield: Greenleaf Publishing Ltd, pp.11–15.

Polman, P. (2014), 'Forward', in K. Muff (ed.), *The Collaboratory*, Sheffield: Greenleaf Publishing Ltd, pp.xii–xv.

Romme, A.G. (2003), 'Making a difference: organization as design', *Organization Science*, **14**, 558–73.

Sowcik, M. and S. Allen (2014), 'Getting down to business: a look at leadership education in business schools', *Journal of Leadership Education*, **12**(3), 57–75.

van Aken, J.E. (2004), 'Management research based on the paradigm of the design sciences: the quest for field-tested and grounded technological rules', *Journal of Management Studies*, **41**(2), 219–46.

Wulf, W. (1989), 'The national collaboratory – a white paper towards a national collaboratory', unpublished report of a NSF workshop, Rockefeller University, New York, 17–18 March.

Wulf, W. (1993), 'The collaboratory opportunity', *Science*, **261**, 854–5.

Index

Printed and bound by CPI Group (UK) Ltd, Croydon, CR0 4YY

23/04/2025

14660985-0003